1991

...aser

Our Changing Cities

D1359439

DATE DUE			
JUN 2 1 '93 S			
JUL 1 2 '93 S			
AUG 0 2 '93 S			
AUG 3 0 '93 S			
SEP 2 7 1993 S			
APR 0 8 1997			

OUR CHANGING CITIES

OUR CHANGING
Cities

Edited by John Fraser Hart

Cartographic design by Gregory Chu

The Johns Hopkins University Press
Baltimore and London

© 1991 The Johns Hopkins University Press
All rights reserved
Printed in the United States of America

The Johns Hopkins University Press
701 West 40th Street, Baltimore, Maryland 21211-2190
The Johns Hopkins Press Ltd., London

The paper used in this book meets the minimum requirements of
American National Standard for Information Sciences—Permanence
of Paper for Printed Library Materials, ANSI Z39.48-1984.

Library of Congress Cataloging-in-Publication Data

Our changing cities / edited by John Fraser Hart ; cartographic design
by Gregory Chu.
    p.   cm.
  Includes bibliographical references and index.
  ISBN 0-8018-4087-2 (alk. paper). — ISBN 0-8018-4088-0 (pbk. :
alk. paper)
    1. Cities and towns—United States—Effect of technological innovations
on. 2. Cities and towns—United States—Growth. I. Hart, John Fraser.
HT123.087 1991
307.76'0973—dc20   91-9226

Frontispiece: Aerial view of Minneapolis.
© 1990 Bordner Aerials

To John R. Borchert, who has been able to
"find tongues in trees, books in the running brooks,
sermons in stones, and good in everything."

—*As You Like It*, 2.1.16–17

300023

CONTENTS

PREFACE

American cities have gotten too big for their britches since World War II. In 1950, metropolitan areas in the United States were home to 85 million people, of whom 49 million lived in their central cities. In 1980, these self-same metropolitan areas had 142 million people, but only 58 million lived in their central cities. These simple numbers merely highlight the well-known fact that our cities have sprawled far beyond their political boundaries, which have turned into nooses. Many of the more talented and more affluent members of society have decamped to the suburbs, leaving the central cities short of leadership and cash as they grapple with their legacy of outdated structures and outmoded institutions.

Cadaverous old factories, stores, and office buildings still stand as silent sentinels of the past. Some few with monumental pretensions have been embalmed for posterity, but most have fallen from grace, victimized by newer structures in more favored areas. Quietly they slip down the vacancy chain from obsolescence to abandonment to inevitable demolition. The land on which they stood will long lie idle, unripe for development, but littered with urban debris. The antique water mains and sewers beneath them are potential hazards to human health, and the streets, sidewalks, and bridges, and all of the other infrastructure of the central city, clearly show their age; they are ever more costly to repair and maintain. Furthermore, the ills of the deteriorating central city are slowly starting to infect some of the older inner suburbs that lie just beyond its boundaries.

Institutions developed in years gone by to serve a vastly different city are gasping for breath as they struggle to stretch shrinking budgets to serve the changing social needs of the central city. Paradoxically, the increasing concentration of less fortunate members of society within the limits of central cities is giving them more political influence and greater power to challenge outmoded institutions, and to demand income redistribution, greater social equity, and improvements in education, health and other human services, housing, streets, and other services both public and private.

John Borchert has shown that the fabric of American cities and the character of their institutions are products of the era in which they were established, the eras in which they have flourished or famished, and the functions they have served in the national urban system. It is clear that our urban system is entering a new era—an era of far greater complexity than those that have preceded it, an era in which the structures and institutions of our cities are becoming increasingly difficult to understand.

In 1988–89, the Department of Geography at the University of Minnesota organized a yearlong series of lectures on the future of the American city. We invited twelve of the most distinguished students of the geography of our cities to share with us their best ideas and latest thinking about the ways in which our urban system is changing, to explore the geographical transformation of our cities. Properly mindful of the old saw that anyone who lives by the crystal ball must learn to eat broken glass, our speakers were wisely reluctant to make major prognostications. They were equally mindful of the dictum that we cannot begin to guess where we might be going until we know where we are and how we got there, however, and they were quite willing to talk about the ways in which our cities have evolved and how they are changing.

The papers they presented were so stimulating that we want to share them with the larger community of scholars; they are the substance of this book. The papers by Morrill, Ford, and Berry deal with cities in general. Morrill challenges three widely held views about what the ideal city ought to be. Many public officials and members of the citizenry at large seem to believe (1) that high urban population densities are better than low suburban densities, and "sprawl" is an abomination, (2) that rail transit systems are good, efficient, and necessary, but automobiles and expressways are bad, and (3) that regional governance and regional planning are good, but fragmentation of local units of government is bad. Morrill draws on his experience as a scholar and consultant to expose these views as myths that do not jibe with normal human behavior in the real world, despite their appeal to those who assume that the fundamental realities of our cities and of modern life are bad. He does not argue the opposite—that high densities or trains or regional governance are bad—but merely asks that we should try to understand our cities and our world as they are, instead of trying to force them to be what someone thinks they should be.

Ford argues for the creation of better models and theories to help us understand the changing internal structure of particular American cities in the postindustrial era of urban development. Most existing theoretical frameworks, he says, lack complementarity and emphasize internal elegance at the expense of empirical testing. He proposes a metatheory that stresses the linkages between levels and types of theory, and relates theory to places. His metatheory integrates a variety of theoretical approaches at three distinct levels of analysis. At the macro level, scholars use macroeconomics, Marxism, and any other approach that considers the larger economic and/or social environment of the city to help us understand when and why certain things were built. At the meso level, scholars explore the identity and the role of the managers and gatekeepers who make the decisions that control urban change. At the micro level, scholars focus on the perceptions and behavior of individuals to understand how they become the aggregates that influence decisions. Individual scholars usually work at only one level, he says, but in order to understand particular places they must work at all three. The understanding of a particular place also requires knowledge of its physical site, its form, and its architectural history, each of which is related to each of the three levels of analysis. Ford identifies four stages in the transformation of industrial cities to mature postindustrial cities. In the final stage, the downtown area is clearly bounded and generally perceived to be complete, so any major change is difficult and controversial.

Berry postulates a long-wave theory of technological succession to explain the epochs of American metropolitan evolution that Borchert identified in his 1967 paper. Berry argues that prices rise and fall in fifty-five-year Kondratiev waves; the upslopes and downslopes of each Kondratiev wave are twenty-five- to thirty-year Kuznets cycles of economic growth. The nation suffered major depressions in the 1840s, the 1890s, and the 1930s, when Kuznets growth troughs coincided with Kondratiev price troughs. Businesspeople are cautious on the upslope of a wave after such a double trough, and invest in the technologies that were established during the downslope of the previous wave. The peaks of Kondratiev waves, when inflationary rates are at their maximum, have coincided with Kuznets growth troughs to create the stagflation crises of 1814–15, 1864–65, 1919–20, and 1980–81, when the no longer new technologies had saturated the market. After a stagflation crisis businesspeople seek new products, and the upswings of Kuznets growth cycles on the downslopes of Kondratiev waves have involved high rates of investment in the development of new technologies, which mature on the upslope of the following wave. Berry concludes that the replacement of the infrastructure and capital equipment of our cities has a fifty-five-year phasing, and the epochs of American metropolitan evolution reflect these waves and cycles of technological succession.

Harvey looks at cities from a Marxist viewpoint, citing the central moral failure of capitalism as its rejection of all values that are not measured by money. Money supplants all other forms of imagery, such as religion and traditional authority, yet fails to provide a social identity to replace them.

Harvey believes that a sense of common purpose and community protects the masses against the travails of capitalism and the dissolving effects of money, but this protection breaks down during periods of rapid change, as in Haussmann's Paris, when the city is reconstructed and traditional sites are eliminated. When the familiar city is replaced, he says, the masses lose their sense of collective identity and seek a new social identity through institutionalized spectacle that replaces their collective memory. He finds a deep continuity in the perpetual dialogue between the emptiness of money values and attempts to construct an image of community in urban settings.

Vance and Hudson shift gears to focus on a specific technology, the technology of transport. They consider the impact of changes in the technology of transport on the fabric of our cities and on the viability of agricultural trade centers. Vance describes the ways in which changes in human mobility have affected the fabric of cities. The form of cities, he concludes, is strongly influenced, if not actually determined, by the dominant medium of transportation at the time when the cities were laid out. Most workers lived in crowded tenements near their workplaces in the pedestrian and later horse-car city. After electric streetcars were introduced in 1888, even working-class people could afford their own homes in strips along the trolley lines, and the streetcar city grew radially. The automobile, which had replaced the streetcar by 1925, permitted residential infilling between the radial spokes of the streetcar city. The arterial streets eventually became so clogged with traffic that limited-access highways had to be developed, and, after 1945, they facilitated the shift of retailing, wholesaling, and manufacturing out of the central city to suburban sites, which have become new foci of growth. The metropolis has recrystallized into a set of urban realms. Each realm has its own nucleus, few ties with the traditional core of the city, and virtually none with other realms. Attempts to develop rapid transit systems centered on the central city, which is no longer central, have failed because they have misunderstood the geography of the multicentered modern metropolis.

Hudson describes the competition between transport modes for the grain trade of the agricultural heartland since 1950, and the impact of this competition on the cities and small towns that serve the agricultural areas where the grain is produced. He rejects conventional wisdom about the origins of trade-center towns, and argues that they were created by railroad companies with the single-minded goal of capturing traffic in agricultural produce, especially grain. Trucks and barges began to compete with the railroads for the grain trade in the 1950s and the loss of business seriously weakened the railroads, which had to trim branch lines and reduce their services to small places. After deregulation in 1980 the railroads were able to recover some of their lost grain traffic by developing unit trains. Large subterminals have been developed that can take advantage of unit-train rates, because the old trackside elevators in trade-center towns were too small to do so. The new subterminals have conferred little benefit on the small towns in or near which they are sited, and Hudson concludes that changes in the technology of transporting grain have deprived small trade-center towns of their primary function as nodes in a grain-collection network.

The papers by Adams, Clark, and Golledge examine three specific critical issues in contemporary urban society: housing, civil rights, and the needs of special populations. Adams uses the Twin Cities of Minneapolis and St. Paul as a case study to describe housing submarkets in American metropolitan areas. Residential areas differentiated by socioeconomic class radiate from the center of the metropolis. Radial streetcar lines encouraged the sectoral development of residential areas, but circumferential highways are rapidly blurring it. The character of each sector was determined by its original residents at the edge of downtown. Each sector grows outward by the construction of new suburban housing, which depresses the relative values of the older houses in its inner segments. Upper- and lower-class sectors are more stable than middle-class sectors, which have long vacancy chains reaching from the zone of new suburban construction to the inner city. A vacancy chain originates when a family moves outward to a new house, leaving an older and cheaper house to be occupied by a second family, whose move creates a third vacancy. Adams says that the baby boom generation raised prices when it entered the housing market in the 1970s, and the baby-bust generation will depress housing prices in the 1990s.

Clark reviews the legal history of school desegregation, open housing, and voting rights. He concludes that many efforts to reduce racial discrimination have been counterproductive, in part because they have not adequately considered the geography of cities. The landmark decision of *Brown vs. Board of Education* in 1954, for example, ignored geography. In 1971 the Supreme Court established the principle of busing, which clearly has a geographical component, but the courts generally have not required desegregation programs to cross school district or political boundaries. The 1965 Civil Rights Act prohibited discriminatory election procedures, but immediately raised geographical questions, because the creation of voting districts dominated by minorities might also create minority school districts. Recently, emphasis has shifted from attempts to eliminate discrimination toward affirmative action, but any integration strategy faces problems resulting from migration, individual preferences, and the geography of cities. Our society is inherently mobile, and court-ordered busing has amplified "white flight" to the suburbs. Whites prefer to move to neighborhoods that are at least 80 percent white, whereas blacks prefer neighborhoods that are 50-50. Income differences between the races may be a barrier to integrating the suburbs, and attempts at integration may actually have encouraged white flight and increased the segregation of affluent white suburbs from poor black central cities.

Golledge ventures beyond the bounds of "normal" human behavior in "normal" situations to investigate the navigational abilities of special populations, such as the mentally retarded and the unsighted. His experiments indicate that moderately retarded people can learn to find their way around in the everyday world, but have difficulty making maps that show sequences and distances along routes. Unsighted people are able to estimate distances and reproduce turn angles fairly well, but navigational tasks that require the integration of these abilities are difficult for them. The concentration of special populations in cities contributes significantly to contemporary urban problems, because such people may unwittingly violate community legal codes, they may be easy victims for other violators, and they place a heavy financial burden on community institutions. The siting of unpopular public facilities, such as group homes or halfway houses for the mentally retarded, often produces community conflict. Golledge asserts that geographers should identify the factors that influence neighborhood acceptability of different types of facilities, and argues that the study of facility siting must transcend normal Euclidean space; it requires consideration of geographic space transformed by the attitudes and perceptions of local residents.

Wolpert and Scott and Paul examine specific aspects of recent economic growth in our two largest metropolitan areas, New York and Los Angeles. Wolpert sees the mixed blessings of rapid regional growth in northeastern New Jersey in the 1980s after a period of economic stagnation in the 1970s. During a period of decline different levels of government may adopt growth strategies that can have negative effects if they persist into the subsequent period of economic growth. Wolpert identifies some of the untested assumptions underlying growth strategies in the framework of the Tiebout hypothesis, which states that the diversity of its fragmented suburbs gives a competitive advantage to a major metropolitan area because individual suburbs can cater to the particular needs of individual firms. He has amassed data for 179 municipalities in northeastern New Jersey, and concludes, on the basis of preliminary analysis, that rapid growth has favored the places that had developable land and made autonomous land-use decisions, but it has created problems that have revived interest in environmental and equity issues at the regional level.

Scott and Paul describe the growth of manufacturing in Southern California between 1970 and 1987. They argue that this region, which has become the nation's leading manufacturing area, is the model for a shift from mass production to a more flexible industrial structure. They identify three major ensembles of industries in the region: mass production industries, specialty craft industries, and high technology industries. Employment is declining in the mass production industries, but it is growing rapidly in the other two. The growing industries are fragmented into many small firms that maintain flexibility by subcontracting heavily. They cluster in new technopoles in areas that previously had little manufacturing. They do not offer stable employment, but rely heavily on temporary and part-time labor. They employ large numbers of female and immigrant workers, many illegal, in low-wage, nonunionized jobs. Craft specialty firms employ more immigrants and women, high technology firms more Asians, and low technology firms more Hispanics. The mass production firms that remain are unionized and employ more African-Americans. Scott and Paul identify five clusters of policy issues in the region: small firms do not command the capital necessary for innovation; society will have to accept greater responsibility for training workers; the region depends excessively on government contracts; the fragmentation of firms inhibits cooperation; and political fragmentation inhibits the provision of an adequate infrastructure.

Borchert wraps up the volume with his usual flair by tying together many of the apparently disparate ideas that have been presented in other papers into his vision of the future of American cities. He identifies our metropolitan centers as major nodes in our national circulation system. Their size and function have been sensitive to changes in the technology of transportation and communication, and each node has age rings that reflect its variable growth during the Wagon, Iron Horse, Steel Rail, and Automobile epochs. The Satellite-Electronic-Jet Propulsion Epoch that began in the 1970s will weaken mass production and defense-oriented nodes, but will benefit air transportation, research and development, and amenity nodes. Each metropolitan center will spawn a new ring that will be more complex than earlier rings. The new ring will have a variety of new housing, worse suburban gridlock, expanded or relocated airports, salvage yards and dumps, and controversial electric generating plants. The 1920–70 automobile ring will be firmly in the middle of vacancy chains for all types of use. Pre-1920 rings will be ripe for redevelopment, but they will have many unimproved tracts. The increasing complexity and continuing political fragmentation of the metropolis will create major problems for public officials who will be forced to plan and operate sophisticated new management systems.

ACKNOWLEDGMENTS

I wish to acknowledge with gratitude the hard work and dedication of those without whose efforts the success of the lecture series and the publication of this volume would have been impossible: each of the contributors, who shared so graciously of their time and ideas; Richard H. Skaggs, who exercised his admirable administrative skills in his usual wise and self-effacing way to ensure that everything went smoothly; John S. Adams, Roger Miller, and Eric Sheppard, who organized and led the superb Saturday morning seminars that were one of the most serendipitous aspects of the series; Margaret Rasmussen, who sacrificed precious weekends to the retyping of manuscripts with nary a word of complaint; Liz Barosko, who entered a seemingly interminable stream of editorial changes and corrections into the word processor; Philip Schwartzberg, Yang Yu, and Carlos Ruiz-Rodriguez, who drafted most of the maps and graphics; and A. N. Other, who has drafted most of the maps and graphics; and George F. Thompson, publishing consultant to the Johns Hopkins University Press, who has supported the project so enthusiastically from its very inception to its appearance in print.

I cannot thank them enough.

ONE

Myths about Metropolis

Richard L. Morrill

Most students of the city probably view themselves as social scientists, dedicated to learning objectively about the city, yet there is scarcely a subject on which these students actually hold or have accepted normative views of what the ideal city ought to be. These ideal images may or may not conform to the reality of human behavior. Although this attitude may be more characteristic of the educated public—and of planners, whose very purpose is often to pursue normative goals—it is also prevalent among urban geographers, but much less common among urban economists (Burns 1988). Like most geography students, I began graduate study with strong images of the way the city ought to be. In the summer of 1956, for example, I worked as a planner for the city of Billings, Montana, and proposed abolishing trailer courts as undesirable. Over the ensuing years as a professor and consultant, I have become increasingly involved in the everyday real world evolution of cities, and thereby increasingly aware of the incongruity between the normative images expressed by people—both professionals and the citizenry at large—and the real nature of the city and the revealed behavior of its residents. In this chapter, I look briefly at three central pillars of what I call the Mythical City, speculate as to why these not-really-true images are so fiercely held, and comment on the effect of this mismatch of the ideal and the real on the cities we have built and on the utility of urban geography.

The first myth is that high density is "better" than low density. Its corollary is the conventional wisdom that "urban sprawl" is the epitome of "bad." The second myth is that rail transit is "good" and efficient and necessary to solve urban transportation problems, while the automobile is "bad" and inefficient. The third myth is that governmental fragmentation is "bad" and that regional governance and regional planning are "good." By discussing these, I am by no means saying that their opposite is true—that high density is bad, or that trains are bad, or that regional planning is bad. What is wrong is the normative a priori labeling of fundamental realities of our cities and of modern life as bad, rather than questioning why the world is like it is and what may be the advantages and disadvantages, costs and benefits of alternative ways of organizing our urban environment or of organizing our lives in the face of that urban environment.

My purpose then is to contrast the actual and possible city with the mythical city—what many think a city ought to be. What is a city? It is a built environment and a center of employment and exchange, of housing of different types, and of transport networks connecting these economic centers and housing areas. It is a large interdependent labor market and community, but it is also a collection of competing jurisdictions and socially diverse neighborhoods, and it is people of varying interests, preferences, and incomes. It is a social space, constructed out of the highly unequal power of individuals, groups, and firms (Knox 1987). What, in particular, is the late twentieth-century American city? It is, with the exception of a few inner cores, of moderately low residential density, averaging about three thousand persons per square mile, about half what it was at the beginning of the century. Its area consists predominantly—about two-thirds—of single-family, owner-occupied houses, as it has for a long time. The majority of residents are middle class, with perhaps as much territory but fewer people in upper-class areas, and greater densities in lower-class areas. Almost 90 percent of households have cars, and we have not quite reached one car per driver's license. Shopping areas have long since been dispersed around the spreading metropolis. Employment has decentralized almost as much, typically creating the multi-centered city that Ullman and Harris already knew more than forty years ago (Harris and Ullman 1945; Erickson 1986). Most metropolises have an impressive degree of functional as well as jurisdictional fragmentation. Collective and individual and corporate choices have somehow created this kind of metropolis.

The mythical city is an image derived in part from our European heritage, and in part from architectural and planning theory of the metropolis, but it certainly does not follow from our formal urban theory (Mills 1987; Richardson 1988). The mythical city is efficient; it has vastly higher density than the real city, without the real city's vacant space, and makes a clean break with a productive countryside, without the unsightly and inefficient sprawl. It has one dominant economic and cultural center. Whether it has class or racial segregation is not addressed by the myth; at least it must not be very contentious or problematic. Perhaps it is subsumed in the diverse but supportive neighborhoods of the mythical city. It has a nonpartisan regional government, but respects communities. Of course, no such place exists, not even Tokyo, Moscow, or Stockholm, and certainly not London, Paris, or any American city. And yet many urban scholars, as well as the educated citizenry, seem consumed with guilt that we do not have such cities, although we often make planning and investment decisions based on that vision.

The real city has quite variable but average low density, because consumer demand has made it that way; the real city seeps into the countryside because so many people like a presumed rural existence and because farming cannot compete (Lowry 1988). In the real city jobs are not so concentrated, because many activities are more efficient outside dense concentrations, and because many people prefer shorter suburban to longer commutes downtown (Muller 1981). In the real city cars have displaced rails and even buses, because the latter could not serve an increasingly dispersed populace. The real city starkly reflects the class and racial divisions of society; the real city is politically fragmented, because citizens and businesses both fear and distrust large government (ACIR 1962; Johnston 1982). But neither the real nor the mythical city should be viewed as inherently "good" or "bad." It was not an oil or automobile company conspiracy, but wider class and corporate interests and our own preferences, that created the real city. The mythical city is the image of one set of expressed preferences, and the real city is the product of revealed preferences, albeit unfolding within a complex structure of powerful constraints. The real city is not nearly as bad as the idealist critics suggest. It cannot help but reflect the imperfections and failures of our society, but to transform it in the direction of the mythical city would not necessarily lead to higher levels of economic and social well-being or of environmental integrity.

DENSITY AND SPRAWL

Residential densities are low because more than 80 percent of the population prefers single-family housing or low-density garden-type apartments, and most of these people, even many of the poor, have been able to act on that preference (Dillman 1979). When asked why, people speak about private spaces, having some sense of attachment to nature despite living in the city, and a deep-rooted idea of a healthy environment for children. All these may be myths as well, but they are myths people work to realize. It was only possible to achieve this low density because of the use of the automobile and because median incomes have grown high enough to afford substantial investments in housing and transportation. Thus, it is no surprise that as real incomes have risen in Europe, its cities have been experiencing the decentralization typical of American cities.

Many urban scholars believe that high densities are "better" and more "efficient" because (1) less pressure is placed on agricultural or other resource lands or on open space; (2) the cost of providing roads, water, sewers, police, fire, and other urban services is argued to be lower per capita; (3)

people will be induced to shift to more efficient public transit; and therefore (4) pollution will be reduced. Particularly excoriated is the exurban settlement form we have come to call urban sprawl—that zone of interspersed small subdivisions and homes strung out along arterials (Real Estate Research Corporation 1974).

Many scholars would like to believe that there is an optimal density, but that notion is as atheoretical as is the question of an optimal size city. Our theory, and the reality of the landscape and certainly of the market, actually says that there should be a continuum of densities from very high to very low, depending on household trade-offs between accessibility and space. In a relatively free society, if high-density housing and low-density housing and even exurban sprawl exist, then somehow each type must be a competitive equilibrium result. Each form is optimal in its niche, unless one can demonstrate that one type is the outcome of market failure to incorporate externalities or that another type is sustained only by subsidies. Planning and zoning are in fact legitimate responses to such market failure, but low density on the urban fringe specifically has not been demonstrated to be an example of such failure or subsidy. Nor, in the absence of growth management and zoning restrictions, was exurban settlement biased toward the affluent.

Contrary to the arguments of the famous study, *Costs of Sprawl* (Real Estate Research Corporation 1974), which was based on hypothetical and not real measures, higher density is not more efficient than lower density in the correct meaning of efficiency—that is, the maximum productivity of resources. If we look only at the simplest numbers—the proportion of income spent on local government services in relation to the size and density of jurisdictions—we find an intriguing result: essentially a flat line with a rise at either end. Real per capita costs rise precipitously at the extremely large and dense end, in places like Boston, New York, Philadelphia, and San Francisco, and at the extremely small end, where densities fall below 100 per square mile (Perry 1988). In short, it is no more costly to the local household or to the wider regional society to sustain those exurban homes and miniclusters, or that inner-city high-rise or inner suburban subdivision, because there are compensatory but different higher and lower needs and higher and lower costs in each kind of settlement. A small semirural subdivision may need minimal police service and provide its own water and sewer service. The public subsidies of the paved road (originally for farm and forest access) are not greater than the subsidies of the city buses for which the rural folks probably help pay. Infrastructure costs in very high-density areas are in fact amazingly high—consider just the costs involved if elevators are required.

Let us turn to the preservation of farmland and forests and consider the adverse effects of sprawl on resource production. The economist argues that if the land were really needed for resource production, that use would outcompete the residential use. But even if we agree on market failure with respect to competition, we cannot ignore the strength of residential demand

and the social costs of constraining the land supply. The voters of Seattle and King County recently approved sixty-five million dollars in bonds to purchase the development rights from county farmers. This at least demonstrated tacit honesty. The voters were prepared to pay suburban land prices for open space they wanted, and could no longer pretend that serious farming and forestry could really compete on the urban fringe (Platt 1985).

A major topic rather neglected by geographers (Walker and Heiman are an exception), but widely studied by economists and planners, is the area of growth management, and in particular the currently popular and very geographic policy of an "urban growth perimeter," designed to prevent further urban sprawl and to foster urban infilling (Walker and Heiman 1981; Dowall 1984; Landis 1986; Frieden 1983; Adams 1987). Certainly an urban growth boundary represents a signal to the rational landowner to withhold land from the market speculatively, thereby raising the cost of land and housing. This occurred, for example, in King County (Seattle), as opposed to the neighboring counties that did not impose a growth boundary, and around Vancouver, British Columbia, and San Diego. Who is hurt most through planning efforts to force infilling and prevent sprawl? Not the rich, who can readily win a hearing variance, but the poor, who are faced with higher prices and reduced supplies of housing. An urban perimeter is a simplistic product of the high-density myth, and one that imposes excessive social costs for marginal environmental benefits. But it is a highly seductive policy, because it seems so right.

A currently popular product of this image of the mythical city is the idea that urban growth is a net cost and burden to society, and, at best, a necessary evil that must pay for itself in advance through "development impact fees" (Connerly 1988; *JAPA* 1988). The proposition is ahistorical and economically incorrect. Where are the urban historical geographers to point out that if such a view had prevailed across history we would have no cities about which to worry? Many forms of development in many places and at many times undoubtedly received unnecessary subsidy and could have paid more of the initial costs, but the trend toward pay-as-you-go new housing, and even overt antigrowth policies, ignores the long-term return on urban investments in human shelter and neighborhood, and risks a severe deterioration of housing opportunities, especially for the less affluent.

RAIL TRANSIT AND THE CAR

One of the most pervasive and persuasive metropolitan myths has to do with the efficiency, the mystique, the very inevitability of rail rapid transit as a solution to urban traffic congestion. Many of the largest American cities have instituted light and heavy rail networks in the last twenty years, in an effort to relieve congestion and ease commuting to central business district jobs (UMTA 1988; Pisarski 1987). It is astounding how many otherwise hardheaded businesspeople are prepared to encourage the spending of billions of dollars for rail rapid transit, without considering costs and alternatives they would devote to a personal or corporate investment. Perhaps it is a romantic nostalgia for what they thought were the virtues of rail systems at the turn of the century, or a feeling that a rail system is a necessary hallmark of a real world-class city, like a stadium or aquarium or convention center. The problem is that our images have led us to confound the advantages of a rapid transit system with the particular technology of fixed rail.

The urban transportation problem is how to accommodate increased travel demand without increasing the number of vehicles on critical corridors, as by increasing the average occupancy per vehicle and by constraining traffic on congested routes (Kemp 1982). The severity of the problem is in part because of the incongruity between the real and the mythical city. The real city has great suburban decentralization of residences, well served by cars, but planners, city officials, and downtown landowners have worked together to maintain relatively high concentrations of jobs in central cities and especially downtown, creating a form of geographic incompatibility (Pisarski 1987; Lowry 1988). Somehow large numbers of dispersed workers and consumers must be brought to dense business centers, but no one has been able to invent an affordable technology to accomplish this task effectively. Cars are effective at the suburban residential end of the trip, but they lead to severe congestion and pollution in the central city end; commuter trains and subways are great at peak hours at the dense jobs end, but their large capacity and theoretical efficiency evaporate in their redundant capacity at all other times and in their inability to get close to many suburban and even city residents.

Contrary to another myth, the choice is not between rail and automobile. The problem is to find the most effective combination of structural and nonstructural transportation strategies, which include a number of less dramatic and monumental but more effective policies. First, accept the decentralization of jobs to where people are living, to reduce the demand for long-distance suburb-to-downtown commuting. Second, improve traffic flow on the arterial system by more grade separation—better separation of through traffic from pedestrians and local traffic, and the like; after all, this is where more than 98 percent of the demand actually is. Third, raise average occupancy per car, through incentives for carpooling and vanpooling, and disincentives for parking in congested centers. Cars carry 90 percent of people, and the leverage from increasing average occupancy from the current 1.35 to 1.5 persons per car, which seems tiny, is much greater than probable potential diversions to transit. Fourth, create a rapid public transit system on major commuter corridors. Rapid transit is a critical part of meeting travel demand, but the most effective technology by far turns out to be the lowly bus and not the train, whose main asset is its romantic image (Kain 1988). The key to attracting people from cars to transit is not the fixed guideway or even the capacity of the vehicle, but the freedom from congestion offered by controlled access rights of way.

A bus system is preferable to rail in the typical low-density multicentered American city for four reasons. First, flexibility: rubber-tired vehicles are able to pass each other, interface easily with feeder buses and park-and-ride lots, and serve major origins and destinations directly. Second, size of network and timing: networks that can be made available for noncongested HOV (high-occupancy vehicle) use for the same cost are far greater, probably fourfold, and they can access a far larger proportion of the population far sooner than a conceivably affordable rail system. Third, cost and subsidy: the road system is built and maintained by car user taxes. Bus rapid transit HOB (high-occupancy bus) lanes can be subsidized 70 percent by carpool/vanpool use. Many of the lanes already exist, whereas the real capital cost of a new rail system is enormous—probably five times as much per mile. All rail systems built in the last twenty years have far fewer riders than forecasted—averaging about half—and cost much more to build—averaging about twice as much; their performance is only one-quarter as good as the forecasts used to justify their construction. Typically 70 to 90 percent of the real costs per ride (e.g., nine dollars on the Metroliner) must be subsidized, compared to 30 to 40 percent for buses. Fourth, ethics: a skeletal rail system is mainly intended to bring affluent white-collar suburban workers to downtown office jobs. This high subsidy represents a substantial and unconscionable transfer of income from the less affluent nonriders. Tying up so much capital and operating costs to serve the affluent few will lead to underinvestment in the less dramatic systems that serve the less well-off.

In reality the automobile and truck have proven to be an incredibly effective and liberating technology, and are utterly indispensable to high productivity and income. Their door-to-door flexibility provides vast time savings and raises the accessibility of much more territory than fixed or high-capacity systems. A final surprising figure is that, taking into account all capital and operating costs, the automobile, with an average of 1.5 persons, has lower costs per passenger mile than any form of public transit on corridors with up to fifty thousand trips per day—a number that exceeds ridership on most recently built rail lines. Akin to trying to force higher density, constructing rail systems in inappropriate places will not achieve the intended purpose of a better environment or a more efficient city, but will have the perhaps unintended consequence of constraining the prospects of the less powerful and less affluent.

POLITICAL FRAGMENTATION

Inefficiency and inequity are associated with jurisdictional fragmentation (Barlow 1981; Morrill 1989; Dahl 1961). Many metropolitan areas have a central-city-versus-suburb dichotomy; the central city has inordinate hu-

man services responsibilities for the poor, the homeless, or the deinstitutionalized, whom many suburbs have been able to exclude (Danielson 1976;
Smith 1979; Dear and Scott 1981). Rival jurisdictions lead to overcompeti-
tion and overbuilding (Cox and Mair 1988). Problems like transportation,
sewers, solid wastes, and air pollution do not stop at or respect local boundaries. What geographic generalization is more basic than that the metropolis
must be seen as an interdependent whole?

On the other hand, perhaps half the people in U.S. suburbs are not in
affluent, exclusive areas. Millions are not even in incorporated places. When
people have a choice, they overwhelmingly opt not to annex to a large central
city, but to incorporate for themselves, or, particularly in the West or South,
not to incorporate at all.

No real regional government exists in the United States (Morrill 1989).
As far as I know, no voters anywhere have voluntarily chosen even fairly
limited regional governance. Most regional governance has been imposed by
legislatures or created by agreements among officials. We need to ask why.
For several years, I have been a member of the Washington State Boundary
Review Board (for King County), a quasi-judicial body concerned with an-
nexations and incorporations and disputes among cities and with special
districts. I have discovered that the real world, and its mix of motivations, is
far more complex than our simple images suggest. There is a pervasive distrust of large, general-purpose governments—exemplified by central cities or
even large suburbs—because of a perception of higher taxes and regulation,
of crime and insecurity, and of an inability to control one's living environment
(ACIR 1962). In many metropolises this distrust is undoubtedly related to
fears of racial mixing. Even where race is less important, as in Seattle and
Minneapolis-St. Paul, the preference for smaller jurisdictions is pronounced.
In the West, at least, millions prefer the weaker mechanism of special-purpose
districts to provide essential services.

Public-choice theorists suggest that fragmentation is the result of people
of varying interests and capabilities competing for space, but that within such
controlled spaces, they exercise precious autonomy (Bish and Kirk 1974). A
structural perspective suggests that it is in the interest of large industries and
landowners to encourage fragmentation, because they can more easily ma-
nipulate smaller jurisdictions (Clark and Dear 1984; Gottdiener 1986; Clark
1987). Both these perceptions are true. If ordinary citizens and the corporate
elite both like fragmentation, but for different reasons, it is not surprising that
it is so pervasive.

Fragmentation is not simply a structure that hurts the poor or minorities
unequivocally (Williams 1982; Hoch 1984). In central cities and in non-
affluent suburbs, beset with problems as they may be, at least the poor and
minorities have been able to gain some degree of participation and political
power. In most metropolitan areas, if there were a regional government,
suburban and downtown business interests would usually bury inner-city

people interests. Does anyone believe that the poor and minorities are better off in Indianapolis after the Republican legislature imposed a merger with Marion County? Will a regional government overturn exclusion and implement a fair distribution of lower-income housing and social services (Baer 1986)?

Yet we must deal with regional problems. The American solution is to create special limited-purpose functional entities—often public corporations—first for airports and ports, then for sewers, and perhaps for the water supply, public transit, and parks and recreation. Noticeably absent in the United States is coordinated or regional land-use planning, or the dispersion of public housing or other human services. This corporate authority or utility approach to regional integration not only avoids dealing with social problems, but it also concentrates effective power in the hands of a technical elite. Thus, it increases the risks of capital-intensive approaches, and even of systems that are more regionally integrated than necessary (Bish and Kirk 1974).

Real regional government is not possible in the United States because virtually all classes and interests appear to derive more benefits—or avoid more risks—from fragmentation (Johnston 1982). The regional frameworks we are able to construct can meet the pure utility needs of a region fairly well, but they fail to deal with human issues. Although some ingenious structure of regional governance may be buildable in the mythical metropolis, in the real world it is clear that serious approaches to human problems, including any redistribution of real income, must come, as it long has, from higher levels—the state and federal governments. The Twin Cities' progress in regionalism, which is the most advanced in the nation, is a case in point (Harrigan 1976).

The real city is a product of competing interests and cooperating coalitions, ever adjusting to changing technologies, populations, and external structural forces. It is an imperfect place. One could argue, in contradiction to this chapter, that low density, and thus the lack of a viable rail transit, and fragmentation impose extra hardships on the less well-off. For example, minorities and the poor have severe problems of accessibility to suburban jobs, shopping, and recreation (Knox 1987; Hoch 1984). Many central cities have deficient tax bases and high service burdens, but the purported answers—higher density, rail, and regional government—are either unachievable, irrelevant, or even counterproductive, just as were earlier forms of spatial engineering, such as urban renewal (Johnston 1982). The reason lies in the structure of power and inequality in the city. Real progress depends on mobilization at higher levels of government that are better able to consider locally impossible policies of redistribution and empowerment.

Consider how much of the agenda of the planned mythical city—high density and concentration of activities, dependence on rail transit, and unitary regional governance—actually serves the interests of the elite and powerful. Given the reality of social and economic inequality and racial and other social discrimination, the less advantaged may be better off with a less-planned land and housing market that makes trickle-down possible, without costly rail systems, and with a fragmentation that permits some autonomy.

The role of geography. Perhaps I malign the academic community as well as planners and geographers. The literature does not in fact support the mythical city. Indeed, excellent research in regional science, urban economics, political science, and increasingly in planning addresses these issues. The urban geography literature, however, seems sparse, despite the intense territorial nature of the issues and their significance to human well-being—the very look and life of the urban landscape. The most disturbing problem is how impotent and irrelevant the academic community is in dispelling or even questioning the power of the myth in the public mind and among local officials and in influencing public policy. Has the research not yet pervaded the curriculum? Perhaps this should not surprise, but it should remind us of the immense power of the urban elite—a fact that should not stop us from undertaking critical research and arguing in the public arena.

REFERENCES

Adams, J. S. 1987. *Housing America in the 1980s*. New York: Russell Sage Foundation.

Advisory Committee on Intergovernmental Relations (ACIR). 1962. *Factors affecting voter reactions to government reorganization in metropolitan areas*. Washington, D.C.: ACIR.

Baer, W. 1986. The evolution of local and regional housing studies. *Journal of the American Planning Association* 52: 172–84.

Barlow, M. 1981. *Spatial dimensions of urban government*. New York: Research Studies Press.

Bish, R., and R. Kirk. 1974. *Economic principles of urban problems*. Englewood Cliffs, N.J.: Prentice Hall.

Burns, E. 1988. Land use planning and urban spatial structure. *Urban Geography* 19: 209–16.

Clark, G., and M. Dear. 1984. *State apparatus: Structures and language of legitimacy*. Boston: Allen and Unwin.

Clark, W. A. V. 1987. Urban restructuring from a demographic perspective. *Economic Geography* 63: 103–25.

Connerly, C. 1988. Social implications of impact fees. *Journal of the American Planning Association* 54: 75–78.

Cox, K., and A. Mair. 1988. Locality and community in the politics of local economic development. *Annals of the Association of American Geographers* 78: 307–25.

Dahl, R. 1961. *Who governs? Democracy and politics in the American city*. New Haven: Yale University Press.

Danielson, M. 1976. *The politics of exclusion*. New York: Columbia University Press.

Dear, M., and A. Scott, eds. 1981. *Urbanization and urban planning in capitalist society*. New York: Methuen.

Dillman, D. 1979. Residential preferences, quality of life and the population turnaround. *American Journal of Agricultural Economics* 61: 960–66.

Dowall, D. 1984. *The suburban squeeze: Land conversion and regulation.* Berkeley: University of California Press.

Erickson, R. 1986. Multinucleation in metropolitan economies. *Annals of the Association of American Geographers* 76: 331–46.

Frieden, B. 1983. The exclusionary effects of growth controls. *American Academy of Political and Social Science* 465: 123–35.

Gottdiener, M. 1986. *Cities in stress.* Beverly Hills, Calif.: Sage Publications.

Harrigan, J. 1976. *Political change in the metropolis.* Boston: Little, Brown.

Harris, C., and E. Ullman. 1945. The nature of cities. *Annals of the American Academy of Political Science* 242: 6–17.

Hoch, C. 1984. City limits: Municipal boundaries and class segregation. In *Marxism and the metropolis.* Edited by W. Tabb and L. Sawyer. New York: Oxford University Press.

Johnston, R. J. 1982. *The American urban system: A geographical perspective.* New York: St. Martin's Press.

Journal of the American Planning Association. 1988. Symposium: Development impact fees. 54: 3–78.

Kain, J. 1988. Choosing the wrong technology, or how to spend billions to reduce transit use. *Journal of Advanced Transportation* 21: 197–213.

Kemp, M. 1982. Improving public transportation in a changing financial environment. *Public Management* 64 (7): 2–5.

Knox, P. 1987. *Urban social geography.* New York: Longmans.

Landis, J. 1986. Land regulation and the price of new housing. *Journal of the American Planning Association* 52: 9–21.

Lowry, I. 1988. *Planning for urban sprawl: A look at the year 2000.* Washington, D.C.: Transportation Research Board.

Mills, E., ed. 1987. *Handbook of urban and regional economics.* New York: North Holland.

Morrill, R. 1989. Regional governance in the United States: For whom? *Environment and Planning C: Government and Policy* 7: 13–26.

Perry, G. 1988. Size as related to efficiency in United States counties. Masters Thesis, University of Washington.

Pisarski, A. 1987. *Commuting in America.* Westport, Conn.: Eno Foundation.

Platt, R. 1985. The farmland conversion debate. *Professional Geographer* 37: 432–42.

Real Estate Research Corporation for Department of Housing and Urban Development. 1974. *Costs of sprawl.* Washington, D.C.: Real Estate Research Corporation.

Richardson, H. 1988. Monocentric vs. polycentric models. *Annals of Regional Science* 22: 1–12.

Smith, D. M. 1979. Inner city deprivation. *Geoforum* 10: 297–310.

Urban Mass Transit Administration (UMTA). 1988. *Status of the nation's local mass transportation* (Report to Congress). Washington, D.C.: UMTA.

Walker, R., and M. Heiman. 1981. Quiet revolution for whom? *Annals of the Association of American Geographers* 71: 67–83.

Williams, P. 1982. Restructuring urban managerialism: Toward a political economy of urban allocation. *Environment and Planning A.* 14: 95–105.

TWO

A Metatheory of Urban Structure

Larry R. Ford

Over the past few decades social scientists have generally concentrated on developing universal theories and models to describe the processes and patterns of urbanization. An important and continuing dimension of geographic work, however, has been to differentiate cities and to speculate about the differing impacts of process on place. Although universal trends may be at work and universal theories may be used in order to understand those trends, urban places still differ. "American Metropolitan Evolution," for example, demonstrates concisely how the internal structure and landscape of American cities vary with era of establishment, growth, and functional specialization (Borchert 1967). Models of city structure should be modified to fit the exigencies of place if they are to tell the whole story. Similarly, "Major Control Points in American Economic Geography" uses capital accumulation and entrepreneurial aggressiveness to flesh out traditional notions of central place and entrepôt locations (Borchert 1978).

In this chapter I examine some of the trends and tendencies shaping American cities today, as well as some of the theoretical frameworks for understanding those trends. I also recognize that American cities are affected differentially. Place matters. More specifically, I hope to demonstrate, at least tentatively, some procedures for identifying differential trends that shape the internal structure of American cities. Eventually, given enough effort, classification systems of the type John Borchert has pioneered can be developed that could give important clues to the processes affecting city centers.

Borchert's argument that American cities vary internally with era and function still holds true, but it is clear that new trends have arisen over the past two decades. Although such epitomic cities as Charleston (South Carolina), Cleveland, and Phoenix are still classic sail/wagon, railroad/ industrial, and auto/amenity cities, respectively, the classification of other cities is more difficult. For example, some "younger" cities, such as Seattle and Dallas, are developing much stronger downtowns than older cities, such as Buffalo and Richmond. Central population densities in "new" cities, such as San Diego, however, sometimes greatly exceed those in much older cities, such as St. Louis (Ford 1988). Some of our stereotypes about teeming older cities and sprawling newer cities obviously no longer apply. At the same time, control points may be sending accumulated capital elsewhere to take advantage of hot real estate markets and other perceived opportunities at the expense of the local environment.

In dealing with such topics as trends in downtown office space and retailing and changes in inner-city population and housing, it is difficult to obtain accurate, meaningful, place-specific data without actually visiting a city, and even then it is sometimes frustrating. The census is out of date before it is published, and definitions of *downtown* vary greatly from city to city and over time. Aggregate data by central city and even by tract often mask differing trends and thus offer little insight into process. In addition, the areas of cities often vary so greatly as to make comparisons meaningless. Newark and Oklahoma City, for example, have roughly the same size populations, but Newark has only 24 square miles and Oklahoma City has 621. Studies monitoring change in central-city populations, therefore, are necessarily difficult to interpret. The problem of comparison is equally difficult when dealing with Standard Metropolitan Statistical Areas (SMSAs).

In order to begin at least to monitor the processes of change in inner-city housing supply and population, I identified "core areas" of roughly twelve square miles for ten American cities and examined changes in a number of characteristics between 1960 and 1980 (Table 2.1). In 1960, most of the traditional generalizations about inner-city population densities held true. The older, more compact cities of Boston, Buffalo, San Francisco, and St. Louis had far more people in their inner rings than did Seattle, Denver, San Diego, or Phoenix. In 1980, Boston and San Francisco remained high density, but Buffalo became more like Columbus, San Diego surpassed St. Louis, and Cleveland joined Phoenix as the least densely populated, although for very different reasons. Era was no longer a good predictor of internal structure.

These diverging trends have a wide variety of explanations. For example, cities with strong overall housing markets, such as San Francisco and San Diego, might be expected to have stronger core housing markets as well. Architecture might also play a role. Quaint, older housing in cities such as Boston and newer, modern housing in cities such as Denver both do better than "industrial era" housing in cities like Cleveland and St. Louis. Other

TABLE 2.1   Population and Housing Units in Core Areas of Selected Cities (in thousands)

	1960		1980	
	Population	Housing Units	Population	Housing Units
Boston	216	92	192	92
Buffalo	201	72	124	57
Cleveland	125	40	63	27
Columbus	162	54	104	44
Denver	125	57	88	52
Phoenix	76	31	57	26
St. Louis	200	72	88	41
San Diego	98	51	104	55
San Francisco	278	150	249	139
Seattle	113	63	84	56

factors, such as strength of the downtown job market and degree of ghettoization, are also important. Where do we start our analyses once comparable areas have been identified?

Even at the scale of twelve-square-mile core areas, however, overall trends masked important internal variations. In Columbus, for example, the core area included at least three different trends—massive decline in population and housing units in the heart of the black ghetto, modest population loss and housing unit stability in historic districts, and significant growth in housing units and population in the Ohio State University area. In addition, several thousand people were eliminated from the core-area population count with the closing of the Ohio State Penitentiary. Clearly such changes are not well described by the phrase "flight to the suburbs."

Similar interurban differences appear when we examine trends in downtown office space construction (Table 2.2). New York City remains the major control point and office center in the United States. More than 73 million square feet of office space were built in Manhattan between 1970 and 1983, in spite of a serious economic crisis in the mid-1970s, but the pattern beyond New York is complex (Pygman and Kately 1985). Some cities, such as Chicago, Houston, and San Francisco, have had immense amounts of office space constructed in gleaming downtown towers, but others, such as Miami and Detroit, have had relatively little. Still others, such as Akron and Fresno, have been skipped entirely by this boom. Skyline differences reflect this situation, as well as different proclivities for housing office space in monumental and expensive towers as opposed to more modest structures.

Once again, a myriad of explanations are possible. Major control points such as New York and Chicago might be expected to have massive skylines, but the situation elsewhere is complex. In some cases, era of growth is important. Older, traditional cities have more focused downtowns than have newer cities, such as Phoenix, regardless of the number of major firms located there. Neither the size of the metropolitan area nor the number of important corporations tells the whole story. In many cities, urban design policies have been developed and implemented which either encourage or discourage skyscraper construction and downtown redevelopment. Houston, for example, has encouraged skyscraper construction to show off its newfound "world city" status. Others, such as Washington, have discouraged it. Having the capital to play with is not enough. Downtowns are diverging, and no one explanation is adequate.

THE NEED FOR NEW THEORIES

Before we examine trends in the structure of urban core areas, it is useful to review the kinds of words, phrases, and perceptions we use when considering the American downtown. For example, we may have been missing the point due to our mode of analysis. We nearly always measure the success of downtown and the central city in general in terms of absolute and relative growth vis-à-vis the metropolitan area. We bemoan the fact that central cities have lost population and have only a minuscule percentage of total metropolitan retailing. We continue to refer to a Central Business District even though it obviously has become something else. We not only do not know what we have, we do not know what we want. We decry both teeming cities and population loss, unsightly mixed-industrial land uses and industrial decentralization, congested streets and empty streets, too little change and too much change. We need a bigger picture, a larger framework to which we can relate our findings.

TABLE 2.2   Number of Office Towers More Than 500 Feet Tall

New York	117
Chicago	31
Houston	26
San Francisco	15
Columbus	5
Detroit	3
St. Louis	3
San Diego	0
Phoenix	0

Three obvious obstacles to an understanding of American cities include (1) outdated models and perceptions, (2) the data explosion coupled with a need to be immediate and current, and (3) an overemphasis on demand-side interpretations, that is, the idea that trends develop as a direct result of existing demands—for suburban housing, shopping centers, and so on. The first has been much discussed, and I will not dwell upon the idea that many of our traditional models of urban structure were time-specific (and perhaps place-specific). The real problem is that we continue to see and to write about inner-city rings and sectors even when they may no longer exist. Worse, we may have contributed to a self-fulfilling prophecy. Sometimes the very institutions funding studies of "urban decay" were busy buying up the land in question (Fusch 1980). In the long run, social scientists may have been duped.

A second problem concerns the myopia that results from a felt need to analyze current data immediately, coupled with the incredible explosion in the availability of such data. I have called this a data explosion rather than an information explosion because it is often difficult to convert the former to the latter. One year Houston is booming, the next year it is declining—Sunbelts, Rustbelts, Frostbelts, and Matchbelts appear as possible explanations for trends that may actually be no more than short-term pulsations (Sawyers and Tabb 1984). Here, too, our analyses are constantly out of date or are premature. We need a bigger picture.

A third problem is our emphasis on demand-side interpretations of changes in urban structure. We need to devote more effort to understanding the role that, for example, housing reformers, religious leaders, appliance and automobile manufacturers, and others played in creating and selling the suburban dream. We also need to know more about the role that large corporations, civic leaders, and designers, from Daniel Burnham to Robert Moses, played in creating and selling the concept of what a proper downtown ought to be. Did people in the Boston of 1840 sit around saying "I would really like a house in the suburbs," or was the idea developed and sold to them? A supply-side orientation may make the development of theoretical frameworks more manageable.

THE POSTINDUSTRIAL TRANSFORMATION AND SOCIAL THEORY

A useful analogy for understanding the American city today is the medieval/baroque transition in European cities between the fifteenth and nineteenth centuries (Vance 1977, 1990). Cities that had evolved haphazardly and piecemeal with a variety of small spaces serving as workshops and centers of production were redesigned during the baroque transition as larger-scale, monumental places of display and consumption. From Florence to Bath, small buildings containing a mixture of artisans and merchants were replaced by palaces, city halls, and theaters. Tourism and conspicuous consumption played increasingly greater roles in the structure of cities such as Paris, Rome, and Bath. Much the same thing is occurring in American downtowns today. The central city is no longer a central business district based on maximum accessibility, but rather a center of display based on maximum visibility. Similarly, the inner city—at least in those cities going through this postindustrial transformation—is no longer a place for teeming masses laboring in the workaday world, but rather a place for "dazzling urbanites" to promenade and seek a style of living.

Just as in Haussmann's Paris, the scale and function of the American central city are changing. A qualitative change is difficult to monitor quantitatively—by total retail sales, for example. Although greatly speeded up by eighteenth-century European standards, the changes are nevertheless gradual, and short-term crises need to be viewed accordingly. Also, as in the baroque transition, the rate and direction of change in the postindustrial transformation are often controversial, and the purpose of change is suspect. The most oft-used justifications for change may not be the real underlying ones. Finally, as had happened in Europe centuries before, the uneven diffusion and acceptance of a new type of central city is serving to differentiate American cities. In the future, the classic industrial American city, along with the various attempts to model such places, may be seen as a brief aberration in the history of urban form. Paris was right.

An increasing number of social scientists, geographers among them, have realized the inadequacies of short-run attempts at description, modeling, and process analysis, and they have sought out long-run "cosmic" explanations such as Weberian structuralism and Marxism (e.g., Smith 1984; Smith and Williams 1986; Smith and Feagin 1987; Gregory and Urry 1985). In spite of the data explosion, however, much of the writing in these areas is data-thin, if not totally devoid of empirical testing. Still less of it is place- and time-specific enough to answer certain questions: Why now? Why Seattle? Geographers need to ask these questions.

Another problem with the development of theoretical frameworks for understanding real places is the lack of interaction and complementarity between the emerging frameworks. Some theoretical views emphasize internal elegance rather than empirical testing, and they essentially become belief systems that brook none of the confusion or complexity that could result from allying them with other modes of analysis. To be of maximum utility, theories should live up to the empirical testing associated with scientific advance, and they should complement and inspire the development of other theoretical approaches.

In recent years, several writers have begun to bemoan this state of affairs. Martin Cadwallader, for example, discusses the basic tenets, attributes, and weaknesses of Marxist, institutional, and behavioral perspectives and attempts to demonstrate the utility of combining them. Although many have argued that it is theoretically inconsistent to combine, say, Marxist and non-

Marxist approaches in order to employ some insights and not others, Cadwallader maintains that theoretical pluralism should be encouraged. He states that "by focusing on the interstices between the various approaches and emphasizing their complementarity, we can, however, begin to construct more thorough explanations of urban phenomena" (Cadwallader 1988, 228).

A vast literature discusses and debates the merits of the various theoretical approaches. One of the problems, in my view, is the lack of proposed applications of such theories. The emphasis on understanding the finer points and internal elegance of such approaches leads to diminishing returns as well as exclusionary tendencies—rather like current debates in Israel over who is a Jew. My purpose here is only to suggest some major trends in American city structure and to encourage a greater emphasis on hybrid theory in seeking explanations for those trends. In other words, I feel we should develop a better understanding of the linkages between levels and types of theory and between theory and place-specific contingencies.

A MODEL OF APPLIED HYBRID THEORY

Let us first ponder a schematic conceptualization of ways in which hybrid theory might be used to study particular places (Figure 2.1). There is a real danger in suggesting such a schema, because it could be viewed as an update of the "desk-drawer" approach used by some regional geographers earlier in the century (i.e., a little of this and a little of that). No one should attempt to do it all, but rather, by understanding the linkages, individual scholars should work toward complementary studies and cumulative results.

Attempts to describe the changing structure of any particular city should at least touch base with a variety of theoretical approaches instead of using one to the exclusion of all others. I have suggested three levels: macro, meso, and micro. In addition, we should recognize three levels of place-specific contingencies that can greatly modify processes of change—a touch of the realist approach. Let us work through the model in the abstract and then apply it to some particular cities. A scholar interested in a particular aspect of urban change, such as the construction of large apartment and condominium projects in a downtown area, could select approaches from the model.

At the macro level a scholar might use macroeconomics, Marxism, or any other approach that considers the economic or social structure affecting a city. Capital accumulation, capital circuits, international controls on capital flows, and class, gender, and racial divisions might be considered. Some cities are major control points that have accumulated immense amounts of capital through banking, insurance, and industrial endeavors. Some may be investing this capital locally while others may be "redlining" local endeavors and sending capital elsewhere. A few cities may be attracting significant foreign capital because of political, economic, or social contacts. Other cities may be largely devoid of capital investments for a wide variety of reasons. Similarly,

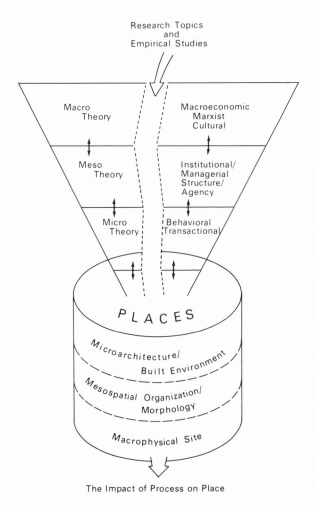

FIG. 2.1   Theory, place, and trends in central city structure.

racial and class divisions may channel capital to reproduce existing relations. We can no longer examine urban change as if it were locally driven and organized. We cannot understand Los Angeles without understanding Japanese investment in high-rise buildings. We cannot understand San Diego without acknowledging the flight of capital from the ailing Mexican peso to San Diego real estate. Similarly, we cannot understand Akron without recognizing that such things are not happening there.

We must realize that capital flows and circuits change over time. The crisis of consumption during the 1930s was largely ameliorated by suburban growth from the late 1940s to the early 1970s. People were sold houses, cars, lawnmowers, television sets, and other consumer goods, and low-interest loans were made available to facilitate such purchases. Surplus capital was easily absorbed and there was no reason to look toward the inner city. By the late 1970s some changes were afoot. The energy crises of the mid- and late 1970s took some of the bloom off the car culture, and the increasing cost of urban land, coupled with greater community resistance, slowed freeway construction. In existing suburbs, everyone already had plenty of televisions, cars, and lawnmowers. Capital sought new outlets, and the inner city was conveniently unredlined. Office towers, galleries, renovated warehouses and harbors, "quiche and spider plant" cafes, gentrified housing, and large condominium projects absorbed capital and redirected its secondary circuit. Quality art became de rigueur. Millions of dollars flowed into the embellishment of urban homes. As certain real estate markets became hot, foreign investors poured money into land and buildings regardless of local demand. All of this and much more has affected the internal structure of the American city in the 1980s. Theory at the macro level can help us understand when and why certain things are built—how the internal structure of the city is modified.

I am obviously not trying to provide a complete guide to Marxism, neoclassical economics, or anything else in this brief account. I am only suggesting that capital circuits have a tremendous role in differentiating some cities from others, and geographers need to pay more attention to theoretical approaches that help explain who controls change. Various theoretical approaches, including Marxism, can provide insights, especially if they are viewed as complementary to other approaches and not as internally elegant belief systems. Not all the macro variables are economic. Significant realities—for example, gender, race, and demographics—might also be considered, especially if they involve the definition of *labor* (i.e., are women and blacks participants in the consumer society and in the labor force?).

A problem with theory at the macro level is that it purposely excludes people—individual actors in the urban scene. Although certain forces may be leading us inexorably down one path or another, in reality, most such forces are controlled by real people who sometimes, if not always, have economically irrational and whimsical notions of what cities should be. Sometimes such people have considerable power. By adding meso approaches we can examine the increasing role (power) that various "managers" and "gatekeepers" have in directing urban change (that is, the "institutional" approach derived from Weberian sociology).

The number and type of urban managers change constantly. We have perhaps seen a deconcentration of power over the past few decades from highway engineers and urban renewal agencies to a wide variety of people involved in urban design, neighborhood revitalization, community control, and social services. Planners, politicians, community leaders, representatives of senior citizens, ethnic groups, homosexuals, real estate agents, merchants, and traffic engineers are all geared up to compete for attention and capital investment. In some cities, certain managers have tremendous power and authority and can direct change with a solid political base and a clear image of what the city should be. In other cities, a power vacuum may exist and no consensus image will have been formulated. Similarly, in some cities, the political system may encourage the dissemination of information to a wide variety of groups or classes. Still others may channel information selectively, through an established network.

Although *enlightenment* is difficult to define without opening up a Pandora's box of biases, it could be argued that new directions in urban change are at least partly a result of more mature, pro-urban training and policies associated with the managers. Lynch, Appleyard, and Jacobs have given some American planners and designers a better idea of what cities ought to be (Lynch 1960; 1972; and 1981; Appleyard 1976; Jacobs 1961). We could examine the diffusion of various ideas by the educational paths and contacts of major players in a particular urban scene as they relate to the topic under study (such as condominium construction). In short, we need better understanding of information flows as well as capital flows. By studying the backgrounds and biographies of those who have shaped the city, we can better understand differences between individually authored landscapes and those largely shaped by a more impersonal economic system (Samuels 1979).

Important movers and shakers, however, are not the only people involved in the life of the city. Individuals of all types and levels operate daily, and their mental constructs of how a city works are important. Micro theoretical approaches focus upon individual decision making and perceptions. Such approaches could be lumped together under the traditional heading of behavioral geography, although plenty of recent offshoots, such as transactionalism, can contribute to the effort (Aitken et al. 1989). Much of the literature on recent inner-city change, for example, has emphasized the emergence of "dazzling urbanites" who appreciate and want to be a part of urban revitalization. Often bunched together as yuppies or gentrifiers, those who move to large central-city condominium projects, for example, do so for a variety of reasons involving everything from self-image to access to work and cultural amenities. Theoretical constructs using such factors as cognitive distance, perception of environmental quality or danger, locational trade-offs, and landscape tastes can be employed. We need to know more about how people (as individuals) picture and use space—how they search for housing, where they re-create, how they develop neighborhood turfs, and how they move through and remember urban environments. How are urban subcultures created and reinforced at the individual level? How do certain people come to see that living and working in the center of the city makes more sense (for them) than do long commutes to suburban retreats? How do people become interested in certain modes of consumption—theater seats versus lawn chairs? How do people learn about cities? We know that cities have changed as they have become home for new kinds of people—college-educated, world-traveling professionals—but we speak of this change largely in the aggregate. We must study individual behavior to understand how people become aggregated into groups.

Although many scholars operate largely at one level, it is difficult to do so and really understand places. Individual real people inhabit the world, even though they may, in the aggregate, obtain information from gatekeepers in various ways and reproduce themselves unknowingly for the capitalist system. When we say "lots of new condos are going up in city X," the need for all three levels should be apparent.

It is hard to know what is going on in a particular city without some knowledge of its physical site, spatial organization, and architectural history. The lower section of the model (Figure 2.1) refers to the place-specific aspects of city structure as macro, meso, and micro. Perhaps the most "macro" aspect of a particular place is its physical setting. The description of physical site characteristics was long a mainstay of urban geography, especially in Europe, where the evolution of medieval cities was inextricably linked with topography. With industrial and modern cities came sluicing, terracing, and leveling, and urban geographers came to believe that sites were there to be conquered. Perhaps more important, the analysis of physical site came to be associated with environmental determinism, and it was meticulously excluded from most newer theoretical orientations. Site matters. It can be integrated with each of the three theoretical levels. For example, capital often flows to resources when scarcity ensures profitability. The incredible cost of land in Manhattan and San Francisco is related to scarcity, but the boom and bust real estate market in Houston is not. In Manhattan and San Francisco (and increasingly in Los Angeles, San Diego, and many other sites) capital flows to the construction of high-rise office and residential buildings regardless of short-term demand. All of this would seem too obvious to belabor if it had not been largely ignored in modern urban theory.

There are other attractive site characteristics aside from scarcity, however, and the roles played by individual actors (meso-level theory) in creating and selling site attractiveness are worth examining. Image making based on site characteristics played an important role in prompting people to move to cities like Los Angeles and Miami, and in getting them sorted out in intraurban space from Beverly Hills to Miami Beach. Individual entrepreneurs also played major roles in developing transportation and other infrastructural improvements that facilitated the selling of the "view" as an important American landscape taste. At the micro level, individual spatial behavior can also sometimes be related to site. At the most obvious level, the imageability of cities is almost always related to physical setting.

Similarly, all three levels of theory can be related to the morphology and architectural stock of cities. We cannot tell the stories of Boston and New York City without discussing the attachment of the elite to the Boston Common and Central Park. Studies of private and municipal investment strategies, the ideas of designers and planners, and the perceptions and transactions of individual users can all be employed productively. Architecture is also important (Relph 1987; Boyer 1985; Fusch and Ford 1983; Goss 1988). Particular styles have been intertwined, not only with the varying fates of neighborhoods, but with more basic aspects of the building stock as well. For example, compared to older, more compact European cities, American cities were initially underbuilt. That simple fact explains much. It explains why houses were overused as too many people, in order to be close to work, squeezed into them in lieu of larger apartment buildings. It explains investment strategies that encouraged the gradual decay of old houses as speculators awaited the possibility of higher and better uses. It explains the necessity for community organizations to battle for the preservation of certain types of urban housing, and it explains the perceptions of architectural disharmony, which are common when large apartments are put up in older neighborhoods. Different types of buildings have had different socioeconomic histories, a fact that has too often been ignored in urban theory (Fusch and Ford 1983).

In summary, various levels of theory must be used to examine unique aspects of places in order to uncover the processes affecting the internal structure of cities. More specifically, macro-, meso-, and micro-level theory can be applied in the analysis of the physical site, spatial organization, and architectural stock of a city in order to explain its transition toward postindustrial form.

STAGES IN THE TRANSFORMATION OF CITIES

I have arbitrarily identified four stages in the transformation of cities from industrial to postindustrial. San Francisco epitomizes the fourth and most mature stage.

San Francisco: Stage Four

During the baroque transition, some cities were gradually rebuilt at a larger and grander scale. Many of these cities, Paris and Vienna among them, are seen as having reached a stage of completion, and further massive change has been difficult or controversial. Most new construction in central Paris, for example, must conform to the height, bulk, and aesthetic characteristics of the "traditional" city, regardless of the demand for space (Kain 1981). Buildings that do not conform, such as the Pompidou Center, are unusual and controversial. In American cities, on the other hand, change has been constant and overwhelming. San Francisco may be the first large American city to reach a comparable level of completion, that is, to become a mature postindustrial city.

In order to illustrate some of the trends in San Francisco, I will concentrate on downtown dynamics and inner-city housing. I will not go through all of the theoretical considerations step by step, but I will simply describe some changes that are afoot in the city with theory implicitly embedded in my explanations.

Downtown San Francisco epitomizes the trend of restructuring the American economy toward businesses and professional services and away from manufacturing. Over the past three decades San Francisco has experienced a tremendous office building explosion, nearly all concentrated in the compact Central Business District (CBD). Seventy million square feet of downtown office space constitute the fourth largest concentration in the nation. The San Francisco skyline is a result of the creation and concentration of office jobs, the concentration of domestic and foreign capital in buildings, and urban design policies. None of this makes San Francisco unique; what is unique is its stage of completion.

A major problem with the American downtown over the past century has been indecision over where, in the central area, to put it. Lacking a permanent consensus core focused upon a cathedral or plaza, American CBDs have migrated considerable distances over time. This mobility has shaped our notions of what downtowns are, complete with zones of discard, zones of assimilation, skid rows, peak land value intersections (PLVIs), CBD extensions, and subcenters. As long as the CBD was free to roam, a constant expectation of change was focused on the possible abandonment of existing cores and the redevelopment of new centers. In San Francisco over the past century the CBD has moved from its point of inception near Portsmouth Square to Market Street, down Market Street, and then back to the north at California and Kearney.

The migration of downtown San Francisco has been stopped. A number of factors—such as the difficulty of the physical site, with the CBD enclosed by water and steep hills; the completion of massive urban renewal projects with non-CBD uses, such as the residential sections of the Golden Gateway Project; increasing community resistance to CBD expansion coupled with a political situation that gives power to such resistance; and a maturing sense of urban aesthetics that gives high priority to the preservation of small-scale historic architecture—all have played a role in hardening the boundaries between downtown and adjacent neighborhoods. The migration of downtown has been blocked in all directions, and there is no place to go but up.

Given the increasing scarcity of downtown space and the tremendous concentration of local (e.g., Bank of America) and foreign (Hong Kong and Japanese investments in property) capital, there would seem to be no limit to the number and height of towers that can be built. In San Francisco, however, the "urban managers" have gained considerable power. The 1971 Urban Design Plan for the city included strict height and bulk regulations. Office towers completed before 1972 remain the tallest and largest in the city (San

Francisco Dept. of Planning 1971). During the early 1980s, restrictions were gradually placed on the total amount of office space that could be constructed during a year—currently less than five hundred thousand square feet (less than half the size of the Bank of America Building)—and some of this space is reserved for small rehabilitation projects (ibid 1981). The managers, backed by much of the populace, have decided that the CBD is not only bounded, but full. New permits are based on an urban design competition, and only the best proposals are approved. In addition, the design guidelines require new buildings to have a tapered, pastel appearance that fits the accepted look of the city (the Paris syndrome?). The downtown and its skyline are nearing a stage of completion and permanence that change the dynamics of growth significantly. In recent years other American cities, from Boston to Seattle, have discussed whether the downtown area should be declared bounded and full. Such centers may house a decreasing percentage of total regional activity, and they are not really *the* central business districts any longer, but they are all that they can be or, perhaps, should be.

Although many of the new controls are based on infrastructural limits—transportation, water, trash removal—public pressure for limits has often revolved around the imageability and usability of downtown landmarks, nodes, and paths. When residents perceive too much change they become upset and take action. Social and aesthetic arguments have become more persuasive.

The neighborhoods just beyond downtown are also changing. The latest population estimates indicate that a number of American cities are now gaining people even if they have been unable to annex new territory—something that has not happened for forty years. Boston, New York, Chicago, and San Francisco, for example, are listed as having more people in 1986 than in 1980 (World Almanac 1989). If this trend continues, San Francisco will have nearly one hundred thousand more people in its forty-nine square miles at the 1990 census than it had in 1980. In neighborhoods close to downtown the turnaround is even more pronounced.

Americans assume that few people want to live in the inner city, and that they will flee to the suburbs given half a chance. Population statistics over the past three decades certainly support this notion, but some important supply-side factors have not been given adequate attention. Most American cities did not have appropriate urban housing until very recently—they were under-built and overused. Only a few of the largest cities had proper apartment buildings, and as recently as 1960 they were common only in New York (Ford 1986). In addition, since housing was lowest on the bid-rent totem pole, it was under continuous pressure for change in use or complete redevelopment. Houses built for single-family occupancy were often too small and space-extensive for a central-city location, and over the years they were converted to boarding houses, tenements, and businesses. Jerry-built additions in back-yards and over garages were also common. By the postwar years many of these houses were worn out and unattractive. There was no option but to leave the central city.

San Francisco has a relatively urban housing stock of row houses and apartment buildings from the early decades of the century. The city's central area population declined slowly relative to that of many large American cities. Still, few new housing units were constructed in and around downtown between 1950 and 1970, but a housing boom has begun in recent years. Since 1980, tens of thousands of new housing units have been constructed within a mile or two of the PLVI; the strict bounding of downtown coupled with the arrival of luxury condominiums have made housing the most profitable form of capital investment in most neighborhoods (San Francisco Dept. of Planning 1981). In spite of sky-high prices, the central city is being repopulated as new housing is provided. The socioeconomic status of the population is changing as well. Even ragged former single-room occupancy (SRO) hotels were being converted to luxury condos before a city ordinance controlled such conversions.

These housing and population changes have been described as gentrification by yuppies, but they go far beyond that. Housing change in San Francisco is a result of a hot California housing market, the physical site of the city, business connections and capital flows, government policies that encourage housing construction, deindustrialization and the recapturing of disamenity areas, changing ethnic relations, changing demographics, transportation developments, and a maturing urban aesthetic involving an appreciation of views, architecture, and human contact. San Francisco could thus be "explained," by using a variety of theoretical frameworks, as a city that has undergone the postindustrial transformation (perhaps along with Boston, Seattle, and New York City—or at least Manhattan).

San Diego: Stage Three

Some cities are restructuring their cores with comparatively little help from the office building boom. The redevelopment of the central city through the construction of office towers can be viewed as both demand-side and supply-side activity. The restructuring of the urban economy requires a certain amount of new space—prestige space that facilitates face-to-face interaction. Much office construction is supply-side, that is, corporations and developers create prestige buildings and then cajole potential occupants out of older space (often creating zones of discard in the process), but there is still a real demand for prestige space in cities such as San Francisco. In downtown housing and shopping, the demand-side dimension is less evident.

Although downtown San Diego has its share of medium-sized, speculative office buildings, the city has few corporate headquarters and no massive redevelopment schemes focused on office construction. With neither local nor international corporate patrons to invest in the center city, other options were needed. They were housing and amenities. Hence, downtown San Diego is being revitalized with an emphasis on supply-side amenities.

As recently as the mid-1970s, downtown San Diego was a marginal place. There were no department stores, few jobs, and the only residences were SRO hotels. Since then, the waterfront has been redesigned as a park, a marina, and a specialty shopping area. Part of the former skid row has been spruced up as the Gaslamp District. Much of the excess space in the under-built CBD is being developed for a variety of housing. Currently, nearly thirty projects are completed, under construction, or planned, with three thousand housing units ranging from new SRO hotels, rehabilitated loft structures, subsidized and unsubsidized apartments, and condominiums of every price. Downtown is gradually becoming a residential neighborhood.

The creation of downtown housing in San Diego was, at least during the initial stages, a totally supply-side endeavor, and one that illustrates nicely the institutional/managerial theoretical framework for understanding urban change. A group of planners and political leaders familiar with the works of Lynch, Appleyard, Jacobs, and others (indeed, Lynch and Appleyard were flown in for a quick appraisal of the urban scene in 1974), was determined to make downtown livable. At first, there were few takers. Land was cleared and units were constructed, but even at subsidized prices and interest rates most remained empty. Eventually the combination of a very hot housing market in San Diego and the continuous pushing of downtown as an amenity-filled and livable place by city planners has increased demand. Now most projects have waiting lists, and units are sold before they can be advertised. The image of downtown as a place to live has changed, and the downtown population is growing and diversifying. Everything snowballs; as low- and mid-rise housing begins to take up acres of downtown space, a perception of scarcity develops that makes property look better to office and hotel developers, especially if it is close to the waterfront. In addition, downtown property becomes increasingly attractive to, for example, wealthy Mexican nationals looking for a safe place to invest pesos.

Several other American cities have experienced significant downtown revitalization with a minimum of corporate towers. Chief among them are San Antonio and Cincinnati, although a number of smaller cities such as Charleston and Savannah have paved the way. Each city, however, has developed its own "shtick."

Columbus: Stage Two

The problem with downtown Columbus, as with most American cities, is that it is too extensive. The city has had its share of new office tower construction near the PLVI, but much of the area within the inner belt remains lightly developed. Only so much office space can be absorbed, and there is little demand for new, high-density housing because housing in the suburbs is affordable and accessible. Throughout most of the twentieth century, American downtowns spread along major streets in search of cheaper prestige locations. With the development of the skyscraper and vertical compaction, coupled with suburbanization, the downtown was simply too large. In order to harden the edges of downtown and thus eliminate the expectation of change that has threatened near-downtown neighborhoods for decades, Columbus planners, developers, and community groups have designed a series of massive gateways that signal clearly where downtown begins. Just beyond the gateways, historic preservation of older housing and commercial complexes has been encouraged through the formation of new ordinances and strong community-based leadership. Eventually these boundaries may create the sense of scarcity that has become common in California. There is still a lot of space to be developed, given the level of investment in the city, but the task is within the realm of possibility.

Cleveland, St. Louis, and Phoenix: Still at Stage One?

Most of our attempts to describe and analyze the problems of central cities have avoided important place-specific dimensions. For example, the core areas of St. Louis, Cleveland, and Phoenix have not progressed as far toward postindustrial maturity, but for very different reasons. In Cleveland, for example, the downtown has remained fairly vibrant, with much activity in a compact, well-defined space. More than eighty-eight thousand people worked in downtown Cleveland in 1980, making it one of the strongest CBDs in America. The central area is lightly populated primarily because huge areas are given over to industrial uses that are still seen as constituting a landscape of disamenity. In St. Louis, on the other hand, much of the downtown and the surrounding neighborhoods were cleared and depopulated as a direct result of political decisions—to clear the waterfront for the Arch, to clear neighborhoods for public housing, to clear the public housing, and so on. Vague forces such as regional restructuring and capitalism did not clear St. Louis; people did. In Phoenix, on the other hand, the lack of a consensus downtown site deterred the creation of a viable urban core. Massive efforts will be necessary if these cities are to experience the postindustrial transformation.

Geographers should develop a mutually supportive set of theoretical frameworks for understanding the processes shaping cities in general, and for understanding the processes that give each city unique characteristics. We should link three levels of theory and three levels of place-specific contingencies in order to differentiate, classify, and understand American cities. By viewing cities as progressing, in the long run, toward a postindustrial transformation, we can develop a meaningful purpose for linking these theories and contingencies.

ACKNOWLEDGMENTS

Research for this chapter was supported by NSF Grant no. SES87-20597, NIH Grant no. PHSEY07022-01, and a John Simon Guggenheim Foundation Fellowship.

REFERENCES

Aitken, S., S. Cutter, K. Foote, and J. Sell. 1989. Contemporary research in environmental perception and behavioral geography. In *Geography in America*. Edited by G. Gaile and C. Willmott. New York: Merrill Publishing.

Appleyard, D. 1976. *Planning a pluralist city: Conflicting realities in Cuidad Guyana*. Cambridge, Mass.: MIT Press.

Borchert, J. R. 1967. American metropolitan evolution. *Geographical Review* 57: 301–32.

———. 1978. Major control points in American economic geography. *Annals of the Association of American Geographers* 68: 214–32.

Boyer, C. 1985. *Manhattan manners*. New York: Rizzoli.

Cadwallader, M. 1988. Urban geography and social theory. *Urban Geography* 9: 227–51.

Ford, L. 1986. Multiunit housing in the American city. *Geographical Review* 76: 390–407.

———. 1988. Housing and inner city population change in Columbus and San Diego. *Yearbook, Association of Pacific Coast Geographers* 50: 105–15.

Fusch, R. 1980. A case of too many actors? Columbus. In *Back to the city*. Edited by S. B. Laska and D. Spain. New York: Pergamon Press. 156–72.

Fusch, R., and L. Ford. 1983. Architecture and the geography of the American city. *Geographical Review* 73: 324–40.

Goss, J. 1988. The built environment and social theory. *Professional Geographer* 40: 392–403.

Gregory, D., and J. Urry. 1985. *Social relations and spatial structures*. London: Macmillan.

Jacobs, Jane. 1961. *The death and life of great American cities*. New York: Random House.

Kain, R. 1981. *Planning for conservation*. London: Mansell.

Lynch, K. 1960. *The image of the city*. Cambridge, Mass.: MIT Press.

———. 1972. *What time is this place?* Cambridge, Mass.: MIT Press.

———. 1981. *A theory of good city form*. Cambridge, Mass.: MIT Press.

Pygman, J., and R. Kately. 1985. *Tall office buildings in the United States*. Washington, D.C.: Urban Land Institute.

Relph, T. 1987. *The modern urban landscape*. Baltimore: Johns Hopkins University Press.

Samuels, M. 1979. The biography of landscapes. In *The interpretation of ordinary landscapes*. Edited by D. W. Meinig. Oxford: Oxford University Press.

San Francisco Department of City Planning. 1971. *The urban design plan*.

———. 1981. *Guiding downtown development*.

Sawyers, L., and W. Tabb. 1984. *Sunbelt/snowbelt*. Oxford: Oxford University Press.

Smith, M. P. 1979. *The city and social theory*. New York: St. Martin's Press.

———. 1984. *Cities in transformation*. London: Sage Publications.

Smith, M. P., and J. Feagin. 1987. *The capitalist city*. Oxford: Basil Blackwell.
Smith, N., and P. Williams. 1986. *Gentrification of the city*. Boston: Allen and Unwin.
Vance, J. 1977. *This scene of man*. New York: Harper and Row.
———. 1990. *The Continuing City: Urban Morphology in Western Civilization*. Baltimore: Johns Hopkins University Press.
World almanac and book of facts 1989. New York: Pharos Books.

THREE

Long Waves in American Urban Evolution

Brian J. L. Berry

The transformation of the United States from a rural to an urban nation was not smoothly continuous. The urbanization curve is marked by a succession of surges (Figure 3.1). In a seminal article, John Borchert (1967) associated these surges with the emergence of successive transportation technologies and energy sources that produced well-marked epochs of urban evolution and regional growth: (1) Before 1830, the location and spread of cities was primarily influenced by wagon and sail technology. Eastern seaports dominated, and centers rising in importance were on the inland waterways. (2) From 1830 to 1870, the rivers and canals, the steamboat and the iron-based railroad were the dominant innovations. Ports with large rail territories grew to dominance. (3) Between 1870 and 1920, the major influences were the steel rail and the ocean-going vessel, combined with industrialization. The Northeastern Industrial Belt lay at the heart of a national rail network, with processing centers at rail nodes. (4) After 1920, cities were reshaped by the automobile while air travel and long-distance communications began to recast regional relationships.

Subsequent authors have modified the Borchert scheme. For example, Edgar S. Dunn, Jr. (1980), hypothesized five rather than four evolutionary epochs, although he retained the central idea that technological change is the driving force: (1) Before 1780, a European growth impulse established mercantile centers as trading outposts along the Atlantic seaboard. Their growth was based on the clipper fleet. (2) Between 1780 and 1840, population, commercialized agriculture, and trade were extended into the interior by river boats and barges on navigable waterways. (3) Between 1840 and 1870, steam was applied to the development of a national transport system, and the cost of transport dropped dramatically. (4) Between 1870 and 1910, railroads replaced inland waterways as the major determinant of urban growth. Large-scale manufacturing became an alternative to commerce in city building, and the American Manufacturing Belt took form. (5) Between 1910 and 1940, urban regions were reorganized internally by electric power, automobiles, and trucks. Streetcars created radial extensions from urban cores.

Others have focused on particular transitions. Of special consequence for this chapter is Richard Walker's (1978) essay on the transformation of U.S. urban structure in the 1840s. Walker argues that the period from 1790 to 1842 was an epoch of "presuburban cities at the petty commodity mercantile stage of accumulation" (Walker 1978, 173). The principal sources of the nation's economic growth were southern cotton, western settlement, and mercantile fortunes made in international trade. An overwhelmingly rural society had only a few large trading centers. These centers were predominantly "walking cities," with little reason for space between work and home, between social classes, or between races. There was little functional separation of land uses, production was uncentralized, and there was little social segregation. The only foci of activity were ports and docks, and desirability of location decreased with increasing distance from the center, where churches, public buildings, and the homes of the most prominent citizens were clustered. To be sure, scattered dam-site mill towns were built in the 1820s and 1830s as the domestic textile industry grew, bringing a different building

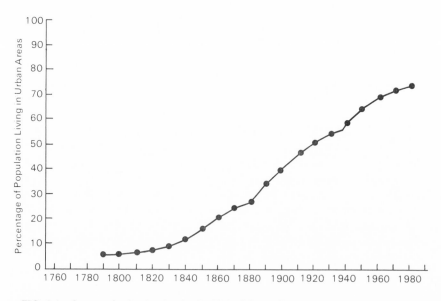

FIG. 3.1 Surges of urbanization in the United States between 1790 and 1980.

pattern and a largely paternalistic social order, but it was the growth of the manufacturing economy in the period 1842–96 that transformed urban structure. Manufacturing replaced cotton as the nation's leading growth sector in the years between 1842 and 1859, and as the full U.S. Industrial Revolution unfolded the national market was broadened by canals and railroads, factory organization of production beyond the textile industry, and the replacement of a self-sustaining peasant economy by commercialized agriculture. Accompanying urban impacts included concentration of production and circulation around central business districts, separation and specialization of land uses, and the outward thrust of residential areas of the high-status groups, first to country seats and later to garden suburbs, leaving behind the working classes in the inner city. With prescience, Walker (1978) argued that

> two major cycles can be discerned from the multitude of lesser fluxes and general "background noise" in the business climate. The first cycle is that of the Kuznets waves, lasting from fifteen to twenty-five years. It has been identified in a wide variety of economic indicators and by a wide assemblage of eminent economists and other investigators. The second, and more controversial, period of growth is the fifty- to seventy-year movement first discerned by Kondratiev for which I prefer the name "stage of accumulation." (170–71)

The periods 1780–1842 and 1842–96 were, Walker argues, successive Kondratiev waves, each with a distinctive style of urbanization, and with the transition between them occurring in the "Kondratiev trough" of the mid-1840s.

> The era centering around 1840 marked a dramatic hastening of capitalist industrialization which deserves to be recognized as a qualitative shift in the mode of production from a domination by petty commodity production to domination by modern industry. Coinciding with this came the change from an urbanism made up of mill towns and mercantile ports to one characterized by the classic industrial city. Focusing on this pivotal era allows us to see more clearly that the pattern of urbanization in this country has not been a smooth evolution to the conditions of the present, but has been marked by major transformations from one kind of city to another. (1978, 203)

The Kondratiev wave idea is of particular importance. "A finer lens," Walker says, should "force us to look further at the steps of development marked out by the Kuznets cycle, without which the story must necessarily sound hollow" (Walker 1978, 171). Walker is unable to make this extension, which I have accomplished in my work on long waves (Berry 1991). This chapter summarizes the knowledge of synchronous Kondratiev-Kuznets fluctuations.

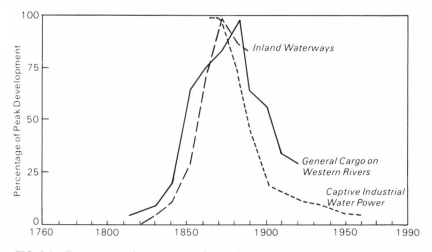

FIG. 3.2 Expansion and contraction of waterborne transportation and industrial waterpower.

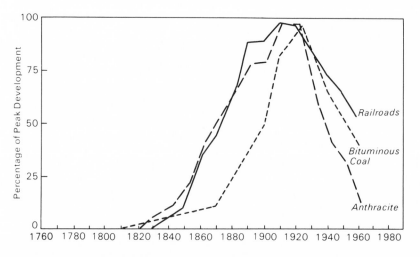

FIG. 3.3 Growth and decline of railroads and coal mining.

THE DRIVING FORCE OF TECHNOLOGICAL INNOVATIONS

No one disagrees that technological innovation is the principal mechanism underlying the successive epochs of urban evolution. In the words of Becker, Mills, and Williamson, "The central engine of city growth is not the

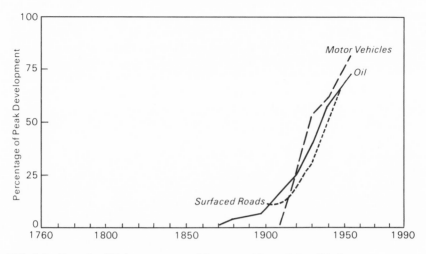

FIG. 3.4   Growth of highways, automobile ownership, and the oil industry.

demand side through Engel's effects but rather the supply side through unbalanced productivity advance. Whenever productivity advance is strongly prourban biased, a disproportionately large share of the new jobs are urban, immigration responds, and city growth takes place" (1986, 30).

Borchert supported his formulation with graphs that showed the deployment and ultimate replacement of each major transportation mode and energy source. Development of the inland waterways and western rivers, together with industrial use of captive waterpower accelerated in the early decades of the nineteenth century, slowed down after mid-century, reached maximum extent soon after the Civil War, and declined thereafter (Figure 3.2). Railroad development and coal use began in earnest after the 1840s, accelerated into the last decades of the nineteenth century, peaked soon after World War I, and declined thereafter (Figure 3.3). Surfaced road development and use of petroleum began in the late nineteenth century, but the real acceleration came in the 1920s, and the process was not ended when Borchert wrote his essay (Figure 3.4). Later evidence reveals that highway deployment and petroleum usage did not peak until after the Vietnam War (Figure 3.5).

Successive technologies ascended in the late nineteenth century, when coal-railroad deployment surpassed water usage, and at mid-twentieth century, when the internal combustion economy surpassed coal-railroad deployment (Figure 3.6). Borchert dated his epochs to begin, as they should, well in advance of these successions, because the acceleration phase of new technology deployment precedes dominance, and the force of transformation has the greatest vigor in this acceleration phase.

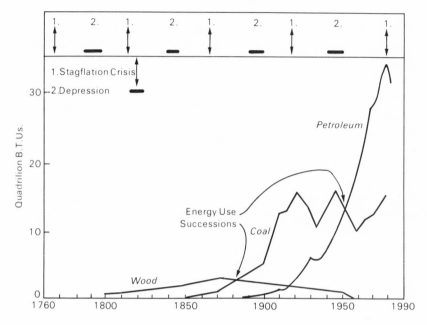

FIG. 3.5   Successions of energy use in relation to stagflation crises and depressions.

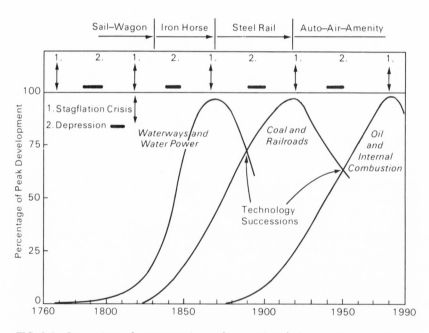

FIG. 3.6   Successions of transportation and energy in relation to economic crises and Borchert's epochs of American metropolitan evolution.

THE TIMING OF TECHNOLOGICAL CHANGE

If the epochal transitions are technology-driven, what determines the timing of technological change? There is a tantalizing hint in the fact that the growth of each successive technology began to accelerate after one of the nation's major stagflation crises (Figures 3.5 and 3.6). These crises have recurred at roughly fifty-five-year intervals: 1814–15, 1864–65, 1919–20, 1980–81. Each reached peak deployment in the subsequent stagflation crisis. Technology and energy-use successions occurred during major depressions, which also occurred at roughly fifty-five-year intervals, halfway between the stagflation crises, in the 1840s, the 1890s, and the 1930s. There is apparently a relationship to the longer rhythms of economic growth—to the fifty-five-year Kondratiev waves, and perhaps to the twenty-five- to thirty-year Kuznets cycles that occur in the intervals between each stagflation crisis and depression. What is this relationship? What does it tell us about technological growth and succession? These are the questions that I probe in order to generate a long-wave theory of technology successions and urban growth that is a logical outcome of Borchert's pioneering work.

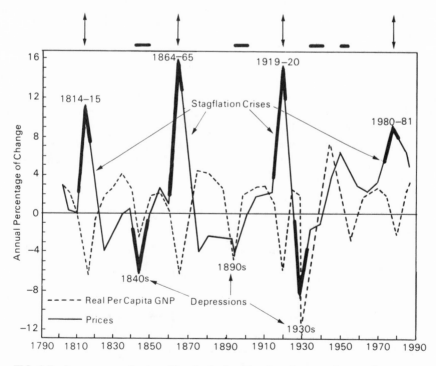

FIG. 3.7   Long waves of prices (Kondratiev) and cycles of economic growth (Kuznets) in relation to stagflation crises and depressions.

Long-Wave Rhythms

Two interdependent rhythms are revealed if the average annual growth rates of U.S. wholesale prices and of changes in real per capita gross national product are computed from 1790 to the present and if the shorter fluctuations of seven- to eleven-year Juglar cycles and three- to four-year Kitchin cycles are smoothed out with a ten-year moving average (Figure 3.7).

Price increases accelerate to reach maximum rates of inflation in the years 1814–15, 1864–65, 1919–20, and 1980–81, and slide from these peaks to reach maximum rates of deflation in the 1840s, the 1980s, and the 1930s. Each trough-peak-trough segment averages fifty-five years, and is named a *Kondratiev wave* after Nikolai Kondratiev, the first scholar to study the phenomenon systematically.

Growth fluctuates with a rhythm that is twice as fast as the fifty-five-year Kondratiev wave. The growth rate is at a maximum midway between every peak and trough of prices. Each price peak and price trough coincides with a trough on a growth cycle. The growth cycles thus average twenty-five to thirty years. They are named *Kuznets cycles* after Simon Kuznets, who was the first to identify them. Richard Walker wrote that each Kuznets cycle in the nineteenth century repeated a "familiar mode of growth: steadily expanding output capped by a burst of overaccumulation showing up as: fixed capital formation; especially intense railroad building and residential construction; land speculation; pyramiding of credit; and, finally, a financial panic led in every case by a failure of railroad securities. The expansion of output was associated with rapid population growth, the assimilation of waves of new migrants from farms and foreign lands, and growth of the industrial wage labor force (which was increasingly employed in factories and located in cities)" (Walker 1978, 184) (Figure 3.8). Kondratiev waves and Kuznets cycles are synchronized in alternating stagflation crises—when inflation rates are at a maximum but the economy is in a growth trough—and deflationary depressions—when a growth trough coincides with a Kondratiev trough (Figure 3.9).

For convenience, I will call the growth cycles running upwave from depressions to stagflation crises Type-A Kuznets cycles, and those running

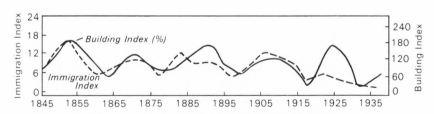

FIG. 3.8   Kuznets cycles in waves of immigration and city building.

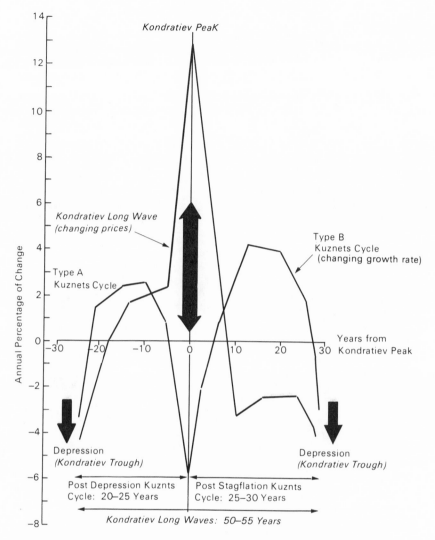

FIG. 3.9   Schematic relationship of Kondratiev waves and Kuznets cycles from one depression to the next, with a stagflation crisis between the two depressions.

downwave from stagflation crises to depressions Type-B Kuznets cycles. Type-A growth takes place in an inflationary environment. Type-B growth is deflationary. Because the deflationary growth involved high rates of innovation and technical progress, American historians have given distinctive names to the upswings of the Type-B cycles: The Era of Good Feelings (1815–25), the Gilded Age (1863–73), the Roaring Twenties (1921–28), and the Reagan Era (1982–88).

The Long-Wave Clock

Another way of appreciating the synchronized cyclicity of prices and growth is in the form of a long-wave clock (Figure 3.10). This clock not only combines the dynamics of Kondratiev waves and Kuznets cycles; it also includes the rhythms of the stock market (Dow Jones (DJ)) averages. At "high noon" in a Kondratiev-peak stagflation crisis, a deflationary Type-B growth cycle begins. It accelerates during the next decade to a peak that is signaled by the crash of a long bull market. As growth rates top out, a financial crisis is accompanied by a turning-point recession that ends in a DJ trough, shifting the economy from acceleration to deceleration. During this growth deceleration a secondary price recovery is accompanied by a modest bull market that peaks and crashes as the recovery runs out of steam. Growth, prices, and

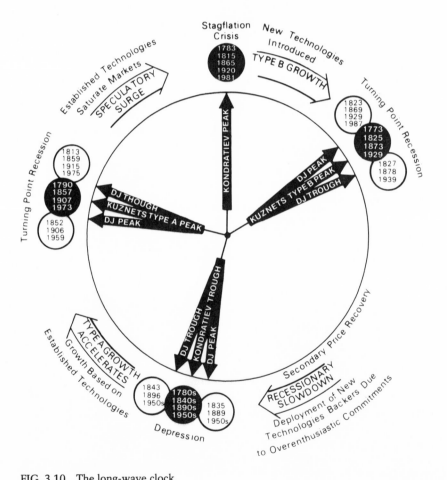

FIG. 3.10 The long-wave clock.

stocks then slide in a synchronous descent into a depression. The time from stagflation peak to depression trough is twenty-five to thirty years.

The end of the depression is signaled by another DJ trough. Growth, prices, and the stock market then accelerate upward with the onset of a Type-A growth cycle. The end of the acceleration phase of this cycle is again signaled by a stock market peak. Once again, there is a financial crisis and a turning-point recession as the economy shifts from acceleration to deceleration. The end of the recession is marked by another DJ trough, but at this juncture prices begin a speculatory surge as growth sags. The forces leading to another stagflation crisis are set in motion. That crisis occurs some twenty-five years after the trough depression, after which another long wave begins.

The whole cycle takes an average of fifty-five years, and involves the repetitive sequence: Kondratiev peak; Type-B Kuznets growth acceleration, turning-point crisis and deceleration; Kondratiev trough; and Type-A Kuznets growth acceleration, turning-point crisis, and deceleration. What is important for this discussion is the relationship to technological change. Technological advances have been concentrated in Type-B Kuznets cycles:

1815–25; 1825–42	Canal construction; steamboat invented; mill towns built; surge of textile production; embryonic railroad development; telegraph and undersea cable invented.
1865–73; 1873–96	Street and electric railways introduced; steel, chemicals, and electricity industries emerge; skyscrapers, elevator, telephone invented.
1920–28; 1928–54	Wave of automobile growth and highway development; aircraft industry and airlines develop; electronics industries (sound films, television, FM radio, xerography, radar, the computer) emerge, as does broadcasting.
1982–	Personal computer, photonics, and fiberoptic networks emerge; growth of biotechnologies.

On the other hand, growth in Type-A Kuznets cycles has arisen from deployment of established technological initiatives:

1842–57; 1857–65	Fifty percent of national railroad network built; manufacturing replaces cotton as nation's leading growth sector.
1896–1907; 1907–20	Street and electric railways built; coal-steel-railroad economy advances to peak deployment.
1954–73; 1973–81	Interstate highway system built; jet aircraft reinforce growth of national and international airline network.

A THEORY OF THE LONG WAVE

What accounts for these Type-B:Type-A contrasts in technological progress, and therefore of the technology transitions that have produced successive epochs of urban evolution? This chapter is a simple overview of the fuller development of the explanatory long-wave theory that appears in *Long-Wave Rhythms in Economic Development and Political Behavior* (Berry 1991). The whole process is endogenous (i.e., internally determined); each phase of the cycle is a consequence of the phases that have preceded it. I begin the sequential description at one of the junctures where there is clear and unambiguous synchronicity.

Synchronization in the Depression

Growth, prices, and the stock market are synchronized when they reach their maximum rates of decline in a severe depression. Old industries serving saturated markets have been in decline since the last stagflation crisis; in the depression, their remaining excess capital is pruned through plant closures and physical depreciation. Excess debt load in new growth industries is cleared out by the defaults and bankruptcies of those least able to survive extreme price competition, but these new growth industries clearly now dominate as sources of future growth. Commodity prices and land values are at their nadir. There is a banking crisis as loans made on the basis of inflated asset values cannot be repaid. Unemployment soars, real-estate markets are saturated, rents and property values decline, and real wealth shrinks along with the value of assets. Because investors overreact, excessive pessimism leads to underestimation of needs, and the stage is set for change—a simultaneous upturn of growth, prices, and the stock market.

Type-A Growth Acceleration

The turnaround comes as those who have survived the crash see assets that can be acquired at bargain-basement prices, and as newly elected public officials seek ways of alleviating distress and getting the economy moving again by addressing problems of rock-bottom prices, massive unemployment, excess capacity, and insufficient demand. As orders increase, existing machines are put back into operation, underutilized resources are brought back into use, and the slack in the economy is reduced. With portfolios and asset values at their nadir, little capital is available for venturing. Businesspeople disavow the search for new alternatives that had characterized the previous growth surge, preferring the security of the products and technologies proven by that surge's innovators and entrepreneurs. The venturers' question of marketability does not arise. Thus, the growth that takes place is not in the older industries and technologies that had reached market saturation a quarter-century earlier. It is in the industries and technologies that experienced their first significant burst of growth after the stagflation crisis, and were confirmed as the leading edge of the economy by the pruning effect of the depression, but for which growth opportunities have not yet been exhausted. Thus begins a Type-A growth cycle.

Increased utilization of existing capital stock results in rising profits, and the prospect of future profits attracts credit and produces orders for new capital equipment. As empty space is filled, rents rise and plans are laid for new building. As the upturn continues, growth moves ahead of prices. Both are led by growing confidence about the future, expressed in a rising stock market. Improving fortunes in the regions housing the new-wave industries signal opportunities to migrants, and an infrastructure and building boom begins.

As the upsurge continues, consumer goods industries expand and further stimulate growth of the capital goods sector. Demand begins to move ahead of supply, and pressure on resources and labor begins to push up prices and wages. Prosperity returns to agriculture and to raw materials producers. With further price increases, competition heats up for control of high-cost resources in inferior deposits or in more remote areas. Wage pressure produces filtering: more workers are drawn into the labor market and occupational mobility increases. Rising labor costs promote adoption of labor-saving technologies and stimulate growth among producers of these technologies. Labor-intensive industries relocate to low-wage areas and contribute to their economic growth.

The boom is lengthy. It is generalized among industrial, agricultural, and raw material producing areas, and reaches down into the labor market. Type-A growth cycles last for some twenty years. An initial fifteen years see progressive acceleration of the rate of economic growth, moving well ahead of the rate of growth of prices. Stimulus is provided by a general expansion of credit, justified by growth and rising asset values. Lags between capital orders and completion produce profit signals that result in upwave optimism and additional investment. The public mood becomes enthusiastic, upbeat, "can do," and expansionary. Growth justifies further growth. Opportunity seems unlimited.

This growth acceleration does finally come to an end, however, as new capital stock comes on line and begins to erode profits. The stock market senses the change, peaks, and then begins to decelerate. Capital orders are cut back. Companies whose investments were financed by more expensive capital are unable to meet their commitments, and the bad loans result in a banking crisis and a turning-point recession. Yet the boom psychology persists among investors. A change in the upwave dynamic occurs as mass psychology becomes the driving force behind aggrandizement. Optimism about investment opportunities switches from the growth industries and the stock market to a search for credit-financed profits in scarce commodities and in physical assets such as land. Profits are assured by rising prices driven by the demand pressures made possible by easy credit. The stage is set for a speculatory surge.

The Speculatory Surge

Speculation first occurs in the growth industries and in the stock market. Signs of a profits squeeze appear as excessive new capital commitments come on line. Speculation then shifts from production to land and property markets and from stocks to commodities as continuing—albeit slower—growth leads to resource shortages and rising prices.

The agenda shifts to expansion into new markets as existing markets are saturated, and to the control of resources as scarcities drive up prices. Resource contention among the major powers makes this the most war-prone epoch of the cycle. Initially, the atmosphere is one of personal satisfaction and generalized prosperity, but speculators' gains grow at the expense of ordinary workers, and inequality increases.

Public leaders take a more aggressive stance, and private greed is fed by spending that increases the money supply, nominal incomes, prices, and profits. Such spending, justified when demand had to be stimulated, fires inflation when the slack in the economy is long past. Speculative gains become self-fulfilling prophecies, and inflation is kicked into full gear, fed by additional borrowing justified by inflationary gains. Speculators leverage to the limit. Greed leads some to feed the spiral further by "kiting" schemes, but contention for loanable funds drives up interest rates, and this in turn drives up the cost of capital, drying up investment. A full-blown stagflationary spiral results, in which all of the worst of excessively rapid acquisition of new wealth is manifest: arrogance, self-righteousness, materialism, and corruption. It is at this time that the nation is most likely to go to war, and the resulting deficit spending to finance war expenditures provides the final impetus to the stagflationary spiral.

The Stagflation Crisis

During the stagflation crisis the economy grinds to a halt. There is nothing left in which to speculate. Bank failures accompany the crisis, many the result of swindles promoted by greed. Once again a group of growth industries have saturated their markets. Cost and wage inflation have driven up prices and eroded the values of fixed incomes and assets. The party in power is defeated and replaced by political leaders who promise to cure inflation, to get the economy back on track and the government out of the economy, and to foster traditional values. Money supply and credit contract sharply. With the economy in the doldrums, prices and wages come tumbling down. Agricultural regions and raw materials producers are severely affected. Many investors' bank accounts are full, but speculatory profits in commodity and land markets have been wiped out. Unemployment shoots up. Defaults mount in housing and property markets. Opportunity vanishes, growing numbers of families drop beneath the poverty line, and homelessness increases. For many, it is the worst of times.

Type-B Growth Acceleration

The solution comes because investors' bank accounts are full. As interest rates fall, the search for investment alternatives turns back to industry and to stocks, but profits have vanished in the main growth sectors of the recently ended cycle; instead, saturated markets and excess physical capital result in plant closings and bankruptcies. A venture-capital industry emerges as investors look for profit opportunities in new and untried technologies: the available pool is the accumulated stock of unexploited inventions, experiments, and early trials. Declining costs, including the lower capital costs made possible by falling interest rates, permit experiments that hold out the possibility of substantial gains, although venture capitalists know that perhaps one in ten of their carefully selected investments will succeed. The growth that begins to unfold is concentrated in the new technologies that effectively substitute for older industries, overcome infrastructure constraints or resource scarcities, or open up new markets. Older industrial regions continue to decline along with the raw materials producers who supplied them. Agriculture is particularly depressed; farmers are unable to meet obligations as commodity prices and the value of land decline.

The initial products are experimental and high cost. Those that attract attention are quickly routinized and imitated. Costs and prices come tumbling down as supply moves out more rapidly than demand. Almost the entire ten- to twelve-year period of growth acceleration is also one of disinflation or deflation. Demand increases first for technically sophisticated workers who can design and maintain the new systems. Rapid deskilling also increases demand for minimum-wage workers who can perform the tasks left for humans. A dual labor market results. There are demands for the highly skilled and for the unskilled, but not for workers in the middle range. At the first sign of pressure on the minimum wage, labor-intensive industries move to low-wage regions. The investment sequence is repeated: high profits attract investment; there are lags between capital orders and deliveries, so profits signal opportunities to new investors for some time after decisions have been made to add capacity that will erode profits. The result is investor overshoot. New jobs and rising incomes in new regions signal opportunity to prospective migrants. There is an infrastructure- and property-building boom that also ends in overshoot.

The entire Type-B growth acceleration is led by an enthusiastic bull market that gets caught in its own speculative frenzy before a crash that signals the bottoming-out of price declines and the topping-out of the growth upswing. There is the usual banking and financial market crisis at the turning point. The growth impulses benefit investors rather than workers, whose earnings have been under considerable pressure, and the prevailing attitudes turn from conservatism to protectionism. Narrower self-interest comes to dominate both the public and the private agenda. Untoward protectionist intervention during the crisis can be disastrous: the Smoot-Hawley Tariff Act of 1930, together with the Fed's restrictive monetary policy, helped kick the 1929 turning-point recession into the Great Depression.

Secondary Price Recovery

Absent panic intervention, decline is not immediate. The transition is gradual. Although the growth rate slows, there is another ten to fifteen years of slackening economic expansion. A secondary recovery of prices and the stock market begins when resource contention develops for the materials demanded by the new growth technologies.

Downwave Psychology Takes Over

Downwave psychology finally takes over. Declining growth pulls down prices and the market in a synchronized descent from the doldrums into a depression. The final coup de grace is administered to older industries and technologies as the newly adopted set of mutually supporting infrastructure and energy technologies rejects alternatives. These "gales of creative destruction" are central to economic development. The next Type-A growth acceleration will begin in these new technologies.

And begin a new cycle will. As Nikolai Kondratiev wrote in his original paper on long waves: "each consecutive phase is a result of the cumulative process during the preceding phase, and as long as the principles of the capitalist economy are conserved, each new cycle follows its predecessor with the same regularity with which the different phases succeed each other" (Kondratiev 1984, 99). Long waves result from accelerations and decelerations in the rate of economic growth; they embody synchronized twenty-five-to thirty-year Kuznets and fifty-five-year Kondratiev rhythms; at work is a complex drive oscillator whose frequencies are harmonics of Kondratiev waves and Kuznets cycles.

DISCUSSION

Embedded in my theorized description are two important ideas: (1) growth impulses come in quarter-century swings, and (2) infrastructure and capital equipment accumulate and are ultimately replaced with fifty-five-year Kondratiev phasing.

Walter Isard (1942) was the first to point out the twenty-five-year transport-building cycles between 1830 and 1933 (Table 3.1). These are readily recognizable as Kuznets cycles (Figure 3.8), with the exception of 1864–78 and 1878–1900, which are a single cycle. The first cycle witnessed the emergence of the canal. Canal construction surged around 1825 with the completion of the Erie Canal, reached a peak in the early thirties, and continued until the early forties. The next three cycles were associated with the irregular emergence of the railroad network. Railways were embryonic from 1830 to 1843, but beginning in 1843 construction of track increased rapidly to a peak in 1856, after which it slumped and touched bottom in 1861. The next two surges were in the 1860s and 1880s. The next transport innovation was the street and electric railway, which started to develop rapidly in the late 1880s, was checked by the depression of the 1890s, accelerated after 1897, reached a peak around 1906, and thereafter declined. The last cycle before the Great Depression was the first wave of automobile growth, beginning in 1918, peaking in 1925, and falling to a trough in 1932.

Many related series have similar swings. There were strong waves of foreign immigration between 1830 and 1930 (Table 3.2). City building was not smooth and uniform, but occurred in a similar series of growth impulses, as evidenced by the composite indexes of construction and of real estate activity (Table 3.3). The periodicity of growth is that of the Kuznets cycle. The upswings and downswings in growth of real per capita GNP (Figure 3.7) have been the outcome of waves of transport and city building, of population growth, and of industrial production, moving in harmony and synchronized by periodic depressions.

The pattern of the technology- and infrastructure-accumulation curves (Figure 3.6) is a five-phase product life cycle in which the phases are introduction (innovation), growth, maturity, saturation, and decline (Figure 3.11). These S-shaped life cycles can be fitted with logistic curves that yield both the

TABLE 3.1   Transport-Building Cycles

	Trough	Peak	Trough	
Before	1830	1836	1843	Canal construction
	1864	1871	1878	Railroads 2
	1878	1890	1900	Railroads 3
	1900	1909	1918	Street and electric railways
	1918	1925	1933	Automobile 1

TABLE 3.2   Cycles of Immigration

Trough	Peak	Trough
1844	1854	1862
1862	1873	1878
1878	1892	1898
1898	1907	1918
1918	1921	1933

TABLE 3.3   Cycles of City Building

Trough	Peak	Trough
1825	1837	1843–44
1843–44	1852–53	1861–64
1861–64	1871–72	1878
1878	1889–91	1897–99
1897–99	1905–7	1918–19
1918–19	1925	1933

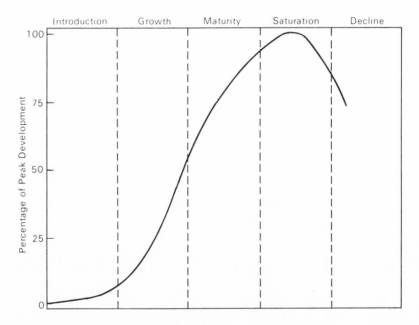

FIG. 3.11   A five-phase product life cycle.

saturation points and what some technology-forecasting mavens call "time constants" (the time required to go from 10 to 90 percent of the saturation level). Time constants of fifty-four to fifty-nine years have been calculated for U.S. railroad development, construction of the Western Union telegraph system, building of the surfaced road network, and crude oil, petroleum, and natural gas pipeline systems. Each of these major infrastructures was built between a stagflation crisis and a depression in the second half of a Kondratiev wave by a Type-B Kuznets cycle. The time from saturation to technological succession lasted another twenty-five to thirty years, during a second Type-B Kuznets cycle, as the old technology faded under the onslaught of the accelerated growth of a new technology. Type-B growth cycles are dominated by investment in new technological alternatives. Type-A cycles push established alternatives to market saturation. After the stagflation crisis, the market-saturated technologies decline: newer technologies then take over, offering investment opportunities that have been exhausted in the older lines. The market-domination crossover comes in the following depression, when the new technological alternative substitutes for the old.

Borchert was prescient when he associated the major epochs of urban evolution with successive periods of new-technology growth and of technological succession. His epochs are recognizably related to the long-wave rhythms. New technologies move from growth upswing following one stagflation crisis to market saturation fifty-five years later, following the next. These crisis-to-crisis intervals are the boundaries between Borchert's urban growth epochs, as they should be if the transforming force of new-technology growth is important.

Likewise for Walker's essay. After a quarter century of growth, new technologies force aside the old in a depression, dominate markets, set the agenda for a full long wave, and are forced aside in turn by yet newer technologies fifty-five years later in the next depression. This kind of depression-era transition is the basis of Walker's essay on the nineteenth-century transformation of urban structure. His essay, too, is recognizably long-wave in character.

Dunn's hypothesized epochs present problems. His second epoch does run between the depressions of the 1780s and the 1840s. The next two epochs were a barely recognizable 1840–70 and 1870–1910, however. Charitably, 1870 is close to the turning point on the 1865–73/1873–96 Type-B Kuznets cycle and 1910 is close to the turning point on the 1896–1907/1907–20 Type-A Kuznets cycle, but he dated his fifth epoch 1910–40, the end of which is unidentifiable as a turning point on the next (1920–1929/1929–54) Type-B cycle. Dunn simply got his technology history wrong. Economic development has been marked by twenty-five-year growth cycles and fifty-five-year price waves and technology transitions. To recognize this reality is to acknowledge, as Borchert did, the technological bases of the distinctive epochs of American urban evolution. Generations of urban scholars will surely be grateful for the foundations that Borchert laid both for analysis of the transformations that have occurred already, and for insight into the transformations that are yet to come.

REFERENCES

Becker, C. M., E. S. Mills, and J. G. Williamson. 1986. Modeling Indian migration and city growth, 1960–2000. *Economic Development and Cultural Change* 35: 1–33.

Berry, B. J. L. 1991. *Long-wave rhythms in economic development and political behavior*. Baltimore: Johns Hopkins University Press.

Borchert, J. R. 1967. American metropolitan evolution. *Geographical Review* 57: 301–32.

Dunn, E. S., Jr. 1980. *The development of the U.S. urban system*. Baltimore: Johns Hopkins University Press.

Isard, W. 1942. A neglected cycle: The transport-building cycle. *Review of Economic Statistics* 24: 149–58.

Kondratiev, Nikolai. 1984. *The long-wave cycle*. Translation of the 1926 essay by Guy Daniels. New York: Richardson and Snyder.

Walker, R. A. 1978. The transformation of urban structure in the nineteenth century, and the beginnings of suburbanization. In *Urbanization and conflict in market societies*. Edited by K. Cox. Chicago: Maaroufa Press.

FOUR

The Urban Face of Capitalism

David Harvey

In *The Painting of Modern Life: Paris in the Art of Manet and His Followers*, T. J. Clark (1985) makes the following observation:

> Capital did not need to have a representation of itself laid out upon the ground in bricks and mortar or inscribed as a map in the minds of its city dwellers. One might even say that capital preferred the city not be an image—not to have form, not to be accessible to the imagination, to readings and misreadings, to a conflict of claims on its space—in order that it might mass produce an image of its own to put in place of those destroyed. On the face of things, the new image did not look entirely different from the old ones. It still seemed to propose that the city was one place, in some sense belonging to those who lived in it. But it belonged to them now simply as an image, something occasionally and casually consumed in spaces expressly designed for the purpose—promenades, panoramas, outings on Sundays, great exhibitions and official parades. (36)

Clark's account whets the appetite, but its meaning remains elusive. He offers, to be sure, some immediate clarifications. To begin with, he calls this mass-produced image "the spectacle" and insists that Haussmann's rebuilding of Paris "was spectacular in the most oppressive sense of the word." The spectacle, however, "is never an image mounted securely and finally in place; it is always an account of the world competing with others, and meeting the resistance of different, sometimes tenacious forms of social practice" (36). In Haussmann's Paris, Clark claims, the spectacle "was not a neutral form in

apitalism incidentally happened; it was a form of capital itself, and
of the most effective." It was "an image put in place of a city which had
lost its own means of representation" (59–60).

In this instance, it is the city itself that appears lost; command over its
spaces and social practices becomes either so weakened or so confused that
the "modes of political, economic, and ideological representation in which
the city had once been constructed, as a contingent unit in and through other
social practices" (49), are dissolved. The dissolution of the city as an affective
and knowable community is the central loss. That city was replaced, in Clark's
account, by a city imaged by capital solely as a spectacle, to be consumed
passively by the populace at large. It was through the transfixing power of the
spectacle that the city itself was made to vanish, as it were, since the city as a
truly knowable community "was precisely a site of unfixity—uncontrol—in
the previous social order: it was a horizon of possible collective action and
understanding, and all such horizons must be made invisible in societies
organized under the aegis of the commodity" (50).

Several aspects of Clark's account deserve amplification. To begin with,
the word *spectacle* is used in the very special sense arrived at through the
theoretical enquiries of the Situationists. Debord, perhaps the most persuasive theorist of that group, argues that the spectacle is much more than a
collection of images; it is "a social relation between people mediated by
images" (1983). The spectacle presents itself as "an instrument of unifica-
tion" that, under modern capitalist conditions of production, becomes "the
common ground of the deceived gaze and of false consciousness." The real
consumer, under the social relations of capitalism, becomes "a consumer of
illusions."

This argument harks back, of course, to Marx's theory of commodity
fetishism, a brief recapitulation of which helps grasp more precisely the sense
in which both Debord and Clark wish to deploy the concept of the spectacle in
analyzing the dynamics of daily life in urban settings. Commodities, Marx
(1967; 1973) argued, are produced through social labor and come to us
through a process of market exchange. The act of market exchange obscures
the myriad social relations that enter into commodity production, transport,
and marketing. In the end, we exchange one thing—money—for another
thing—the goods we purchase. Nothing in that physical exchange reveals
anything about the processes of production or the conditions of labor of those
doing the producing. The market draws a veil over or imposes a mask upon all
those basic activities of social labor that serve to reproduce daily life. Under
such circumstances it is impossible, Marx insists, to establish social meanings
and relations through simple inspection of market exchange. Marx calls this
masking effect the fetishism of commodities. The fetishism becomes ideological if we either fail to inquire into the social relations that lie behind market
exchange or if we represent the world as if what we observe in the marketplace is all there is.

The Situationists use the concept of spectacle to refer, then, to a condition in which commodities themselves become the means of representation. If the signs, codes, and signals we use to interpret the world are produced as commodities, they also become subject to fetishistic readings. It is Clark's primary contention that (1) the city is itself a form of representation (the place of primary sociality and self-expression as well as the physical milieu of collective memory and tradition) and (2) this means of representation became so commodified in Second Empire Paris that the mass of the population was deprived of those creative avenues of collective action and understanding that would allow them to participate as active agents in the creation of their own history.

It is useful to take the argument back one step further. Capitalism acknowledges one and only one measure of value, and that is given by money. This sign is used to place value on all things traded; it is the sign to which all of us have to conform in the marketplace; it is a social construct that returns to dominate us in innumerable ways. The trouble, as Simmel (1971; 1978) pointed out, is that there is something profoundly unsatisfying about money, "with its colorlessness and indifferent qualities," becoming the denominator of all values. Money dissolves all manner of human activities into "free-floating processes," which "hollow out the core of things, their specific values and uniqueness and incomparability in a way which is beyond repair." Everything seems to float "with the same specific gravity in the constantly moving stream of money" (1971, 330).

Deeper problems derive from the singular role of money in capitalist society. Money is a form of social power that permits individuals to appropriate the results of the whole world of social labor. As such, it becomes the object of the fiercest desire and the primary means of alienation and class division. Control over money power means control over the fruits of the social labor of others. Money, furthermore, breaks the bonds of personal dependency, dissolves the traditional sense of community, and, in so doing, defines a new kind of community—a community with objective rather than subjective dependency relations between individuals who relate to each other instrumentally through commodity exchanges, market prices, and money transactions (Marx 1973, 146–78). It was Simmel (1971) who most clearly saw how the metropolis of capital in formation in the latter half of the nineteenth century was itself a particular manifestation of this new kind of community of money.

Money hardly satisfies, then, as a means to represent the manifold complexity of human wants, desires, and values. "We see in the nature of money itself something of the essence of prostitution," says Simmel (1978, 377), and Marx (1973) concurs. Freud took things even further, picking up on our penchant to describe money as something dirty and unclean ("filthy lucre" and "filthy rich" are common expressions). "It is possible that the contrast between the most precious substance known to men and the most worthless . . . has led to the specific identification of gold with faeces," he wrote, and shocked his Victorian readers by treating gold as transformed excrement and exchange relations as sublimated rituals of the anus. Money, wrote Ferenczi, "is nothing other than odorless, dehydrated filth that has been made to shine" (Borneman 1976, 86).

Capitalism has a central moral failing: money supplants all other forms of imagery (religion, traditional authority, and the like) but puts in its place something that either has no distinctive image because it is colorless, odorless, and indifferent in relation to the social labor it is supposed to measure, or, if it projects any image at all, connotes dirt, filth, excrement, and prostitution. The effect is to create a vacuum at the heart of capitalist society—a colorless self-image of value that can have nearly a zero purchase upon social identity. It cannot provide an image of social bonding or of community, and fails as a central value system to articulate even the most mundane of human hopes and aspirations. Money is what we aspire to for purposes of daily reproduction; money, as Marx has it, "becomes the community," yet money itself is empty of any positive meanings. The problem in a secular capitalist society is to find an alternative means of representation that compensates for the emptiness, substitutes for the colorlessness, and resists the filthy connotations of money as a measure of value. The problem, of course, is that the alternatives are perpetually in danger of becoming commodified because it takes money power to do almost anything of significance in capitalist society. Zola captures that contradiction quite brilliantly and explicitly in his novel *L'Argent*:

> Mme Caroline was struck with the sudden revelation that money was the dung-heap that nurtured the growth of tomorrow's humanity. . . . Without speculation there could be no vibrant and fruitful undertakings any more than there could be children without lust. It took this excess of passion, all this contemptibly wasted and lost life, to ensure the continuation of life. . . . Money, the poisoner and destroyer, was becoming the seed-bed for all forms of social growth. It was the manure needed to sustain the great public works whose execution was bringing the peoples of the globe together and pacifying the earth. She had cursed money, but now she prostrated herself before it in a frightening adulation: it alone could raze a mountain, fill in an arm of the sea, at last render the earth inhabitable to mankind. . . . Everything that was good came out of that which was evil. (1967, 224–25)

To what degree, then, do the qualities of city life and of urban existence permit the construction of some alternative sense of community, some alternative sense of human values? Here, I think, Clark is on strong ground. His insistence that a sense of a knowable and affective community provides some protection against the travails of capitalism and the dissolving effects of money power is one of the grand themes of urban history. His point, however, is that the protections break down in a radical transformation of urban life (including the renewal of a city's built environment and the reorganization of its spaces to eliminate many of the traditional sites of collective memory and identity). The "creative destruction" of the urban fabric by the unleashing of speculative money power puts even hearth and home, neighborhood and places of collective memory, within range of the dissolving power of money. The resultant sense of loss is serious, primarily for those who suffer it, but also for those who are concerned to maintain social control and the proper functioning of civil society.

The spectacle, defined in the Situationist mode, gains its power and purchase precisely in such a context. The struggle to find a proper representation, a mode of interpretation of an urban society in dramatic transformation (which Second Empire Paris was undergoing) is fought from below, but it is also a pressing matter for the ruling classes. The struggle to impose a new set of representations from above can either be waged explicitly (as, in the Second Empire, through appeal to the Napoleonic legend, the construction of monuments to imperial power, and the organization of religious symbolism to political purposes) or it can be arrived at through the commodification of representation itself. Clark chooses to focus upon this latter thrust, presumably because he believes that the long-term transformations in political consciousness occurred at this deeper level (rather than at the superficial level of imperial imagery). Commodification and money exchange penetrated into every nook and cranny of daily life during the Second Empire. They did so in part because the spectacular transformation of Paris, itself wrought through intense financial speculation, transformed the spaces of collective memory and of affective community to the total obliteration of past patterns of social relations. All that was left was commodified space and overwhelming attention to commodities and money power. It was hard to find a mode of representation of the world that was not constructed in such terms. In this sense, Clark proposes to study how the spectacle so mediated social relations that "true" representation became progressively masked in a veil of fetishism.

So what did the populace of Paris feel they had lost? In what ways could the spectacle of the commodity and the commodification of the city and its spaces and places, its signs and signals, compensate for that loss? The answers to these questions are by no means simple, in part because, in a class-divided and socially segmented society such as mid-nineteenth-century Paris, different people evidently felt they had lost quite different things. On the other hand, the overwhelming sense of loss unified quite distinctive groups and gave them common cause that was most clearly manifest in the odd alliance of forces that joined together to promote the Paris Commune (Ross 1988; Harvey 1985).

The working classes, for example, had multiple grievances. The long deskilling of the craft worker that had begun in the 1820s accelerated during the Second Empire. It was coupled with yet another strong surge of rural migration into the city and the diminution of any collective power over labor-market conditions. Furthermore, the struggle to reverse those conditions through the formation of a social and political republic in 1848 was roundly defeated, first in June of 1848, but even more seriously by the coup d'état that saw workers' organizations proscribed and the working-class leadership put under the strongest system of surveillance. Not only did the condition of the craft workers deteriorate, but the sense of empowerment to do anything about it was likewise lost. To add insult to injury, the reorganization of the city's interior space through Haussmann's works, and the intense speculation in land and property markets that accompanied it, had the effect of expelling the working class from the city center, an emphasis, by physical spatial removal, of their progressive removal from any effective influence over government. With that physical expulsion came the destruction of traditional working-class neighborhoods and of many facets of social organization, paralleled by increasing journey-to-work and social fragmentation. Disempowerment of the worker's movement, deskilling, and expulsion from the city center went hand in hand.

Other strata in society likewise felt a sense of loss, not least those traditionalists (Catholics) who scorned material values and looked to a firm continuation of hierarchy and aristocratic privilege. For them, the activities of the new entrepreneurs, the property speculators and the financiers, were anathema, and to be in no way compensated for by imperial glitter and gloss. Social control over Paris's notoriously fickle and rambunctious population had always been difficult for the forces of law and order, but under conditions of rapid growth and reconstruction it became downright impossible except through a network of street informers and secret police who were almost as uncontrolled as everyone else. Judging from the literature of the time, even those who benefited financially from property development and financial speculation felt a loss of the genuine sense of security that comes with strong social bonding rather than oppressive and authoritarian rule. Symbolic of this problem was the issue of censorship and press freedom and debate in a city where information flow was crucial to business enterprise, where politics had long been fought out in the belief that Paris was both the head and heart of Europe. Press freedom, at least for the entrepreneurs, was vital, but the imperial authorities had every reason to fear it. To cap it all, the lack of self-government for Paris and the seemingly arbitrary and authoritarian rule of Haussmann over the city's daily affairs became the focus of intense discontent. It highlighted the fact that the populace at large had lost political control over the city space in which it lived, at a time when economic and social changes were destroying the traditional urban fabric.

To be sure, there were innumerable compensations, and the various strata sought their own paths to redeem their own particular situation. The workers built the cabaret and cafe into places of political as well as social interaction. They found covert means to preserve traditional, and build new, institutions even in the new spaces of the city being opened up to commercial forces (the new arrondissement system that Haussmann created became a powerful principle of organization in the revolutionary movement of the Commune, for example). The struggle over press freedoms and self-governance preoccupied the professional strata, and the Catholic church constructed elaborate defenses against the inroads of the new order. The empire was also deeply exercised over legitimacy, and used every means to try to find a firm class basis for power coupled with mechanisms designed to secure allegiance.

It used the organized powers of festivals, parades, universal expositions, military events, royal visits, and court life as part of a controlled spectacle designed to deceive the gaze and attract support. Scarcely a month went by without some spectacular event to entertain and divert the populace at large. The monumentality of Haussmann's imperial design for Paris likewise played its role in the promotion of spectacle. The commodification of the city's spaces and intensive speculation in land and property markets altered the visage of the city in innumerable ways as a means of social control through the shaping of collective memory. All that demolition and reconstruction contributed to the sense of spectacle in itself, while the product often took the form of what one might call institutionalized spectacle. The boulevards, the squares, the new "mairies," monuments, and markets were all, in their own way, trans-fixed sites of the spectacle, which contrasted dramatically with the lost neigh-borhoods and places of collective memory for the popular classes.

Beneath all this, and in part through it all, another kind of spectacle was emerging that seemed naturally to compensate for all those other losses. The boulevards spawned a particular style of life—a life of fashion and of street spectacle that, through the exercise of imperial power, was evacuated of any direct political content and promoted the commodity as a means of represen-tation in itself. The transformation of the boulevards into well-lighted spaces for nightlife, the organization of the street cafes, and the coming of the department stores with all their flamboyant gaiety meant the commodifica-tion of daily existence certainly for many of the new white-collar and profes-sional strata as well as for the traditional elite. The demimonde of actresses, prostitutes, entertainers, cabaret entertainers, writers, and artists gave Paris the air of a place of perpetual entertainment, yet the entertainment was itself a part of the extension of commodification. It rested upon the formation of new markets and the manipulation of a wide range of consumption activities for profitable commercial ends. The art market, theater, cabaret, and cafe were no less sites of commodity fetishism than the department stores.

Although these spectacles may have been the focus of many a deceived gaze, they were not accepted without question. By the end of the Second Empire there was an intense struggle in which the contested ideological ter-rain of the spectacle was transformed into something increasingly antagonis-tic to the imagery that had preceded it. The public meetings, the resurgent working-class organizations (such as the Paris Branch of the First International), the strikes and huge funeral processions began to crystallize into a counterspectacle of resistance to the empire and, to some degree, to the new social relations of production and exchange. This movement was to come together to reoccupy the central space of Paris during the Paris Commune of 1871 and to attempt thereby the construction of a quite different social order (Lefebvre 1965).

Two incidents in that spectacular event, which even Lenin subsequently described as the "festival of the people," require commentary. The tearing down of the Vendome column was in many respects an event of great symbolic import, since it sent a message that new forces controlled the central spaces of Paris and that the collective memory of an imposed hierarchical order must be erased in the construction of a new, horizontally ordered society. The column was perceived to be a "permanent insult" and a "perpetual assault" upon the dignity and self-respect of the popular movement (Ross 1988, 4–12). Marx's prediction, made nearly twenty years before, that the contradictions of the empire would split asunder and shake civil society so deeply that the iron statue of Napoleon, that grand symbol of imperial legend, would "crash from the top of the Vendome column," proved only too prophetic (1963, 120). There is no evidence that his remark played any role in the communards' decision to topple the column on a day of grand festival (even with the forces of reaction menacing outside the city's walls), but what is striking is how widely felt was the symbolic oppressiveness of imperial accomplishments and monumentality, and how deeply felt and widespread was the desire to reassert control over the central city spaces and to do it in a manner that countered commodification and imperial power.

The second incident concerns the abolition of night work in the bakeries and the moratorium on rental payments by communard decree. The first directly attacked the most virulent forms of oppressive labor relations and sought to decommodify, as it were, the labor process as well as the labor market in the interior space of Paris, and to return it to a knowable and effective community in which social relations of exploitation were replaced by the federalism of cooperation. The moratorium on rental payments signaled the interdiction of that most fundamental of all processes at work in the shaping of urban spaces. The sorting of land to uses under the maximization of land rent had to be stopped, because it was through the commodification of space that the working classes were being forcibly expelled from their rightful place in the center of their city.

Although the efforts failed, the communards nonetheless organized for much of their life along the lines of a counterspectacle, with the clear intent of instituting a new spatial and social order in the city that would be antihierarchical, democratic, and reasonably egalitarian. The idea of spectacle and counterspectacle caught up in the maelstrom of class struggle is more than a little intriguing. It confirms that the society of the spectacle is not firmly rooted, with the result, as both Debord and Clark insist, that the deceived gaze can be averted or counteracted even in the midst of the crassest commercialism.

Some contemporary versions of this same problem suggest that there is a deep continuity of this perpetual dialogue between the emptiness or filthiness of money values and the attempt to construct a counterimage (no matter how illusory) of community in urban settings. Many of the themes I have examined can be illustrated, for example, by Baltimore's recent inner harbor redevelopment. It has all the hallmarks of the production of spectacle that changed a population's mode of representation through the recommodification of an urban space. Here, as does Clark, I want to stress that the construction of the spectacle was not consciously planned (although some elements within it were thought out in terms of strategies of social control, community reconstruction, and political legitimation in the face of social unrest), but chaotically arrived at in response to the powerful forces that have reshaped urbanization since around 1970 (Harvey 1989).

In one respect, the Baltimore story is one of reassertion of the power of commodified spectacle and the achievement of social control through the fetishistic masking of the socially disruptive counterauthoritarian and countercultural spectacles manifest in the social unrest of the 1960s. The inner-city riots that followed the assassination of Martin Luther King, Jr., in 1968, for example, left several casualties and widespread property damage. The sight of tanks and the National Guard patrolling the streets left an image of the inner city, already rife with unemployment, racism, and deprivation, as uncontrollable, dangerous, and therefore unapproachable for the mass of the population. The viability of the downtown urban renewal of the 1960s was plainly threatened. In the wake of the riots, a broad coalition of civil rights, religious, and community leaders, local politicians, professionals, and academics, with worried businesspeople tagging along behind, got together to think out ways of overcoming the flagrant divisions and of restoring a sense of common purpose and community built upon economic and racial justice.

In this climate, the idea of a city fair took root—a fair that would be built on neighborhood traditions and ethnic differences but would be a celebration of a common purpose. The first city fair was held in 1970. In spite of fears of violence it was a success and drew more than two hundred fifty thousand people over a weekend. It brought divergent factions together—"A City Reborn through a Fair of Neighborhoods," ran the headline in the *Baltimore Sun*. Two years later, nearly two million people attended, but by then several commentators complained that the themes of neighborhood and the celebration of civic unity through difference were being gradually supplanted by the commercialism of commodity exchange and entertainment. Weekly ethnic festivals downtown in the summer months not only taught that money could be made by selling ethnic identity but simultaneously consolidated the sense that the inner city could be reoccupied by affluent suburbanites and that it could once again become the site of capitalist consumerism and property development.

The fair certainly helped renew civic pride in a city that had a national reputation as one of the dreariest urban environments in the United States ("the armpit of the East" was one of the more trenchant comments from out-of-towners). Baltimore had, it seemed, rediscovered the "bread and circuses" formula of ancient Rome to counter seething discontents, promote downtown redevelopment, and recover a sense of civic pride and purpose.

Unfortunately, the economic crash of 1973–75 brought another massive wave of deindustrialization and unemployment to a city whose center had long been in decline as industry, population, and commerce had suburbanized, leaving much of the center derelict and ripe for urban renewal. It was exactly at that moment that the federal government, because of its fiscal difficulties and political leanings, chose to cut back severely on grants to cities to fund social improvements. From that moment on, city government entered into a partnership with business and assumed a much more entrepreneurial posture (Harvey 1989). Its capacities to compete in the international division of labor were limited, and a variety of factors (internal and external) militated against its assumption of a strong role in command and control functions. Urban strategy gravitated inexorably toward exploration of the consumption option. With the crowds pouring in, it was easy to commercialize and institutionalize the spectacle that the city fair had pioneered. The construction of the Maryland Science Center, the National Aquarium, a Convention Center, a marina, innumerable hotels, and pleasure citadels of all kinds quickly got under way, paralleled by burgeoning investments in retail space. The center-piece was first the pavilions of Harbor Place, and later a whole string of interior shopping malls in which the world of commodities could be celebrated under tight security surveillance and control. In retrospect, the officials of the federal Housing and Urban Development Agency came to interpret the spectacle of the city fair, not as a genuine attempt to reassert some notion of community, but as a pure gimmick designed to promote the recommodification of the city's central spaces and, as such, something to be recommended to all other cities in the United States. "Spawned by the necessity to arrest the fear and disuse of downtown areas caused by the civic unrest of the late 1960s," they wrote, "the Baltimore City fair was originated by individuals in city government who seized upon the idea of a country fair in the city as a way to promote urban redevelopment" (HUD 1981). The success of this aspect of the venture testifies how organized spectacle and recommodification of urban space can indeed go hand in hand.

The result has been a radical reconstruction of the image of Baltimore. An architecture of play and pleasure, of spectacle and commodification, emphasizing fiction and fantasy, replaced that of function (although, of course, both function and fiction follow profit). The local television and press produced a grand media-hype to the glories of Baltimore's redevelopment and with the passing of time they had more and more to hype. The mayor was voted the best mayor in the United States by *Esquire* in 1984, and Baltimore hit the front cover of *Time* as "renaissance city," shedding its image of dreariness and appearing as a dynamic go-getting city, ready to accommodate outside capital and to encourage the in-movement of capital and of the "right" kind of people. No matter that the reality is increasing absolute impoverishment in most of the city's neighborhoods, and congressional researchers consider the city one of the neediest in the United States in terms of substandard housing, educational provision, and the like (Levine 1987). There is, as one recent report put it (Szanton 1986), plenty of "rot beneath the glitter," yet the image prevails. Jenkins (1987) conveys the mythology without a single hint of criticism: "Baltimore, despite soaring unemployment, boldly turned its derelict harbor into a playground. Tourists meant shopping, catering and transport, this in turn meant construction, distribution, manufacturing—leading to more jobs, more residents, more activity. The decay of old Baltimore slowed, halted, then turned back. The harbor area is now among America's top tourist draws and urban unemployment is falling fast." It is apparent that putting Baltimore on the map in this way, giving it a strong and coherent sense of place-bound identity, has been successful politically in consolidating the power and influence of a local ruling public-private partnership. It has brought development money into Baltimore (although it is hard to tell if it has brought more in than has been taken out through interest payments, exported profits, and imported purchases). It has also evidently given the population at large some sense of place-bound identity. The society of the spectacle takes over and the circus succeeds even when the bread is lacking.

Consider, as a second example, these same themes as embodied in the intricate history of Times Square in New York City. Built up as a pure piece of real-estate and business speculation in the 1890s and early 1900s, Times Square soon became the symbolic heart of a city in the full flood of disintegration as a knowable and effective community. The stresses of rapid urban growth and successive revolutions in technology, merchanting, building styles, and space relations, all under the overwhelming influence of dominant money power, were dissolving the fragile immigrant and neighborhood institutions of community built up during the early nineteenth century. Times Square rose to prominence at the same time as the modern metropolitan New York City of five boroughs and sprawling suburbs, of rapid mass transit (the subway cross came to Times Square in 1901), of new systems of international and national communication, of information and money flow, of commercialism and merchanting of mass fashions (Buder 1978). Under such conditions of rapid growth and change, many New Yorkers lost their sense of collective identity, in much the same way that Parisians felt the loss of their city some three decades before. The creation of a symbolic heart was a response. Times Square in its earliest incarnation was the source of civic pride—it became the heart of Manhattan, of New York City, and even, at times, the nation. Like Baltimore's Harbor Place, it was a symbolic heart that was simultaneously the site of pilgrimage to the fetish of the commodity, to the production of images and fictions as well as to overwhelming signs of money power. Partly in response to the democratizing and leveling influence of money, it also managed to function, in surface appearance at least, as a classless space of ritual and togetherness. It became the place to which the populace flocked in manifestations of communal unity at times of trauma, celebration, and ritual.

As the center of commerce, fashion, advertising, news, entertainment, and ritualistic and political celebrations, it provided a place where community of some sort could be celebrated amid growing class divisions, alienation, and commercialism (all of which paralleled in intensity the experience of Second Empire Paris). The meaning of Times Square has undergone several successive transformations, however, and much about its history is deeply revealing of the problems that arise when capitalism shapes commodities as a spectacle "in place of a city that had lost its own means of representation."

It is instructive to try to read the contemporary signs of Times Square backward, moving away from the colorlessness of money (hidden within all those reflecting glass towers that lurk in the background of Times Square and that now, given current redevelopment plans, threaten to dominate it more directly) back through all the colorful qualities of commodities to the experience of social labor in the production of those commodities. The signs of commodities abound, of course, in the advertising extravaganza that greets the eye and that has always been central to Times Square. Here, too, the gap between the image of the commodity and the commodity itself adds to the fetishistic inversion of social relations with things. The sign of the commodity, rather than the commodity itself, gets sold, reminding us that political economy is as much about the trading of signs and the stimulation of desire as it is about the trading of things. I do not agree, however, with Baudrillard's (1981) thesis that the trade in signs rather than commodities is a recent feature of capitalism's history and that it demands an entirely new sense of political economy. Capitalism, in its early stages, used the artifices of display and spectacle as part and parcel of its strategies for insertion into daily life. The theater and the circus, for example, were proving grounds for advertising and commodification (Agnew 1986), as were the various universal expositions (the Crystal Palace of 1851, the Paris efforts of the Second Empire, Chicago in 1893, and so on), all of which Walter Benjamin (1973) properly dubbed "pilgrimages to the fetish of the commodity." The selling of signs and images has always been fundamental both to capitalism and to Times Square.

There are, however, no signs of social labor in Times Square. This disguising of social labor is entirely in accord with the whole thrust of capitalist advertising, which has always excluded any reference to the conditions of social labor (except in some ancient or artisanal system of production). The square has everything to do with masking that. Experience of that place socializes us to conditions of consumption, fashion, and taste, but conceals the significance of production. It promotes the fetishism of commodities and the curious qualities of money power as the ultimate measure of value.

Times Square has long assumed the guise of a permanently institutionalized spectacle, but many of the traditional forms of spectacle—fashion innovation or new forms of live entertainment—have either been modified (for example, the transition from live theater to cinema entertainments in the 1920s) or obliterated by subsequent developments. The decline of the square as a viable and interesting point of social interaction must largely be attributed to the advent of television, which came to dominate the production and marketing of signs, fashions, tastes, and images in the postwar period. The crowds that once flocked to Times Square for special events—election results, World Series celebrations, international crises—gradually dwindled to the point where it was plainly recognized that a national institution of ritual had largely been obliterated by the mid-1950s.

The nostalgic anger that greets current proposals to redevelop Times Square, as if it were just another piece of valuable real estate, in part attaches to the collective memory of such spectacles, even though they were fundamental to the socialization of the popular classes to "the phantasmagoria of the commodity" and all of its associated fetishisms. The reaction is particularly odd when it is set against the unquestioned fact that Times Square always was, from the very beginning, a hyperpiece of real-estate speculation. It seems that whoever has seen the circus, experienced the spectacle, seen the bright lights, all too often wants them back again.

The decline of the square from symbol of civic pride to embarrassing netherworld of pornography, prostitution, peep-shows, crime, and drugs is largely attributed to the loss of the activities that made the square so attractive in its halcyon days of the 1910s and the Roaring Twenties. Historical enquiries show only too well (Senelick 1988) that this netherworld was always present and, like the celebrated demimonde of Second Empire Paris, was a vital part of its allure. The New York City underworld has long actively shaped this central space to its own earthy image of a society founded on the pure venality of money power. If many of the social behaviors to be observed there conjure up the ugly psychological connotations of money value (prostitution, degradation, feces, and human detritus), then we ought not in principle to be surprised (although I suspect the antagonism toward such places on the part of the ruling elite derives precisely because of this concordance).

Behind the current nostalgia for Times Square in its halcyon days, then, lies a deeper reality about Times Square. The very name is suggestive. Time is money, we are told again and again, and it is curious that the symbolic heart of Manhattan, center of the world's financial system, should have such a name (different indeed from Moscow's Red Square or London's Trafalgar Square). The origin of that name is even more interesting. It was arrived at through political pressure from the *New York Times*, which moved there in 1905 and promptly invented one of the most significant rituals associated with the square—the welcoming in of each new year, the descending of the famous ball—as a publicity gimmick. The square was named because the *New York Times* exerted its power to have its own named space in which to compete with the *New York Herald*, which had its own headquarters in Herald Square farther south.

Times Square—the center of illusions; the consummate spectacle of commodity fetishism run rampant; the street haunt of tricksters, vamps, con artists, pimps, and prostitutes; the place where almost every secular opiate of the people is up for sale, all accumulated at a crossroads of people (three million a day pass through the turnstiles of the subway station alone), of news and information flowing fast and furious from the four corners of the earth, and embedded in a built environment of debt-bottling plants and trading floors where voodoo economics is daily practiced in soaring towers of glass and steel, seemingly oblivious (save for the interminable flow of people) to the seedy scene that laps around the base of this incalculable money power.

Is there any better way to capture the cultural history of this place carved out of space that we call Times Square than as a centerpiece of pilgrimage to the fetish of the commodity, as a complex tissue of truth and lies, of illusions and of fetishisms that are nevertheless made real by the millions who had in the past and continue to pass daily through this tiny piece of real estate, absorbing its ideological meanings, its illusions, its images, and its subliminal messages?

Yet there is something here that undermines, that seems to threaten the very foundations of the capitalist system, something that burrows away at its base with all the canniness of the worm that threatens the biggest apple of them all. Is this Times Square the true face of capitalism? Baudelaire's exultant poem, written in the context of the dissolution of a clear imagery of Second Empire Paris, appears equally appropriate an epitaph for the history of Times Square:

> Against the lamplight, whose shivering is the wind's
> Prostitution spreads its light and life in the streets:
> Like an anthill opening its issues it penetrates
> Mysteriously everywhere by its own occult route;
> Like an enemy mining the foundations of a fort,
> Or a worm in an apple, eating what all should eat,
> It circulates securely in the city's clogged heart.
> (Translated by David Paul. In Benjamin 1973, 57).

Second Empire Paris, Baltimore's Harbor Place, and New York's Times Square present the history of urban spectacle under capitalism in rather different lights. The commodification of images and urban forms in Second Empire Paris was part and parcel of a deeper implantation of capitalist social relations, and produced its own denouement (however temporary) in the traumatic spectacle of the Paris Commune and the toppling of the Vendôme Column. The spectacle of Baltimore's Harbor Place, on the other hand, arose out of the ashes of destruction and dissolution visited upon the central city in the radical struggles to regain popular political command over the city's spaces during the 1960s. Those years, for all their contradictory ferments, were still about the exploration of possible avenues for collective action and the understanding of precisely the sort that must be "made invisible in societies organized under the aegis of the commodity" (Clark 1985). That Harbor Place makes them so is its principal achievement. The history of Times Square is empty of such direct struggles, but in a sense provides the most interesting case of all—a space that literally dissolves under the weight of fetishism and money power to reveal in the crassest and most vulgar of ways the emptiness and corruption that attach themselves to money as the central value system to which capitalism is inexorably committed.

Capitalism is a contradictory formation, and so we must expect that its urban face, particularly when rendered as spectacle, will be equally contradictory. To read the signs and symbols correctly is, as always, to learn to get behind the mask, the urban face of capitalism, and to penetrate to the deeper forces at work beneath. Money lies at the root of it all, of course, and like Zola's Madame Caroline, we can either resist it or prostrate ourselves before it.

ACKNOWLEDGMENTS

The materials on Times Square are largely drawn from a symposium, "Inventing Times Square," organized by the Institute for the Humanities, New York University, over the academic year 1988–89. Many of these papers will shortly be published in a book of that title.

REFERENCES

Agnew, J.-C. 1986. *Worlds apart: The market and the theater in Anglo-American thought, 1550–1750*. Cambridge: Cambridge University Press.

Baudrillard, J. 1981. *For a critique of the political economy of the sign*. St. Louis, Mo.: Telos Press.

Benjamin, W. 1973. *Charles Baudelaire: A lyric poet in the era of high capitalism*. London: New Left Books.

Borneman, E., ed. 1976. *The psychoanalysis of money*. London: Urizen Books.

Buder, S. 1978. "Forty-second street at the crossroads: A history of Broadway to Eighth Avenue," in *West 42nd Street: "The bright light zone."* New York: Graduate School and University Center.

Clark, T. J. 1985. *The painting of modern life: Paris in the art of Manet and his followers*. London: Thames and Hudson.

Debord, G. 1983. *Society of the spectacle*. Detroit: Red and Black Books.

Harvey, D. 1985. *Consciousness and the urban experience*. Baltimore: Johns Hopkins University Press.

——. 1989. "From managerialism to entrepreneurialism: The transformation in urban governance in late capitalism." *Geografiska Annaler* 71(13): 3–17.

HUD (U.S. Department of Housing and Urban Development, Office of Public Affairs). 1981. *The urban fair: How cities celebrate themselves.* Washington, D.C.: U.S. Department of Housing and Urban Development.

Jenkins, S. "Save our cities: How to bring new life to the urban heartlands." *Sunday Times*, Magazine section, 29 November 1987, pp. 22–27.

Lefebvre, H. 1965. *La proclamation de la commune.* Paris: Gallimard.

Levine, M. 1987. "Downtown redevelopment as an urban growth strategy: A critical appraisal of the Baltimore renaissance." *Journal of Urban Affairs* 9, no. 2: 103–23.

Marx, K. 1963. *The eighteenth brumaire of Louis Bonaparte.* New York: International Publishers.

——. 1967. *Capital.* Volume 1. New York: International Publishers.

——. 1973. *Grundrisse.* Harmondsworth, Middlesex: Penguin Books.

Ross, K. 1988. *The emergence of social space: Rimbaud and the Paris commune.* Minneapolis: University of Minnesota Press.

Senelick, L. 1988. "Private parts in public places: The perception of prostitution and pornography in Times Square, past and present." In *Inventing Times Square.* New York: New York University Institute for Humanities.

Simmel, G. 1971. "The metropolis and mental life." In *On individuality and social form.* Edited by D. Levine. Chicago: University of Chicago Press.

——. 1978. *The philosophy of money.* London: Routledge and Kegan Paul.

Szanton, P. 1986. *Baltimore 2000.* Baltimore: Goldseker Foundation.

Zola, E. 1967. *L'Argent.* Paris: Pleiade.

FIVE

Human Mobility and the Shaping of Cities

James E. Vance, Jr.

One of the truisms of geography is the interaction of transportation with settlement. Any serious practitioner of geographical analysis knows that these two aspects of the human use of space are related, but how does the association work? Does transportation always precede settlement? Is it the activity that really determines where settlement will be, and how it will function? If we know about transportation, are we greatly informed about most aspects of settlement? We all know that it takes transportation to keep cities going, as was shown during the nonurban early Middle Ages when feudalism was in full flower and even small towns seemed doomed to extinction. Can a relationship be known to exist even though its actual operation is not widely understood? This chapter will try to answer these questions.

Starting with a doctoral thesis in the early 1950s, I have earnestly tried to resolve three general questions: in what way is organized transportation brought into existence and transformed over the years; how is the morphology of settlement originated and transformed over the years; and how are these two processes related? In my thesis, I learned a great deal about transportation and its evolution, but hardly that much about its causal relationship to settlement.

Clearly we must look where transportation-settlement relationships have been operative long enough to provide preserved morphological evidence. The historical geography of transportation shows that most of human history has had one dominant medium of transport for the mass of people: the two human legs (Vance 1990). The rich were transported in sedan chairs in Roman times, by wagons, on horseback, or later in carriages, but so few were transported that we may disregard that narrowly available assisted mobility. Only after the transportation revolution of the sixteenth century did matters change significantly. Canals were built in Italy and Flanders, ships were improved and made more seaworthy, and even roads were made better by the earlier engineers for the use of the improved wagons, coaches, and harnessed draft animals available by the year 1500. Still, most people had to walk if they were to have any mobility.

Only during the nineteenth century was assisted transportation widespread. Canals were widely developed in western Europe and eastern North America by the 1830s. Steam railroads were increasingly common in the 1830s and 1840s, and by mid-century most economically developed regions possessed an integrated net affording assisted transportation for those of steady income. Carriages never became common transport, but enlarged versions of horse-drawn vehicles—omnibuses and horsecars—came increasingly into use at the end of the nineteenth century. The development of electrically propelled road vehicles, the trolley in particular, finally offered assisted transport cheap enough so that virtually anyone with regular employment might use it. Between about 1825, the year of the first omnibus line in Nantes, and 1888, the year of the first truly successful trolley line in Richmond, Virginia, human mobility shifted fundamentally. The onset of that period concerns us here, although obviously conditions in the century before 1825 are an example of the millennia of traditional pedestrian mobility before the transportation revolution. Because human mobility was radically transformed during the life of North American urbanization, we may, in fact, use North American cities to study the evolution of the physical city brought on by shifting human mobility, rather than having to examine the past only in Europe, as is so often the case in historical geography.

Although academics often find transportation-settlement relationships interesting and worthwhile, those who use significant impact on "practical existence" as their touchstone regard them with a certain impatience. This chapter will show that such fretfulness is unwarranted, that quite practical people need to know how those relationships work. To demonstrate this practical importance I propose as a basic hypothesis that the physical form of cities, in its many variations, can perhaps best and most synoptically be viewed as a consequence of changes in the level and form of human mobility. At present no synoptic theory of city shaping exists, yet, given the progressive change in city form, there is a real and practical value in being able to follow through the processes of transformation at work in ever-enlarging areas subject to urbanization.

THE SHAPING OF CITIES

If we accept the notion that transportation has been a major force in locating cities in broadscale space, as Christaller agreed in 1933 (under a special expression of central-place theory) and I did in 1970 (as the rootstock of my mercantile model of cities and their location), it seems to follow that transportation will become a strong shaping force within cities as well. We accept the proposition that transportation-settlement interaction exists; we must demonstrate more detail of its variation and transformation and seek to establish the process and its evolution. We should begin with the basal state, human existence in cities during the millennia of pedestrian movement before about 1825 and the introduction of the first significant assistance to the ordinary residents of cities. This basal state of transportation was clearly accompanied by a similar basal form of cities. Certainly not all cities were the same in ancient Rome and medieval France, for instance, but the two times and places shared characteristics that suggest the operation of similar shaping forces. If such forces were present in the basal state, it seems probable that different forces (1) have operated in other stages of transport development, and (2) have transformed the parts of cities laid out while that specific form of transportation dominated. Differential human mobility, as brought about by the evolution in the technology of transportation, can be expected to shape "different cities" associated with the individual stages in that evolution. This ontological evolution within two separate systems—transportation and urbanization—provides the organization we will use here to search for evidence of transportation-settlement relations and of the nature of their change over time. One ontogeny can be considered alongside another, and the resulting generalization of urban form can be tied, in turn, to a class of vehicles and their provision of a specific assistance to human mobility. Coincidence in time and place of change in the evolution of transportation technology and city form can provide compelling evidence of relationship; clear processal interaction of the technology of movement and of urban morphogenesis allows us to propound regularities of that relationship, which becomes the dominant city-shaping force.

HUMAN MOBILITY IN BASAL STATE AND TIME

The cities that were shaped during the long period when human mobility (particularly in cities) was on foot had a specific urban morphology that was widespread. Among its more significant characteristics was a cramping of space for circulation. In the cities in archaic Greece, it was the practice to knock on the inside of a door before opening it outward into the alley, then the nearly universal path through cities, to avoid striking pedestrians in those narrow and winding passageways. Anthropologists often comment on the residential "maze" in Muslim cities, arguing that it protects resident clans and other small social groupings. The passages may have that virtue, but lack of street width and indirect course were the rule rather than the exception in urban circulation before the nineteenth century. Even after Hippodamus, or whoever developed the orthogonal town in ancient Greece, the streets remained narrow even if straight. Only with the onset of the Renaissance did the wide, visual, ceremonial street come into use, and then only selectively. When London burned in 1666, it possessed great numbers of streets too narrow for horse-drawn vehicles. "Wheeled vehicles" for use throughout the city had to be barrows, and human porterage was the only absolutely universal access to all the city.

The modular scale of buildings was equally small, notably as cities increased in population, because space became an increasing luxury. Because most goods were pushed in barrows or borne on the backs of people or donkeys, these porters and animals were given "right of way" over ordinary pedestrians in alleys and other passages. These difficult conditions of circulation made the tightly packed city efficient. Lest these seem merely ancient conditions, we might observe that the central business district before World War II, the financial districts of a few cities even today (New York, San Francisco, London), and prospectively the aisles of the French *hypermarche* are crowded and heavily pedestrian to require compaction.

The first generation of integrated outlying shopping centers were, following Country Club Plaza's original, spread out because they envisaged parking interspersed within the center. After 1945, when parking was ranged around the edge of larger clusters of shops, it became obvious that the extent of a center with interspersed parking could grow beyond the willingness of shoppers to walk. The two-level shopping mall emerged to pack more people and shops closer together, particularly in extreme climates where weather modification was also introduced. Even today the introduction of basal transportation (walking) has a strongly morphogenetic consequence. The city district, central or outlying, that results is of limited radial extent to reduce long pedestrian journeys.

The other characteristics of the city in the basal state and time are too numerous to be detailed, but the differentiation in the use of space when viewed three-dimensionally must be mentioned. Today we talk about land use in cities, meaning the use of the ground space within an urbanized area. In the long history of cities, the distinction has lain more among the uses of various stories within buildings than in simple ground space. For example, in the medieval city the first floor (ground floor) was almost universally given over to a use that brought the household in direct contact with the public. If the occupant were a member of the gild merchant, his ground-floor shop would be used for selling, usually in the combination of retail and wholesale trade, common before the second half of the nineteenth century. If he were a member of an artisan gild, the householder would have his workshop on the ground floor, serving as his own sales agent in addition to making the goods, and doing so where the goods could be observed from the narrow streets (and even possibly displayed in front of his doorway). On the second floor the householder would commonly live with his family. On upper stories journeymen and their families might be accommodated or apprentices lodged. Goods would be stored in the attic, perhaps the driest part of the house, against future sale or fabrication. Under such a system there would be more accurately "story use" rather than "land use," because the ground floor would be nearly universally used in retail trade, possibly combined with artisan manufacture. The result was "occupation districts" where makers of a particular product would cluster along a street, creating a concentration of workspace and shops. For the gild merchant the district would allow for easy access to pedestrians. Because merchants did little but retailing and wholesaling, a maximum flow of pedestrians would be most commercially beneficial to them. Even today, in a central business district or an integrated shopping center where reversion to basal transportation occurs, the value of specific locations on the ground is based on pedestrian flow, as it would have been in or adjacent to the Greek stoa, the Roman basilica, or the *corniere* of the medieval bastide.

Such persistence of shaping forces in places of similar transportation, whether in the medieval marketplace or in the most recent integrated shopping center, gives us confidence in the assumption that transportation-settlement relationships are stable given similar pairings of transportation and urbanization.

A CENTURY OF RADICAL CHANGE

The tendency of general history to treat time as the grand engine of change, working toward that end with considerable consistency, is belied by specialized history, which commonly sees paroxysms of change after long periods of stability. What the American and French revolutions were to feudalism and heritable government, the century of the Industrial Revolution was to occupational practice and privilege. Industrialization transformed the organization of manufacture and trade, and human mobility as well, between 1825 and 1925. This was a century of transportation revolution, most notably in assisted human mobility. Most people still walked at the beginning of that century, but at its close most people in cities enjoyed at least some assistance in their daily movement. For the period 1825–1925, change was rapid, increasingly encompassing a larger society and geography. Each generation during those one hundred years had a fundamental transformation in transportation that advanced human mobility. Since 1925, change has been qualitative, relatively slow, and in no instance as fundamental as were several shifts during the century of transportation revolution between 1825 and 1925. The diesel-electric locomotive, the hovercraft, the jet plane, and high-speed elevators are the transportation innovations of the last two-thirds of a century, whereas the railroad, the airplane, the trolley, the subway, the powered ship, and electric communication were introduced in the previous one hundred years.

This chapter discusses what brought these transportation introductions in that marvellous century, why there were so many, and why they came so rapidly, and then looks at their relationship to human settlement and mobility during the years since 1825.

Before and after 1800, the physical extent of cities changed quite considerably in those countries beginning to experience a rapid expansion of trade and manufacture. The immediate example is Britain, but the United States perhaps is clearer. Up to the time of independence, the American colonies were severely restricted both in the pursuit of trade and in manufacture, but those legal constraints disappeared with peace in 1783. Maritime trade grew rapidly—although largely within the band from Norfolk to Portland, most importantly in New England and New York—and by the middle of the nineteenth century the American merchant marine was the largest in the world. Although American ships carried the trade of others, much of their cargo was laden or landed in U.S. ports, creating the country's first larger cities, places where the physical extent of the city was great enough to make assisted local transport nearly essential. The freeing of the United States allowed it to become, along with Belgium, the second country to have an industrial revolution. Soon after the Civil War, manufacturing activity began to grow rapidly, and by 1890 the United States had surpassed Britain as the dominant workshop of the world, again filling its cities with laborers in great numbers.

It is frequently overlooked that the rapid rise of population in the United States in the late nineteenth century was expressed in the ten largest cities rather than in the expansion of rural and small-city populations. Most places grew only modestly in area, but the big cities spread rapidly, as they had since the beginning of the nineteenth century. When we seek to explain why a transportation transformation began around 1825, this growth of a number of truly large cities in Europe and in the United States is perhaps most important. The generally higher wages and the much freer nature of landholding in the United States led directly to the social and technical advance in urban transit that were first experienced in the larger cities of America.

The concentration of urbanization in the larger U.S. cities combined with land-development practices fast becoming American characteristics to create specific and enlarged demands for urban transportation. By the middle of the last century, emerging industrial nations needed a national housing policy, mainly for the working-class population of cities. Western Europe turned to public housing, but the large amounts of cheap land surrounding most cities in the United States led to "private" provision of decent worker housing. That policy rested on the idea that cheap land allows for reasonable housing, and that peripheral open land was available if reasonably priced intraurban transportation could be provided.

THE HORSECAR: BREAKOUT

With the exception of the first "mass transit"—the omnibus, introduced in 1825—most efforts to provide transport to a wide urban public came first in the large industrial cities of the eastern United States. Although the horse-drawn street railway was introduced in 1832 in lower Manhattan as a way to permit the passenger cars of a steam railroad to be drawn southward from Twenty-third Street (under an embargo of steam-locomotive traction beyond that point), the horsecar lines quickly became widespread and fully divorced from standard railroad operation. By the 1850s, most of the larger cities of the eastern United States had extensive horsecar systems laid out on their preexisting arterial streets. These provided widely usable transit ranging outward from the city center for a distance of one-and-a-half to two miles, enlarging a traditional pedestrian city several times in area by doubling or even tripling its radial extent. The relatively slow speed of horsecars was in many ways an advantage, as it permitted easy stopping and starting, thus furnishing high-density service. The simple infrastructure of these lines meant that they might be ramified extensively within suburban bands, allowing these bands to house a large working-class population on ample areas of cheap land. The combination of the horsecar railway and cheap building sites provided the first private solution to the housing problem of ordinary families in the large cities that were increasingly becoming the homes of Americans.

THE TRADITIONAL CORE PATTERN

The settlement association related to the horsecar (which ruled urban transit in the United States between about 1850 and 1890) was an ever-increasing densification of housing even when ample cheap land was available. The horsecars were slow and relatively costly, so they were not infinitely extensible. Poorly paid workers still had to accept a walking journey-to-work, so extended commuting would be physically taxing. Furthermore, the length of a horsecar ride had to be limited, because the animals could not draw the heavy cars any great distance without a relief team or a substantial period of rest. Separation of workplace from residence for manual and service workers had to be minimized—both factory space and residential space had to be piled up into increasingly larger buildings. The tenement became the most characteristic accommodation. Only the upper middle class and above might live in separate residences.

Beyond these closely clustered (although separated) houses only two specialized groups might live: the wealthy, who were transported to true estates in individual carriages, and the skilled crafts and clerical employees, who might afford daily commuting by train to outlying working-class suburbs. Eastern American cities developed a series of bead-patterns of commuter villages housing the middle class and those skilled laborers willing to accept the time involved in commuting by train. Lower land costs kept housing costs down in such bead-pattern suburbs. The higher cost of railroad commuting kept such housing as expensive as that nearer the city core, but in the outlying town more space per house might be enjoyed.

So long as steam railroads provided the only alternative to walking to work, or traveling there on a short horsecar route, crowding into tenements at the center of the traditional city remained the norm for most people. After the Civil War, the tenement spread grimly in a frame around the traditional city core except where environmental amenities encouraged the similar, although less dense, clustering of the upper-middle- and upper-class apartment buildings. On Chicago's lakeshore and along the Garden City's parkway belts, these "French flats" became a façade of respectability similar to those bounding Central Park in Manhattan, Commonwealth Avenue in Boston, and the squares of Penn's Philadelphia. The earlier American Impressionist painters, such as Childe Hassam in Boston, frequently recorded the functional and geographical association of the streetcar, both horse-drawn and electric, and the apartment in America in the same way Gustave Caillebotte had tied together the boulevard and the original French flats of Paris in his paintings.

The French recognized this American contribution of the horsecar and its associated densification of the upper classes, merely translating the American terms into French, *le chemin de fer Americain* for the street railway and *le gratte-ciel* for Chicago and New York's skyscrapers, which in the two decades following the Civil War offered reasonably comfortable housing along horse-car lines for the well-to-do. In fact, in the hands of Parisians the most stylish and comfortable *appartements* were made, in part because they managed to internalize expansion, substituting a more demanding yet shorter elevation (climbing stairs) for that same muscular demand on a horizontal plane (pedestrian journeys-to-work).

MECHANICAL ASSISTANCE TO HUMAN MOBILITY

The horse was never a fully satisfactory traction for mass transit. It was expensive to buy and operate and was a public health nuisance, producing slippery streets, stench and filth, clouds of flies in the summer, and cacophonous springs with true storms of birds. Efforts were made continually to substitute mechanical assistance—from steam, chemical reactions, compressed air, ropes and cables, and other sources of energy—but none was satisfactory. Experiments in Vermont in the late 1840s had suggested that electricity might be a satisfactory source of energy for traction, but problems of distributing electricity from fixed generating sites constrained its use. In the late 1870s, notably in Germany and the United States, advances in generation and distribution offered new hope, leading Frank Sprague in the United States to an effort to devise an electric streetcar. In January and February of

1888 his experimental installation of overhead wires energizing trolley poles on streetcars proved successful, ushering in the Trolley Era that was matched only by the Industrial Revolution as a time of radically transformed morphogenesis in cities.

The striking transformation of urban fabric resulted from a vast expansion of the measure of space within cities. This expansion grew out of the true mechanization of assisted mobility in cities, and the introduction of a nonlinear cost of transit. The trolley motor was not only fully electric, rather than simply mechanical like some of its experimental progenitors, but it was also based on perhaps the most durable and efficient motor that has yet been devised, possessing acceleration-deceleration qualities that have not been bettered in a full century. A set of unusual circumstances favored a single, low, flat fare within cities or even metropolitan areas. In the next decade, when a five-borough metropolis was created in New York, an integral part of its charter was the requirement that any part of that vast city must be reachable from all parts by a flat fare of five cents on a mass transit system, creating the extreme expression of a cost-uniform if not cost-free daily transit.

That uniformity was rather fortuitous. The Metropolitan Railway in Boston was the first large horsecar system to be electrified, and it was in the late 1880s the world's most extensive horsecar system. Henry Whitney, the Metropolitan's president, decided that only a mass ridership would justify such an investment, and such a ridership could be secured only by keeping fares low and uniform. He was correct as to the best way of obtaining a mass ridership, and at first also seemed correct on profitability. The intake at the fare box expanded rapidly. Income quickly outpaced expenditures when the electric system was new, particularly because most trolley companies failed to set up sinking funds to repay the original debt or to renew the fabric of the system. The rapid growth in gross intake encouraged a sanguine appraisal of the profitability of almost any trolley line. Lines were long (due to the flat fare's encouragement of extension), and service along those lines was extremely high. For these two reasons the trolley built a massive increase into urban transit systems.

Radial extension geometrically increased the amount of development land inside the transit system. This increase, in turn, flooded the market for housing lots, lowered lot prices, and further expanded potential housing locations on a system where unit fares had abolished the economic friction of distance. Never before or since has intraurban transit been so relatively cheap nor the supply of potential building sites grown so rapidly. The trolley-era American metropolis was the first example of the broadly open city, offering the possibility of spacious housing sites to all classes of society, from the modest worker to the corporate titan. This rapid and radical spread of cities, seen by some as the bane of metropolitanism, is commonly blamed on the use of automobiles, while in fact it stemmed from the economically "frictionless space" of the Trolley Era.

THE ARTERIAL PATTERN

In many American metropolises the outer limits of the trolley city were not extended until after World War II, even though trolley commuting had lost its morphogenetic force as much as a decade and a half earlier. The hectic platting of lots, seemingly to the edge of the metropolitan horizon, gave a new basal structure to large U.S. cities. The engine driving that growth was already skipping strokes soon after World War I, when the profitability of electric-traction companies plummeted, maintenance and repairs were delayed or omitted, and the lightly trafficked outer ends of trolley lines faced being put out of service, awaiting a larger developed market for their support. Only slowly did that market grow, and when it did, a different driving engine would have replaced the trolley.

A discussion of that replacement requires an understanding of the morphology of the classical trolley city. Because so much space was introduced into the city, that period saw the rise of the archetypal American suburb, comprised of either single-family or simple detached houses on reasonably open lots in strips along trolley lines. These were turned into blocks by building backward from the arteries. As long as development land remained plentiful it was uncommon for the depth of development to reach farther perpendicular to the arterial than the rough spacing of stops along the trolley line. This "arterial structuring" of housing areas was the most characteristic feature of the trolley-era suburb. Housing was more compact in more equi-dimensional plats at the two polar extremes of income. The dense parceling of small land holdings into tiny lots crowded as many on the original three-to-five acre holding as human decency would allow. The upper middle class sought status through the creation of social strong points large enough to allow them to circle the wagons against social inferiors. Despite these modifications—clusters of two thousand-square-foot lots with twenty-foot frontages or ten thousand-square-foot lots "with trees and amenities in a gracious park"—the arterial structure was basal, both in time and in extent.

In such an arterial structure the construction practice of the era was most at home. As the trolley city spread, the large acreages of land opened to potential housing had to be transformed from agriculture use to mass housing. The notion of platting a parcel into lots for use as building sites by many small builders had already been accepted in the earlier years of the pedestrian city. The plats of American cities, of which John Reps has so splendidly made us aware, clearly demonstrate that from the time of William Penn in the 1680s speculative land platting has been well advanced in America. Small-scale builders have traditionally bought the single lot, constructed thereon a house, and sold it to obtain further capital to repeat the process, thus gaining a reliable wage. The practice continued into the Trolley Era, perhaps slightly enlarged in scale—a few adjacent lots developed simultaneously—but the basic separation of platting from building remained. Platting tended to be in fairly large tracts divided all at the same time and frequently some years ahead of any rationally expectable occupation of those lots by actual houses. The thinking of the land speculator gave the gross morphology to our cities: the traction magnate's plans and accomplishments set up the time pattern of our urbanization.

THE COMPACT PATTERN

It is hard to set as precise an ending for the Trolley Era as for its beginning. The fate of the electric traction industry began to look grim at the close of the First World War. By 1925, the automobile had gained ascendency in shaping geographical increments to cities. The supersession was masked by the areal explosion during the Trolley Era, because there was still a large amount of premature subdivision as late as 1925, but by that year recent building had begun to delineate a morphology of settlement associated with individual rather than mass mobility.

That morphology arrived in two stages, first of crisis and then of response. The trial came when the electric traction industry fell into rapid decline and many lines were abandoned during the 1920s. Those living in the more geographically exposed places, commonly the more peripheral parts of the metropolitan electric traction system, had lost frequency and density of service by the late 1920s; the Great Depression of the 1930s starved most trolley and interurban railway companies beyond survival. After 1925, many workers were forced to accept automobile commuting to maintain their employment. It was an easy step from partial dependence on self-provision of assisted mobility to full personal responsibility for most aspects of the family's mobility. Once the latter stage was reached, the transportation response to the financial collapse of the electric tractions had been set.

Metropolitan areas have been the site of demographic expansion during the automobile era, 1925 to the present, and we can observe several stages with distinctive morphological patterns. For the first ten years after 1925, that morphology had been almost wholly inherited. These were trolley cities with automobiles rapidly taking the lead in urban transportation. Roads became clogged and technologically malfunctioning. Where they had previously been arterial or neighborhood in a local context they now became arterial or neighborhood in a metropolitan frame, forcing the creation of a new form of "superhighway" that was highly experimental throughout the 1930s. The physical separation of opposing directions of traffic, the grade separation of crossing roads, and the creation of continuous flow junctions were early accomplishments. Slower to be seen as a clear necessity was legal limitation of access if regional arteries were to replace local ones. Only in Rhode Island in 1937 was the legal instrument to accomplish that end in a general fashion hammered out, and only in 1940 in California was such a limited-access highway actually constructed. Ultimately these efforts toward the shaping of an evolved superhighway created a second stage of the automobile era with a related urban morphology.

The metropolitan superhighway in the 1930s was becoming an effective instrument of private-car mobility for individuals or small groups of people riding together, thus potentially transforming access to workplaces. It was also establishing the possibility for a new form of residential area. When cars were first used for commuting in the 1920s, the two termini of journeys still were determined by trolley era patterns of workplace and housing location. The arterial orientation of housing was still strong. There was some slight freeing of siting from frontage on the arterial to include short streets intersecting it at right angles, but cars used the same arterials as those used by trolleys. Departure from the arterial for new house lots was constrained by reliance on formerly rural roads—often narrow, rough, unpaved, and unserved by municipal services. It was easier to develop new building sites farther out on the same arterial or on a different arterial than to build perpendicular to arterials.

THE AREAL PATTERN

The fundamental shift to the automobile city, with housing sites different from those of the trolley city, came with the creation of an areal pattern design orientation in housing. Block-like rather than linear housing tracts had been introduced into nineteenth-century cities even in the era of the horse-car, particularly to secure social cachet. It was easier to convey the higher social status of a house in a compact and coherent tract than in an arterial and linear pattern. At first the large supply of lots in linear patterns left over from the Trolley Era masked the increasing desire for class-specific tracts, but the use of automobiles in the journey to work facilitated such a class division, originating toward the top of the socioeconomic stratification. By the Crash of 1929, Babson Parks, Cliff Estates, and St. Francis Woods for the auto-motively mobile were being touted by real-estate operators who increasingly assumed a deliberate morphogenetic role.

THE RISE OF SOCIAL CLASS

In this morphological and social context the American government first began to assume a role in guiding housing development through the adoption of the Federal Housing Act of 1934, the ultimately omnipotent FHA. From its inception, the FHA operated with a contemporary and almost isotatic conception of class as a dominant factor in determining "sound housing." The car had enabled class separation to gain ascendency among the processes at work in housing choice and spatial location. The FHA arrived on the scene when the trolley had lost any significant power to shape cities, and the car had gained adolescent vigor in shaping them. This initial effort to establish a national housing policy accepted class division as part of that policy. When

Homer Hoyt, working for the FHA, published his classic *Residential Structure of American Cities* in 1939, he sought not only to present maps of such a structure based on economic class, but also to justify its perpetuation in the interests of maintaining sound and stable housing in the United States. There was a strong morphogenetic element in creating and maintaining the class-structured FHA suburb of the American metropolis.

In the 1930s, the automobile had become the dominant form of transportation. By being individual it could allow a sensitive differentiation among suburbs on the basis of housing cost and economic status. The mortgage insurance policies of the FHA encouraged housing tracts of narrow uniformity as the most "stable," and a compact net of curvilinear streets "built out" within a short period was the most likely to be acceptable to most house buyers. This pattern of compactness required regular incrementation of later tracts with strong social similarity. Transitions of class between adjacent tracts seemed to require sharp environmental distinctions. Elevated, wooded, or "view" lots increased status level; flat, low-lying sites or tracts adjacent to industry had a lower social level. Under early FHA policy, ethnic and racial uniformity (particularly the latter) was encouraged, and street patterns were expected to shield favored social groups from areas housing the less favored. Automobile transportation encouraged the compact and rapid development of tracts. The superhighways of the 1930s tied increasingly peripheral land blocks to the general arterial system of the metropolis and opened extensive areas for development. The FHA mortgage insurance made the class stratification of tracts more likely because it was based on ability to repay. The size of mortgages was determined not by the personal thrift of the borrower but rather by a bureaucratic classification of incomes necessary to support monthly payments.

THE METROPOLIS IS RE-SORTED

The compact form of the FHA tracts and their differentiation by income created the first stage of fully automobile suburbanization, whose morphogenesis was established before 1945. Since World War II, several subsequent phases of automotive suburbanization and a major re-sorting of other types of metropolitan activity have been shaped by automotive transportation. A major shift of central-business-district-type retailing to suburban locations after 1945 was based almost entirely on the superhighway of the 1930s, which allowed the journey to shop over an increased distance. The suburbanization of shopping reduced the remaining support for commuter rail lines, both steam and electric, and led to new abandonment of rail service. By the mid-1950s, the switch to automotive commuting was nearly complete. Less than a dozen North American cities still possessed functioning rail commutation— Boston, New York, Philadelphia, Baltimore, Pittsburgh, Cleveland, Chicago, St. Louis, Montreal, Toronto, and San Francisco.

The rapid and massive growth of trucking after 1945 encouraged an outward shift of wholesaling and manufacturing activity and further re-sorted use districts in metropolitan areas. The 1930s superhighways, often called "expressways," provided the initial access to outlying industrial and commercial sites. Those routes clogged so rapidly that less than ten years after the war there were calls for a new system of urban freeways patterned on the first such road, which opened in Los Angeles in 1940. In the early 1950s, the federal government began planning a national system of interstate highways, to which was appended a considerable mileage of metropolitan freeways. The first federal funding of urban roads was the authorizing act passed in 1954. When freeways were completed, industry began to move toward the edges of many metropolitan areas. The shift of retailing and manufacturing created massive employment activities in the suburbs.

By 1955 the metropolis had been massively transformed. The suburbs were the fastest growing area in the United States. Increments to housing, although based on automotive transportation, had a different morphogenesis from the FHA stage of 1935 to 1955. Compact tracts of elaborate social stratification, attached to the core by the arterial roads of the automobile era, were replaced by larger tracts apparently predicated on the notion of style. Each year seemed to have its own model house. The new role of style came with mass production of houses shaped from standardized major components that could not easily be transported any great distance. The benefits of mass production required that the market be narrowed to a few models clustered in a small area. "This year's style" encouraged concentration of purchases in tracts enjoying a distinct, if ephemeral, style advantage.

Another transformation grew out of the creation of the metropolitan freeway grid, made up in part of state highways and in part of local components of the Interstate highway system. A new conception of spatial organization grew rapidly when the metropolitan highway system entirely of freeway design was completed. Just as the trolley, with its low-unit fare, had revolutionized space after 1888 by removing the cost friction of distance, the metropolitan freeway system after about 1960 revolutionized space again by removing much of the time friction of distance. Actual commuting distances mattered little, compared with how long it took to get there. The removal of spatial friction proved ephemeral, as in the electric traction industry's history. Cost increases by distance were back in the pricing of metropolitan transportation by 1985. Nevertheless, times for travel were greatly improved while the metropolitan freeways were young. Industries, warehouses, shopping centers, and sports facilities were built toward the edge of the metropolitan area, frequently with the hope that intercity freeways would allow facilities at the edge of one metropolis to serve its metropolitan neighbor as well. When the freeway was youthful it was also usually fast (as the trolley had been at the turn of the century), but speeds declined radically as metropolitan maturity

and consequent morphogenesis filled up the landscape and thereby the freeway integral to it. Decline in speed on the route bore heavily on a much
lengthened urban movement. Given a desire by a greater number of cars to
move an increased distance, any decrease in average speed would rapidly
clog the route.

THE URBAN REALM PATTERN

Until the clogging became too severe, much land was developed under
unduly sanguine speed-of-travel assumptions. Freeway system morphogenesis reintroduced the concept of the near costlessness of distance because it
facilitated journeys to work, to shop, and for other purposes. The cost of
housing had rapidly inflated in the 1960s and 1970s, and people attempted to
lower its costs by moving rather farther from the traditional core, particularly
as employment opportunities multiplied near the edge of the metropolis.
After 1850, when American metropolises had been more extensive than
those in most other countries, the wealthier residents commonly had moved
to the edge, but with a true working class employed near the edge there were
also reasons for modest to even marginal housing at the periphery. In a
number of cities, a new class of "libertarian suburbs" grew up as havens for
those who opposed building codes, planning restrictions, use constraints, and
formally incorporated local government. Horses could be tethered on small
lots, other animals raised in number and kind forbidden in cities, old cars
stored in immobility or semidestruction fully exposed to the world, and an
individualism enjoyed that would have been resented in the older formal
suburbs.

The wider range of social milieux in the era of the post-1960s freeway
network in metropolitan regions shaped a new morphological component
induced by the substitution of the integrated freeway system for the diversity
of public transport. The individual family, even the single individual, now has
a strongly personalized form of assisted mobility, and a multicentered metropolis has become possible, whereas, under mass public transportation (as
in the commuter railroad, the interurban electric system, or the ramified
trolley) a single center had to tie it all together. The great areal extent and
population of many metropolises and a reshaping of land-use patterns has
recrystallized urban structure. The major subdivision of these metropolises is
the urban realm, a major building block of the extended city. Each realm has
its own daily urban activity system, with fewer functioning ties to the traditional core of the city than to activities within it.

The recrystallization of urban activities into the smaller, more functional, area of the urban realm is incomplete. Patterns of mobility based on the
earlier stages of transportation in the long evolution of urban morphogenesis
have not been fully transformed, leaving an awkward pattern of excessively

long daily journeys, or journeys so focused through some bottleneck that mobility rapidly freezes up. Transportation-settlement relationships have had both healthy and pathological processes at work throughout history, commonly at the same time. Today, however, virtually everyone must move in a daily fashion and seldom on a geographical scale that gives many alternative ways of doing so.

The most recent stage of urban morphogenesis based on transportation and human mobility, although not fully delineated at present, seems to depend on the effort to secure individuals' choices in assistance to human mobility. The first choice is probably seeking to confine daily movement within a single urban realm. The Bay Area City, as an example, has several urban realms—the traditional cities on either side of the Bay, Oakland and San Francisco, the central sections of the West Bay and of the East Bay, the Santa Clara Valley focusing on San Jose, and the North Bay focusing on Santa Rosa. These five urban realms, as each has gained ever larger populations, have become the homes both of more housing and more retailing, wholesaling, and industry, each producing enlarging employment. These five realms are components of a metropolitan area of six million people, but they can hardly function efficiently as a single unit. Each individual unit is related in part to one of the traditional core cities, San Francisco or Oakland. Normally, each outlying focus—San Jose or Santa Rosa—has a daily activity relationship only to its urban realm, because it has become a nucleus under the operation of freeway transportation, but all the realms have some daily relationship with the traditional cities, all with San Francisco and those in the East Bay with Oakland.

The Bay Area Rapid Transit System (BART) was conceived in error in the 1960s, based on the notion that the metropolis remained focused on a single city and still depended on flows to and from downtown San Francisco. It is an example of a nineteenth-century urban mass transit system with excessive core-city focus of routes and service. A costly and out-of-date heavy rail transit system was introduced to try to stem the growth of a metropolis of realms. This project, advanced by the merchant group and landowners in downtown San Francisco, as well as those working there, represented a deliberately selfish or at the very least uninformed conception of needs for a metropolitan transit system. The realms, as the vital geographic elements of present-day urbanization, have continued to emerge in the quarter century since BART was floated as the ultimate solution for the daily transportation needs of the Bay Area City. This system was extremely costly to build, and planners misunderstood the growth of their metropolis, but little other effort has gone into improving Bay Area transportation. The freeway network in the area was designed in large part as the metropolitan section of the Interstate highway system aimed at longer-distance movement. Circulation within the individual realms of the Bay Area City has been forgotten to such a degree that automotive traffic flows have become clogged metropolitan-wide. It is difficult to find any solution for the geographical failure to perceive the existence of urban realms and to provide a rational public transportation system for them. In the absence of a realm-transit system, pathology with respect to human mobility has overcome us, creating within metropolises the widespread notion that flight into the countryside, to secure a necessary asylum, is essential.

THE ASYLUM PATTERN

The evidence of an asylum pattern of transportation-settlement relationships is already in hand. Small towns in the penumbra of cities have had the highest rate of increase in population in recent years. The asylum band has been heavily developed to provide a greater choice of housing, particularly oriented toward those seeking retirement or truly exurban living with only occasional contact with the central city. These penumbral towns have become increasingly specialized worker suburbs for those employed at the edge of the continuously built-up metropolis, who now quite frequently drive across an informal "green belt" until they reach the truly satellitic smaller town, frequently deep in the countryside but no farther in travel time from their work than the more traditional suburbs are for core-city workers.

Perhaps the most persuasive asylum is economic. For more than one hundred years there has been a conscious effort to provide reasonably priced worker housing on "cheap land" at the contemporary edge of the city. Because the securing of municipal services may be increasingly more difficult at the edge of the city, and because land has become a primary speculative commodity, it may prove far more satisfactory for many families to abandon the true edge of the city and move well out to the satellite towns and their margins.

I have tried to suggest that cities receive much of their physical organization from contemporary transportation. Because that urban morphology is a quite substantial and determinant feature, it neither changes automatically with transformations of transportation systems nor is it impossibly dysfunctional after a new form of human mobility is introduced. In the absence of any previous development, however, current urban morphogenesis will reflect the dominant current transportation.

Cities more than a century old have a core morphology initially dominated by pedestrian mobility. This traditional pattern continued to arise in large cities somewhat after the introduction of an arterial morphology incident on the horsecar and the electric trolley. The arterial settlement pattern showed modest beginnings (with the horsecar) around 1850 and found a full flowering (with the trolley) after 1888. This arterial pattern was not absolute.

There was infilling of modest depth away from the car lines, but the arterial component remained dominant in additions to the city in the second half of the last century.

The automobile arrived in U.S. cities soon after the turn of the century, but a successor morphological pattern did not become dominant until after the collapse of electric traction around 1918. Throughout the 1920s, the arterial probably remained the most common component of urban morphogenesis, and the successor form could confidently be determined only with the advent of FHA housing in socially stratified tracts. This compact pattern of accretion to the city was based largely on automotive movement and the rise of the housing tract, with an annual incrementation of dozens or even hundreds of tract developments.

The compact pattern became dominant after 1945, aided by the initial phase of freeway movement within metropolitan areas. The freeways were initially so successful that they created a temporary illusion, that the friction of time in urban driving had been conquered. A massive areal pattern of incrementation expanded metropolitan regions rapidly and created extensive areas served almost universally by automotive transportation. This expansion was so extensive that it destroyed not the fabric but rather the function of the single-centered city. First came dispersal of land uses throughout the metropolitan fabric and then the replication of what had earlier been almost exclusively core area functions.

By about 1970, that replication had produced a new metropolis with a realm pattern. The constraints that had existed as the metropolis grew larger lost force once a set of realms began to parcel it out. Growth did not stop with the emergence of realms; instead, for a time it seemed that growth's undesirable features might have been tempered by limiting the average person's daily activity area to a single urban realm. The dispersal of functions among a number of realms helped, but the absence of any form of urban transportation functionally adjusted to the specific scale of the realm allowed most cities to become clogged with traffic. Even its realms seemed affected by a pathological decline in human mobility of the sort that had ultimately constrained all previous stages of transportation-settlement relationships.

A new stage has emerged, an asylum pattern under which those who can move out of the metropolis completely have done so. Some have been able to seek only partial asylum, a place of residence but not a place of work. If past processes are representative, the asylum pattern and its era probably will be subject to congestion and resulting decline in human mobility. There may be a further pattern as yet unperceived. It is also possible that no further pattern will be acceptable, and we will have reached the ultimate restraint of human mobility and the ultimate expression of transportation-settlement relationships. If that proves to be the case, the future is not totally bleak. We can attempt to fill the gap by improving transportation yet again, by finding a way to provide "proper transportation" for the basic needs of cities.

From this evolution there seems little doubt that there are transportation-settlement relationships, that they constitute one of the fundamentals of urban morphogenesis, and that they have done so for most of the era of massive urbanization since 1800.

REFERENCE

Vance, James E., Jr. 1990. *Capturing the horizon: The historical geography of transportation since the sixteenth century.* Baltimore: Johns Hopkins University Press.

SIX

New Grain Networks in an Old Urban System

John C. Hudson

The revolution in grain marketing and transportation has been one of the least noticed of the many changes that have swept across rural America in the last several decades. We know of larger outputs produced by fewer farmers, of cost-price squeezes on the farm, of stagnation or decline in trade-center towns. We know that the agricultural sector has become more export oriented, and that government programs have evolved, however imperfectly, in response to new foreign markets. Linkages between producers and markets also have been changing. The map of American commodity flow has been compressed here and twisted there as the web of connectivity has stretched to cover new patterns of supply and demand (Figure 6.1). These changes have wrought more than merely a restructuring of agricultural flows. The town-and-city network of mid-America was created by nineteenth-century capitalists largely to organize rural hinterlands efficiently. Now this network is being reshaped, and a new logistics has emerged to test the old urban system.

EVOLUTION OF THE TRANSPORTATION SYSTEM

The new nexus has evolved rather steadily since 1950, but it can be viewed as a three-step process of change: first, the original grain-collection system was based on railroad transportation; second, the emergence of inter-modal competition in the 1950s involved truck and barge movements followed by the 1970s export boom; and third, the deregulated transportation environment of the 1980s has fostered new patterns of grain storage and movement. The nodal points in the network, the trade-center towns, initially were a product of the transportation business, but subsequently have had to adjust to each new development.

Stage 1: The Railroad-Based System

It contradicts the conventional wisdom of geographers to claim that the network of trade-center towns was created by men who had the single purpose of forming chains and networks of collection points, but I am convinced that this purpose was preeminent in determining town locations over most of the nation's midsection and even beyond that in areas where agricultural prospects were especially good. Our "central place network" resulted not from many invisible hands working in spatial competition for trading territory. Nor did it arise very often from isolated acts of noble individuals or groups who, for their own purposes, simply founded a town at a particular site. Rather, it was the plan to capture the traffic in agricultural produce, notably grain, that caused railroad men and their associates to build mile after mile of railroad line and to dot those lines with trade-center towns (Hudson 1985). A dense web of evenly spaced towns was the result. Probably 90 percent of the central places in Iowa were founded in this manner, and the percentage is even higher in the major grain-producing regions of the Plains.

The town network was born of efforts to create a grain collection system. Railroad men in the latter half of the nineteenth century were interested in funneling as much grain traffic as they could over their own lines to Minneapolis, Omaha, Kansas City, Chicago, and a half-dozen other centers. Knowing that other railroads shared the same strategy, competing companies built into any territory they could capture. The method of capture was simple, based on the valid assumption that a farmer marketing grain would generally choose to patronize the closest elevator. A townsite platted next to the grain elevator would anchor the farmer's trading habits because the town would offer him the banking services and retail goods he needed. Goods that the farmer purchased would be hauled in by rail, and other farm products, such as livestock, would be hauled out, but the grain business offered the best prospects for a profitable railroad line. The densest networks were built in regions where grain farming was the most profitable.

Anyone looking at a map of towns and transportation routes in Iowa, whether in the late nineteenth century or the mid-twentieth, would see an evenly spaced scatter of small towns served by a crisscrossing web of routes. Anyone, that is, except a railroad official, who would perceive something more like tree trunks with branches; one of those trunks was his, the others, those of his competitors. The layperson's perception of Iowa's map suggests a broad, democratic quality: hundreds of little places set in their own little patches of territory. The corporate perception (the creator's perception, as it were) emphasized branching and hierarchy, position and control. The object was to build an optimal funnel to direct Iowa's abundance toward the market.

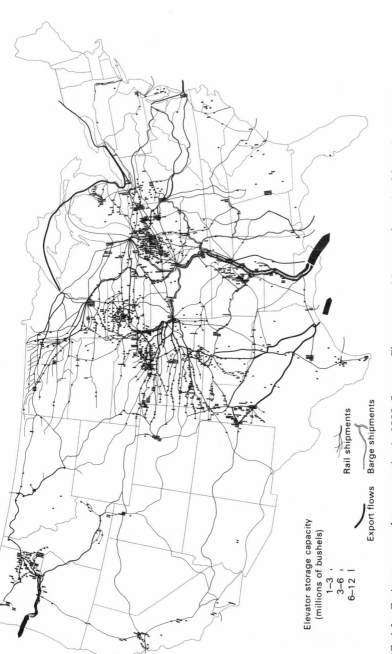

**Elevator storage capacity
(millions of bushels)**

1–3 ;
3–6 ;
6–12 |

Export flows

Rail shipments

Barge shipments

FIG. 6.1 Grain storage and transportation in 1988. Sources: Elevator capacities were determined from the *North American Grain Yearbook*, 1988; from the *Official Railway Guide* "Grain Connection," July-August, 1988; and from data supplied by individual companies. Railway traffic flows were estimated from Association of American Railroads, *The Grain Book*, and numerous other sources including field observations and interviews with railroad personnel (no published data are available for individual railway routes). River, Great Lakes, and waterborne export flows were taken from U.S. Army Corps of Engineers, *Waterborne Commerce of the United States*, 1986, and National Waterway Foundation, *U.S. Waterways Productivity*.

Far-off investors with big schemes dictated the network of towns, but the farmers and townspeople who lived in it were not necessarily aware of the outsiders' role. They rebelled against the rates charged by the railroads and generally distrusted large corporations, but they had little inkling that the towns they came to know and love were the product of simple paper-and-pencil calculations by businesspeople. The typical small-town resident's view of community history even today is some variation on, "our town was founded in 1886 when the railroad came through." An accurate, though heartless, correction would be, "your town was founded by the XYZ Railroad in 1886 to collect grain and fat cattle for shipment to Chicago." What the men who created these strings of towns may have overlooked was that every "place" comes to have meaning to its inhabitants. A social order emerged that differentiated each from the others. Fortunes were made and lost. Communities grew and often declined. And all of these events became, in turn, a community history inextricably linked to the site and ultimately rooted in the belief that some purpose had been served by the generations who labored to make it a good place to live.

Thus today, long after the rusty rails of the XYZ Railroad have been torn up and the town's reason for creation has been lost, its community leaders meet to discuss strategies for survival, looking for a niche in a system that seems to have forgotten the past. The buildings on Main Street are crumbling in disuse or have been converted to uses of which their builders never dreamed. The town is no longer a trade center. Its school buildings are unused, replaced by larger, more centralized facilities serving two, three, or more towns. The forces that have brought about the current low estate include farmers traveling longer distances to shop, children who leave for the city and are not replaced, and other factors not directly related to transportation (Hart 1988). The crops grown outside of town are far more bountiful today than they were a century ago, but even the local grain elevator no longer serves its former role.

Stage 2: Intermodal Competition

This typical, if mythical, place is caught in the grip of changes in the second stage of evolution in the mid-American system. Railroads had dictated the settlement pattern because they offered the only means, at that time, of binding farms, towns, factories, and cities together efficiently. Their monopoly on transportation went virtually unchallenged until the 1950s. Farmers had owned trucks and automobiles long before, but their increased freedom of mobility only had a local impact. They were able to drive farther to shop, and small towns saw a further reduction in the retail trade that, in many cases, never had been adequate because the railroads' competition for territory had created an excess supply of towns. Farmers began trucking grain to town in the 1920s, but their trips were generally no different from those they had made in the era of horse-drawn wagons: they still were inclined to haul to the nearest elevator, beyond which transportation remained the exclusive domain of railroad companies.

The continued improvement of the national highway network and the construction of the so-called Interstate and Defense Highway System in the late 1950s made truck transportation competitive with rail over much of the nation's interior. Trucks were ideal for hauling the rapidly expanding array of consumer durables that a trade center had to offer to remain competitive. Cattle and hogs, formerly shipped live to enormous stockyards in packinghouse cities like Chicago, soon vanished from the list of items hauled by the railroad as meatpacking began its westward shift toward the sources of supply. The effects were seen in the small towns of mid-America, where first the freight house was closed, then the stockloading pens were abandoned, and finally the railroad station was closed. The elevator remained and, until the 1970s, so did nearly every mile of railroad track.

Hauling grain by truck more than thirty or forty miles is not a least-cost solution when railroad rates are based on costs (Won, Thompson, and Larson 1984). Between 1945 and 1960, however, railroad rates on grain nearly doubled (Haldeman 1960b). Rail transportation became a more costly alternative for reaching many terminal markets. If water (barge) transportation is added to the modal mix, then trucking one hundred miles or more can be cost-effective when coupled with the extremely low per-mile costs on the inland waterways. New navigation channels made the Missouri River a natural route for grain traffic south of Sioux City, and the Columbia-Snake was developed west of Lewiston, Idaho. The Arkansas Waterway, from Catoosa (Tulsa) to the Gulf, the long-established Illinois River barge system, plus navigation on the Mississippi south of St. Paul, and on the Tennessee, Ohio, Chattahoochee, White, Tombigbee, and Yazoo rivers began to compete with railroad grain movements.

Illinois, Iowa, and Indiana are the top three corn and soybean exporting states; Missouri, Ohio, Nebraska, and Minnesota are also major exporters. All of those states began shipping export grain down the Mississippi River or its major tributaries. What had been a modest downriver flow turned into a torrent with the sharp increase in U.S. grain exports in 1973. Foreign-bound grain accounted for a substantial share of the 50 percent increase in Mississippi River tonnage during the 1970s. Although U.S. agricultural exports slipped nearly 50 percent from 1981 to 1986, the new patterns of movement were already entrenched (U.S. Department of Commerce 1988).

A typical bushel of eastern Iowa corn used to be consumed by meat animals on the farm where it was raised, or else it was trucked to the local elevator and shipped to Chicago in a railroad boxcar. Today that typical bushel of corn probably is trucked to a river elevator on the Mississippi and is exported from the vicinity of New Orleans. Many river elevators are comparatively small affairs with storage capacities no larger than the country elevators with which they compete for traffic. Some of the larger facilities are equipped to receive grain arriving by rail, but grain trucks are the most common source of supply at the riverbank.

The Mississippi waterway system, with its north-south alignment ideally suited for grain exports through New Orleans, caused a massive crisis for railroads in mid-America. Retrenchments in railroad service to small towns, already underway due to competition from trucks, were accelerated by the loss of grain traffic to barges. Traffic sources of some railroads, especially the smaller and financially weaker companies, disappeared, and they sought protection by merger into larger systems. In 1960, nine major railroad companies served the upper Middle West. By 1980, the nine had been merged down to five, and two of these were in bankruptcy.

The Interstate Commerce Commission (ICC) long opposed merger between parallel railroad companies on the grounds that it would reduce competition. With the competition coming more from trucks and barges than from other railroads, however, the Commission finally gave approval to such combinations. If two merged companies both had tracks running between the same points it was logical to remove one of them to avoid duplication. Further cost reduction efforts by railroads resulted in trimming many branch lines and removing circuits. Towns removed from the system often lost their grain business to the truck competition.

In addition to a ruthless trimming of light-density branch lines, railroad companies tore up tracks even through first-rate cash grain country where business had gone largely to the truck/barge alternative. North-south branch lines paralleling the Mississippi have been almost entirely removed. North Dakota, in contrast, still ships the bulk of its grain to Duluth and Minneapolis over a rail network that has seen only minor abandonment. The same is true for the winter wheat belt of Kansas and Oklahoma where the crop—nearly three-fourths of it destined for Texas Gulf ports and overseas export—moves almost entirely by rail (Fuller, Makus, and Taylor 1983). Railroad abandonment has been most widespread where intermodal competition has been keenest, relatively minor in cash-grain specialty areas farthest from the inland waterways.

Grain elevators in towns left without rail service saw less activity. They still could be used for storing grain, of course, but their locations were no longer strategic. It was a particularly hard blow to many small towns that were carved out of the system just when the long-slumbering grain industry leaped to life under the impetus of export demand. Hauling grain to the elevator was the lone remaining reason many farmers had for patronizing their local trade-center town, the retail trade having already vanished. Some farmers' grain cooperatives reorganized as branches of larger, nearby elevator associations in an attempt to keep their marketing options open.

Rather than invest further in grain storage facilities in town, many farmers chose to construct new bins and flat-houses on their own farms. Some purchased semitrailer trucks to haul grain to terminals fifty to one hundred miles away where the price was attractive. Owning the means of transportation also meant they were no longer at the mercy of railroad companies, which, despite their overcapitalization, never seemed to have enough grain cars available when demand surged—a problem especially serious in the 1970s boom when the rail system failed to move grain fast enough and enormous backups ensued (Barnett, Brinkley, and McCarl 1984).

Confusion reigned in the grain transportation industry in the mid-1970s. Farmers were plunging boldly into the storage and transportation business. The small elevators owned by those same farmers were being bypassed as grain moved to new destinations. Long trains of hundred-ton grain hopper cars were crushing lightweight rails on branchlines built to support nineteenth-century equipment, causing lengthy tie-ups. Railroads were filing abandonment petitions on dozens of lines of track they no longer considered functional yet were too costly to rehabilitate given the prospects for further loss of business. The parade of grain trucks heading for the Mississippi and Illinois river elevators rumbled on. The network for collecting, storing, and moving grain that the railroads had developed was rapidly disintegrating under competitive pressures that were only exacerbated by a regulatory environment more sensitive to transport competition than to the interest of shippers.

Although truck rates on grain-to-inland terminals were competitive with railroad rates, truckers often charged half again as much to haul grain the same distance to one of the new river elevators that had no facilities for unloading grain from rail cars (Haldeman 1960a). Truckers naturally pursued what advantage they had, and there was some sympathy for them, given the increases in railroad grain rates, but it was obvious that the rapidly evolving truckers' monopoly was no more desirable than the old railroad monopoly had been. Farmers could own their own elevators and truck their own grain. They could even mill the flour and bake the bread if it came to that, but a levelheaded appraisal of costs and benefits suggested that a return to a more rational system of public transportation was needed.

Railroads had not always tried only to raise rates, either. There was the infamous "Big-John" grain car case during the 1960s, when the Southern Railway, in an attempt to take advantage of the economies of multiple-car movements, posted a rate on unit-train grain shipments that was about half of what the old single-car rate had been. It was opposed by truckers, barge interests, and an assortment of other industry types who were thriving under the status quo. The rate case was finally settled in the Southern Railway's interest by the U.S. Supreme Court (Nightengale 1967). The ICC, long a target of railroad industry scorn and ridiculed by many professional economists, was increasingly seen as an impediment to effective rate-making because of the cumbersome procedures it imposed.

The ICC was created by Congress in 1887 largely to regulate rate making by railroad companies. Shippers and consumers alike needed protection against excessively high rates ("what the traffic will bear") and from ruinously low rates that eliminated competition. The ICC had an elaborate machinery for deciding railroad grain rate cases, yet there was no federal regulation of interstate truck and barge rates on grain (Ulrey 1967). The Motor Carrier Act of 1935 had explicitly exempted regulatory control of interstate trucking rates on unmanufactured agricultural products. When Congress passed laws regulating inland waterway barge traffic in 1940, it exempted bulk commodity movements from federal control. Truckers and barge operators hauling grain were free to set whatever rates would bring traffic their way, but the railroads were obliged to submit their own rates to ICC scrutiny, to defend themselves at public hearings, and to be subjected sometimes to lengthy litigation—not only to raise rates, but to lower them as well.

Who would oppose reduced rates on hauling grain by rail? Truckers and barge operators obviously would, but grain millers also frequently opposed decreases (Nightengale 1967). Long-established milling centers such as Kansas City and Minneapolis had "transit privileges" on grain shipments. Wheat grown in North Dakota was milled in Minneapolis and shipped as flour to Chicago under the same rate as wheat moved from North Dakota to Chicago. The milling industry had evolved at the rate-break points and was protected by the in-transit rates governing those points. The milling industry sought to preserve transit privileges, and it opposed any rate increases on flour over grain because such a shift would, in location-theoretic terms, pull the industry's Weberian optimal point toward the market, away from its traditional location nearer the sources of supply.

Railway rate decreases were approved where a shift in mode would not upset the industry. Rates on Houston-bound export grain from Enid and Wichita, for example, were lowered by 40 percent between 1957 and 1964, largely to meet truck competition. The northern transcontinental railroads reduced rates on export wheat in the 1960s in an attempt to increase the flow of grain to the Pacific Northwest. Reduced rates were proposed because improvements in railway technology had made it possible to haul larger-capacity hopper cars assembled into one hundred-car unit trains at less than half the cost of single-car movements.

Grain could easily be massed in such quantities, but flour and other milled products were not consignable in large volumes. Storage in the grain industry, as in most industries, is cost-effective at the raw materials end, not at the market. Railroads stood ready to haul trainloads of wheat from Superior to Buffalo, trainloads of corn from Louisville to Birmingham—trainloads of anything that could be moved in such quantity—but millers, truckers, Great Lakes carriers, and barge operators opposed the reduced rates and often succeeded in getting them denied or at least postponed.

The ossified geography of grain milling, protected by the system of in-transit rates, probably was close to a least-transportation-cost solution when the market was concentrated east of the Mississippi and north of the Ohio, but population had shifted toward the West and South. Flour was barged from St. Louis down the Mississippi to Carrabelle, at the easternmost end of the Intracoastal Waterway, and then trucked to the growing peninsular Florida market (Ulrey 1967). Americans were shifting their allegiance from beef to chicken, but the Southeastern "broiler belt" was chronically short of the feed grains that Midwestern farmers produced in abundance. Asian and South American markets for wheat, corn, and soybeans were growing and demanded new transportation solutions. Farmers were held hostage by a tradition that caused the ICC to set railroad rates that allowed all modes of transportation to be competitive instead of granting the lowest rate to the least-cost alternative.

Stage 3: Deregulation

Congressional passage of the Staggers Rail Act (P.L. 96) of 1980 gutted the authority of the ICC and set the stage for the next phase, popularly known as deregulation. The Staggers Act set the minimum railroad rate on a shipment at 100 percent of variable costs, beyond which the ICC was to apply a standard of "reasonableness." With the freedom to set rates as low as cost, and with upper limits challenged by all the usual sources, railroads began to recover traffic. The Association of American Railroads claims that railroad grain rates decreased 26 percent from 1980 to 1985 (Association of American Railroads 1986). The depressed export market allowed only a small recovery in railroad traffic during this period, but the railroad share of grain traffic is likely to increase. Railroads can haul more than half the grain forwarded for export if rates are no more than 10 percent above variable costs, but their share diminishes rapidly beyond that point (Fuller, Makus, and Taylor 1983).

It is impossible to say if a Staggers Act ten years earlier would have saved many railroad lines, but deregulation came too late to help the Milwaukee Road and the Rock Island, both major grain-carrying railroads of the Middle West and Great Plains that went bankrupt in 1980. A railroad once removed is almost never replaced, and few grain elevators that lost rail service during the 1970s had any prospect of regaining it. Even communities with their railroad track intact became alarmed if those tracks were not in service. Unwilling to accept what appeared to be yet another assault on their economic viability, they rallied under "Save the Railroad" banners. Buying railroad lines—even idle ones—proved expensive.

Collapse of the Rock Island line threatened rail service across a wide swath of northern Kansas wheat country. Fourteen counties banded together to obtain an 18-million-dollar loan from the Federal Railroad Administration plus 7 million dollars through state bonds and tax liability releases in order to keep the line intact (Bryan 1988). Bankruptcy of the Milwaukee Road line and substantial abandonment plans by the Chicago and Northwestern caused alarm in South Dakota, where most of the railroad system was jeopardized. In 1981, the state levied a one-cent-per-gallon tax on motor fuel to fund a railroad rehabilitation program. Not surprisingly, the plan was thrown out by the state's Supreme Court, but the South Dakota legislature made available 6.9 million dollars from other funds to bring a core system of remaining tracks up to operating conditions (Lamberton 1983). Wisconsin, Michigan, and Oklahoma took similar steps. In all of these cases, grain transportation costs were the main factor that caused state governments to get into the railroad business to try to prevent a truckers' monopoly.

As railroads gained more freedom under deregulation they began to take a hard look at all aspects of their operations. Deregulation made it easier for them to shed unprofitable branch lines and even to sell hundreds of miles of lines if they could find a buyer. The large limbs cut from the corporate tree became known, in the jargon of the 1980s, as "spinoffs," small railroads in their own right, which became the basis for the recent "regional" approach in the railroad business. Mergers in the 1960s had reduced the number of railroad companies, but it had not stemmed the tide that was sweeping them under. Spinning off parts of the system, thereby creating more railroad companies, was the response in the 1980s. Working with fewer employees (often nonunion), the new companies in the Middle West were founded largely on the prospects for grain traffic in the territories they served.

Groups of small-town shippers, including farmers and their elevator associations, saw the possibility of purchasing tracks declared unwanted by the railroad owner and operating the line themselves. Elevators less than, say, twenty miles from a main railroad line, but too far from a river terminal to make the truck/barge alternative feasible, have purchased used railroad locomotives and hired former railroad employees to shuttle grain cars back and forth. Such arrangements earn no money for the local groups because railroad rates, now necessarily based on costs, no longer contain the so-called "rate divisions" that used to favor short lines that generated long-haul traffic for the connecting main-line railroad (Lamberton 1983).

The new short lines are simply the latest effort to keep the local elevator—and hence the local farmers—from being handicapped by the twists and turns of events. They are a wise move for shippers, because railroad companies are increasingly inclined to rip up tracks at the end of a branch line, forcing the traffic to move to a more distant railhead from which the railroad earns the same revenue hauling to market and with slightly reduced costs. The railroads employed exactly the same strategy when they were building lines, not removing them, in the nineteenth century. They constructed fewer miles of track than the farmers wanted, but they knew that farmers would absorb the added hauling costs because they had to market their grain somewhere (Hudson 1985).

GRAIN STORAGE

Increased grain production, periodic swings between export booms and storage gluts, and a greatly modified transportation system have also created new patterns in the grain storage industry. When railroads were constructed, line elevator companies operating out of terminal market cities owned dozens, sometimes hundreds, of individual country elevators along tracks of various railroad companies. The farmers cooperative movement eventually purchased many country elevators from the line concerns. These small elevators at tracks in the trade-center towns of mid-America participated in an annual rush to market in the months after the harvest. Large terminal elevators in Minneapolis, Omaha, Chicago, and Kansas City stored grain until it was sent to millers or exported overseas (Figure 6.2). The system perfectly reflected the first stage of transportation evolution because it was based entirely on the movement of grain by rail to mills and ports.

Grower ownership of country elevators was far easier to secure than control of the terminal markets. Line companies had built nearly all the country elevators, but they discovered that storing grain in small amounts at dozens of isolated locations was not nearly as remunerative as concentrating storage at the terminal. They sold the country elevators to farmers, but kept the terminals for themselves.

The first major breakthrough for farmers came in 1926 when four country elevators in the northern Texas Panhandle founded the Union Equity Cooperative Exchange. In 1930 they constructed a one hundred thousand-bushel terminal elevator at Enid (Union Equity 1988a). As grain production in the southwestern plains expanded, Union Equity gathered more farmer-owned elevators into its federated structure, and, by the mid-1950s, it was the principal agency for exporting winter wheat through the port of Houston-Galveston. Union Equity now markets grain collected at 489 country elevators from northern Nebraska to Texas. Its terminal elevators have a storage capacity of 165 million bushels (Union Equity 1988b), making it the fourth largest in the U.S. grain trade, after Cargill, Continental, and Bunge, all private companies (*North American grain yearbook* 1988).

Union Equity's counterpart in the northern heartland was the Twin Cities-based Farmers Union Grain Terminal Association (GTA) serving local cooperative elevators from northwestern Wisconsin to the wheat-triangle region of Montana. The GTA, founded in 1938, adopted a hybrid form of cooperative structure in 1943 when it purchased the entire line of 135 country elevators owned by the St. Anthony and Dakota Company of Minneapolis (*Farmers elevator guide* 1943). The resulting system of 460 owned or affiliated country elevators shipped wheat—again, almost entirely by rail—to the Minneapolis mills and the Superior docks. By 1981, the GTA served 732 country elevators (604 affiliated, 128 line). It operated eleven feed-manufacturing plants, owned the former Froedtert Malt Company, and operated seven food-grain facilities, ranging from Albany, Georgia, to Fridley, Minnesota, in its Honeymead Products division (GTA 1981). Harvest States Cooperatives, as GTA is now known, still collects wheat and barley at Superior and Minneapolis, but it also loads barges with corn at Savage, Minnesota, and with wheat on the Columbia River, and it fills Pacific Ocean freighters with grain at the port of Kalama, Washington. It is the tenth largest U.S. grain company.

Critics of American farm policy have had an easy time over the past decade—the past five decades, for that matter—ridiculing a system that encouraged more farmers than were needed to produce more grain than was needed, buying the surplus and storing it at public expense. But the critics are silenced in those occasional years (e.g., 1974 or 1987), when production, policy, and demand get into phase, grain sales soar, and the elevators are emptied. Unfortunately, those conditions have rarely been met in recent years.

The 1970s export boom slowly subsided under the shadow of a strong dollar, foreign competition, and a faltering export subsidy program. By 1981, the annual carryover in grain stocks exceeded one hundred million metric tons, and by 1986 the figure was in excess of two hundred million metric tons (USDA 1987). Off-farm grain storage capacity in the United States inched upward every year, from about six billion bushels in 1977 to more than nine billion bushels in 1987 (*North American grain yearbook* 1988).

Stored grain can be thought of as moving toward the market at a (temporary) velocity of zero. It moves when demand dictates, but if the market is either foreign or domestic and the carrier is truck, rail, or barge, then it makes sense to store grain in economical quantities somewhere between the sources of supply and the many points of demand because there is no assurance where, when, or by what mode it will move. Milo grown in Nebraska might be trucked to a local feedlot, trucked to Atchison and barged down the Missouri, or hauled by rail for export either at Galveston or from the Columbia River ports. Where should it be stored?

The industry's solution was the subterminal. The network needed added capacity at points that were locationally "uncommitted" in the sense that they could economically forward grain to more than a single destination. Subterminals are a cross between the country- and terminal-elevator types (Guilfoy 1983). Their storage capacities are larger than the country elevators,

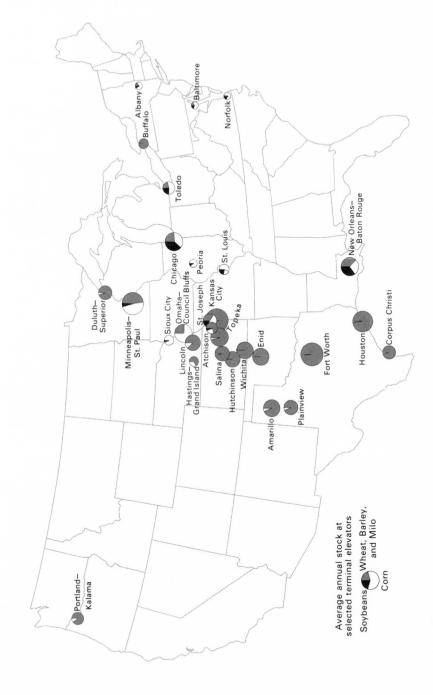

FIG. 6.2   Grain stocks at terminal elevators, computed by averaging February 1 and September 1 listings in *Stocks of Grain at Selected Terminal Elevator Sites.*

but their locations are nearer to producers than to the markets. They are poised to ship grain to several locations without incurring excess transportation costs.

A subterminal boom in the 1970s was fed by increasing grain production and storage needs, and by changing transportation patterns. Subterminals were able to take advantage of unit-train grain rates that railroads were beginning to offer because they were large enough to load fifty to one hundred covered-hopper cars with ninety tons of grain each, which the smaller country elevators were unable to do. Country elevators without rail service were unable to participate in the subterminal/unit train system (Larson and Kane 1979). Their only alternative was to ship by truck, but with lowered grain rates railroads now were the least-cost alternative. Railroads would have to be rehabilitated to serve subterminals, even to serve locations where subterminals could be built. The older, smaller country elevators on lines with little traffic potential would be excluded from the system. With railroad rates based on costs, network-optimizing, least-cost transportation solutions could be worked out so that benefit-cost ratios for every railroad line would be known.

In the mid-1970s agricultural economists at Iowa State University redrew the railroad map of the state in exactly this way (Baumel, Miller, and Drinka 1977). To a remarkable degree, their recommendations were followed. Northeastern Iowa has few subterminals, easy access to the Mississippi, and it has lost most of its railroad system. The intensive cash-grain region of north-central Iowa, farther from river alternatives, has seen fewer reductions. It has retained a network formed from segments that met benefit-cost standards. The tracks are used almost exclusively for moving grain, some fertilizer, and other farm inputs. Track segments of bankrupt companies have been sold to solvent ones and main lines have been spun off to regional carriers. There is little resemblance to the original system.

One Iowa town that kept its rail service is Albert City, now connected to the outside world by several dogleg segments of track that were about to vanish. Albert City's welcoming sign proclaims it "A Small Town Doing Big Things," and with a population of 818, "small" is unassailable. But Albert City's self-promotion is not merely just the usual small-town hype. It is the headquarters of ALCECO, the old Albert City Elevator Company, now grown to a storage capacity of more than nine million bushels that includes elevators at several nearby locations as well. ALCECO is a member of the "Grain 100," in fact, the eighty-sixth largest grain company in North America.

Indiana's railroads were also subject to an eleventh-hour analysis by economists (Hilger, McCarl, and Uhrig 1977), and the state has managed to retain tracks linking the new subterminals with various markets. Scircleville, Indiana, in the midst of corn and soybean heaven on the Tipton Till Plain, had a small country elevator, owned by the Clinton County Farm Bureau, that met local needs until 1968, when grain production began to strain existing facilities. New grain silos were built in 1974, 1976, and 1977. They shipped their first one hundred-car grain train in 1976. Now Scircleville's elevator is called AGMAX, the storage capacity is 4.5 million bushels, and they ship one hundred-car trainloads of corn to Tennessee on a regular basis. Scircleville has fewer than one hundred inhabitants and no retail trade to speak of.

It would be an exaggeration to say that grain is now stored anywhere a place can be found to put it, but the new "surge tanks" in the system, the sites of intermediate storage, are not confined to the likes of Kansas City or Minneapolis. The Farmers Co-op at Farnhamville, Iowa, has room for 9,226,000 bushels of grain, Sunray Co-op at Sunray, Texas, 6,539,000 bushels. The Trumbull Co-op Association at Trumbull, Nebraska, has 4,125,000 bushels stored in eighty different buildings in a radius of twenty-five miles of Trumbull, which they are now reducing by half given drought damage to the harvest of 1988. The co-ops headquartered at Farnhamville, Sunray, and Trumbull are all Grain-100 companies. Farnhamville has a population of 461 and Trumbull only 216; Sunray, an oil field center, has 1,952 inhabitants.

The fact that grain storage still entails delivery trips to grain elevators has done little for the central places containing the new supersized elevators. Many new subterminals have been built in open country, while older elevators that have multiplied by a factor of ten or more have often spread out to cover most of what used to be a trade center. Towns with a lively elevator trade are likely to have retained banks, although often not under local ownership. Coffee shops and cafes still are common, and boutiques have sprouted in many an abandoned storefront. Convenience stores, which have become as ubiquitous in the 1980s as general stores were in the 1880s, occupy highway locations in or near such towns, but that is about all that is left of the trade-center role. The central-place network that resulted from building a grain-collection system has become increasingly redundant even for that purpose.

THE NATIONAL SYSTEM

The maps of grain storage and transportation in the United States today reflect all of these trends and more (Figure 6.1). Textbook economic geographies that stress the importance of Minneapolis and Kansas City, Great Lakes shipping, and west-to-east flow have become dated. Asia now consumes more than two-fifths of U.S. agricultural exports; Japan alone accounts for nearly 20 percent. Western Europe receives a little more than one-fourth, about the same as Latin America and Africa combined. Canada, the Soviet Union, and Eastern Europe receive the rest (USDA 1987). Pacific Coast ports are closest to Pacific Rim markets, of course, but Gulf Coast ports are where most of the export grain is loaded.

No discussion of exporting North American grain to the Pacific Rim countries can proceed very far without mention of Crows Nest Pass. The financially strapped Canadian Pacific Railway took 3.6 million dollars from the Canadian government in 1897 to build a line through Crows Nest Pass in exchange for a promise to maintain 1897-level rates on flour and grain in perpetuity. The rate became a burden for the Canadian railroads and also for the U.S. grain industry after the demands for wheat in the Far East began to expand in the 1960s. Canada soon took over the trade, aided by the low rates. The northern transcontinental lines in the United States engaged in some creative rate-making by setting inverse-distance rates that made it as cheap to ship to the West Coast from the Red River Valley of Minnesota as from western Montana, but it still required a U.S. export subsidy of fifty-eight cents per bushel to overcome the Canadian advantage (Nightengale 1967).

Subsequently the rate map was flattened across the northern plains (Wilson and Koo 1985), and the result, with the aid of export subsidy, has been to drive the Pacific-Atlantic "wheat divide" from Montana east to Minot, North Dakota. The line is not sharp everywhere, and some eastern Dakota wheat does move west (*North Dakota Dept. of Agriculture* 1986), but the western Dakotas are now Pacific-oriented, as are western Nebraska and Colorado. In 1985 the majority of Colorado's export grain movement shifted to the Northwest Coast for the first time. About 45 percent of Colorado's grain moves northwest, 36 percent to the Gulf, and only 10 percent to Kansas City (*Colorado agribusiness roundup* 1987).

Far Eastern markets for feed grains are growing in response to increased meat consumption in those countries. Gulf Coast ports are a least-cost solution for most of the Corn Belt as well as the southwestern plains, but corn is no longer confined to the Corn Belt. Irrigation in the Arkansas and Platte valleys and in the High Plains has made corn profitable where even wheat once was marginal. Low rates on corn moving in one hundred-car unit trains have pulled Nebraska and Colorado into the Pacific Northwest's sphere of influence. Tacoma, which shipped Montana and Palouse wheat to the Orient for more than a century, recently has handled more corn than wheat (U.S. Department of the Army 1987).

Minnesota now ranks fifth among states in feed grain exports. Duluth-Superior and the Mississippi River elevators are the obvious export gateways, but low unit-train rates from country elevators to the Pacific Northwest have resulted in a substantial westward flow of Minnesota corn and soybeans (Fruin and Buschena 1989). Western Minnesota and the southern Red River Valley of North Dakota, once considered peripheral to the cash corn/soybean region of the United States, are now on the front line of supply to the Pacific Rim, given the inverted logistics of westward flow.

No port comes close to rivaling New Orleans in total volume. The New Orleans-Baton Rouge district stores only a fraction of the downriver shipments, mainly corn and soybeans; the bulk of it is poured directly from barges to ocean vessels. Storage in the Mississippi River corn and soybean export trade is concentrated in the grain growing states bordering the river, from northern Louisiana to Minnesota. River levees are not the best places to construct elevators of the multimillion-bushel capacity this trade demands, and new grain storage facilities are more often within truck-hauling distance of the river, on the floodplain.

Twomey Grain Company, headquartered at Smithshire, a village of perhaps two hundred inhabitants in Warren County, Illinois, is already the fifteenth largest grain company in the United States. It is expanding its storage capacities to forty-five million bushels (*North American grain yearbook* 1988). Twomey's large elevator, characteristically adjacent to the tracks, casts a shadow across Smithshire—a townsite platted by the Santa Fe Railroad in 1888 when it built to Chicago—but appearances can be deceiving. The railroad is all but irrelevant. The company trucks nearly all of its grain from Smithshire, and a half dozen country elevators it owns, about twenty miles to the Mississippi River bottoms opposite Burlington, Iowa. Twomey has about ten acres of grain storage buildings, unmarked and unidentified, within easy reach of the river dumping location. It is the riverbottom site, not the country elevators in nearby towns, that gives the company its great size.

The grain map (Figure 6.1) omits elevators of less than one million bushels capacity, but it fairly reflects crop production in the areas that have been caught up in the new export patterns. Large elevators are uncommon in the northern spring wheat, barley, and durum growing area. Few railroad lines were abandoned there, smaller country elevators remain the standard, and farmers have substantial on-farm storage capacities. Three-fourths of North Dakota's grain still moves out of state by rail and North Atlantic markets remain the principal export destination. This pattern contrasts with Union Equity's territory in the winter wheat belt, where million-bushel country elevators are common and farmers store less grain on their farms. Local feedlots are important consumers of High Plains grain, but the major flow is east to long-established terminals such as Hutchinson and Enid, then south to Houston or Galveston for export. Rate changes could make the ports of Long Beach and San Diego attractive for wheat, corn, and milo from the Texas Panhandle, but the shorter rail haul to the Gulf is cheaper in total, even with a detour through the Panama Canal for exports to Asia, given the low cost of ocean transport (Ulrey 1967).

The Indiana Farm Bureau and the Fort Wayne-based Central Soya Company continue to own two of the largest elevators at the Port of Baltimore. Europe purchases nearly half of the U.S. soybean exports (USDA 1987). Soybeans and corn from Indiana and Ohio are "assigned" to Baltimore and Norfolk in a least-cost transportation solution when export demand is brisk; they move to markets in the southeastern United States when it is slack (Hilger, McCarl, and Uhrig 1977). But new areas of soybean production on the Coastal Plain are well situated to serve European as well as domestic markets, and they will make Indiana and Ohio producers depend even more on low-cost rail transport to eastern ports. Chicago, Milwaukee, Toledo, and Saginaw export corn and soybeans by the Great Lakes (U.S. Department of the Army 1987), but this traffic is not growing, consistent with the flat trend in Great Lakes shipping in general.

Old grain milling industries have dispersed away from the traditional pattern and new smaller-scale production facilities have appeared nearer to markets (Figure 6.3). Flour mills in the southeastern states receive Kansas wheat by barges on the Tennessee River system, a reflection of the low rates on raw material versus finished product. Corn processing industries are still concentrated in Illinois and Iowa, but new mills have been constructed in the western Corn Belt. Soybean processing shifted in similar fashion during the 1970s, when new mills were built throughout the expanding area of soybean production. Export demand for milled grain products has dispersed the milling industry away from the heartland, a trend further reinforced by the continued shift of population toward the coastal margins of the nation. All of these factors have operated centripetally and they have broken the old pattern based on in-transit rate privileges for established milling centers.

Grain projections to 1999 suggest that soybean production will expand markedly in Alabama, Georgia, Kentucky, and Louisiana (Lazarus, Hill, and Thompson 1980). Kansas and Nebraska are expected to more than double their outputs of corn. Wheat acreage increases also are projected. Westward shifts are envisioned for wheat and corn production, a reflection of the pull of Pacific Rim markets. The patterns of grain storage and transportation that have evolved in the past decade will be expanded to cover whatever production increases actually do occur, but the next decade should not have to witness frantic attempts to refashion the transportation system as the past one has.

The small towns of the American grain belt—equal sized, spaced at regular intervals along a railroad line—suggest a democratic equality, like the uniform grid of 160-acre farms these towns served. But economically healthy trade-center towns in this tradition are nearly as scarce as 160-acre farms are today. The towns remain physically, more or less, but their present role has little to do with the reasons for their creation. Some of these tiny places, like Fowler, Indiana; Ralston, Iowa; or Fairmount, North Dakota, like those mentioned earlier, have become headquarter "cities" for farmer-owned or family-owned companies dealing millions of bushels of grain in world markets. The fact that such towns spawned colossal developments suggests the continued tradition of local entrepreneurship that has always been important in agricultural industries (Borchert 1987). The small sizes of these towns reflect the irrelevance, not the importance, of their trade-center role.

As the grain business grows and new areas come into production to serve

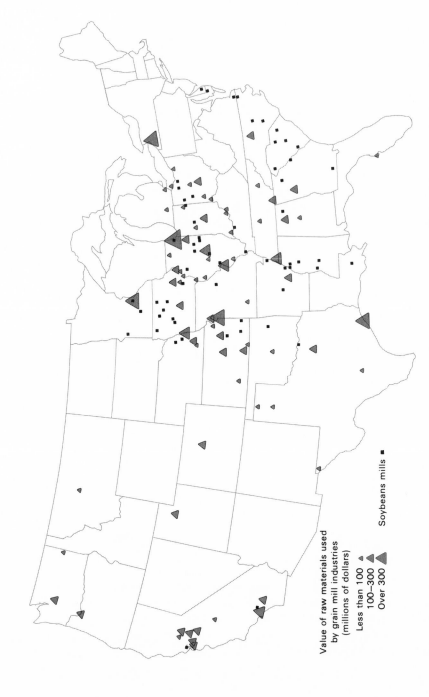

Value of raw materials used
by grain mill industries
(millions of dollars)

Less than 100 ◢

100–300 ◢

Over 300 ◢

Soybeans mills ■

FIG. 6.3   Grain milling industries, based on data in *U.S. Census of Manufactures, 1982,* and *The Soya Bluebook, 1985.*

foreign markets, the relative importance of the old terminal market cities and their milling industries will decline. New patterns of grain supply and product demand have already dispersed the milling industry away from its traditional pattern. The massive grain silos will remain in these cities, but, like other symbols of American industry, they will be eclipsed in utility, if not in grandeur, by a worldwide system of supply and demand in which electronic transactions serve small towns as well as they do the largest cities. The town network and the grain network, once identical, are pulling their separate ways.

ACKNOWLEDGMENTS

Several dozen U.S. grain companies responded freely and in detail to my inquiries about their operations. I would also like to thank James R. Ericson, Union Equity Cooperative Exchange, Enid, Oklahoma; Mary Roy, Transportation Librarian, Northwestern University; the staff of the Steenbock Memorial Library, College of Agriculture and Life Sciences, University of Wisconsin-Madison; and Dave Bassingthwaite, Mike Turner, and Jim Wilson for their assistance. I gratefully acknowledge the support of the John Simon Guggenheim Foundation and the William and Marion Haas Fund.

REFERENCES

Association of American Railroads. 1986. *The grain book*. Washington, D.C.

Barnett, Doug, James Brinkley, and Bruce McCarl. 1984. Port elevator capacity and national and world grain shipments. *Western Journal of Agricultural Economics* 9: 77–89.

Baumel, C. Phillip, John J. Miller, and Thomas P. Drinka. 1977. The economics of upgrading seventy-one branch rail lines in Iowa. *American Journal of Agricultural Economics* 59: 61–70.

Borchert, John R. 1987. *America's northern heartland*. Minneapolis: University of Minnesota Press.

Bryan, Frank W. 1988. Kansas grain hauler. *Trains* 48(12): 48–53.

Colorado agribusiness roundup. 1987. Fall edition. Fort Collins: Colorado State University. Cooperative Extension Service.

Farmers Elevator Guide. 1943. 83(9): 7.

Fruin, Jerry E., and David E. Buschena. 1989. Grain transportation: Adaptation to changing export markets. In *Economic Report to the Governor of Minnesota, 1989*. Minneapolis: Minnesota Council of Economic Advisors.

Fuller, Stephen, Larry Makus, and Merritt Taylor. 1983. Effect of railroad deregulation on export-grain rates. *North Central Journal of Agricultural Economics* 5: 51–63.

GTA (Farmers Union Grain Terminal Association). 1981. *Annual report*. St. Paul, Minn.

Guilfoy, Robert F., Jr. 1983. *The physical distribution system for grain*. Agriculture Information Bulletin, No. 457. Washington, D.C.: U.S. Department of Agriculture. Office of Transportation.

Haldeman, Robert C. 1960a. *Grain transportation in the north central region.* Marketing Research Report, No. 49. Washington, D.C.: U.S. Department of Agriculture. Agricultural Marketing Service.

Haldeman, Robert C. 1960b. *Grain transportation statistics for the North Central Region.* Statistical Bulletin, No. 268. Washington, D.C.: U.S. Department of Agriculture. Agricultural Marketing Service.

Hart, John Fraser. 1988. Small towns and manufacturing. *Geographical Review* 78: 272–87.

Hilger, D. A., B. A. McCarl, and J. W. Uhrig. 1977. Facilities locations: The case of grain subterminals. *American Journal of Agricultural Economics* 59: 674–82.

Hudson, John C. 1985. *Plains country towns.* Minneapolis: University of Minnesota Press.

Lamberton, Charles. 1983. *Restructuring a rail system: South Dakota's experience from 1976–1981.* Bulletin, No. 688. Brookings, S.D.: South Dakota State University. Agricultural Experiment Station.

Larson, Donald W., and Michael D. Kane. 1979. Effects of rail abandonment on grain marketing and transportation costs in central and southwestern Ohio. *North Central Journal of Agricultural Economics* 1: 105–13.

Lazarus, Sherry S., Lowell D. Hill, and Stanley R. Thompson. 1980. *Grain production and consumption for feed in the north central and southern states with projections for 1988, 1990, and 2000.* North Central Regional Research Publication, No. 267. Urbana, Ill.: University of Illinois Agricultural Experiment Station.

National Waterway Foundation. 1983. *U.S. waterways productivity.* Huntsville, Ala.: The Strode Publishers.

Nightengale, Edmund A. 1967. Some effects of recent changes in the railway grain-rate structure on interregional competition and regional development. In *Transportation problems and policies in the trans-Missouri west.* Edited by Jack R. Davidson and Howard W. Ottoson. Lincoln: University of Nebraska Press.

North American grain yearbook. 1988. Shawnee Mission, Kans.: Milling and Baking News.

North Dakota Department of Agriculture. 1986. *North Dakota Agricultural Statistics,* No. 55. Fargo, N.D.: North Dakota State University Agricultural Experiment Station.

Official Railway Guide. 1988. North American freight service edition, "The grain connection." Vol. 121 (July-August issue): 5. New York: Thompson Publications.

Ulrey, Ivon W. 1967. Current problems of transportation in the trans-Missouri west. In *Transportation problems and policies in the trans-Missouri west.* Edited by Jack R. Davidson and Howard W. Ottoson. Lincoln: University of Nebraska Press.

Union Equity Cooperative Exchange. 1988a. *Union Equity: A story of growth and performance.* Enid, Okla.: Union Equity Cooperative Exchange.

———. 1988b. *Annual report.* Enid, Okla.: Union Equity Cooperative Exchange.

U.S. Department of Agriculture (USDA). 1987. *Agricultural Statistics, 1987.* Washington, D.C.

———. 1988. Livestock Division, Livestock and Grain Market News Branch. *Stocks of grain at selected terminal and elevator sites.* Washington, D.C. 63: 1–36.

U.S. Department of Commerce. Bureau of the Census. 1982. *Census of Manufactures, 1982.* Washington, D.C.

———. 1988. *Statistical Abstract of the United States.* Washington, D.C.

U.S. Department of the Army. Corps of Engineers. 1987. *Waterborne commerce of the United States, 1986,* ser. WRSC-WCUS-86. Washington, D.C.

Wilson, William W., and Won W. Koo. 1985. Grain transportation rates and export market development. *North Central Journal of Agricultural Economics* 7: 27–37.

Won W. Koo, Stanley R. Thompson, and Donald W. Larson. 1984. *An analysis of selected changes in the U.S. grain transportation system, 1990.* Agricultural Business Research Report, No. 458. Lansing, Mich.: Michigan State University. Agricultural Experiment Station.

SEVEN

Housing Submarkets in an American Metropolis

John S. Adams

In 1939 Homer Hoyt examined block-by-block variations in residential rental levels in 142 American cities to challenge the conventional explanation that U.S. urban residential property values formed concentric rings, with low values circling downtown and successively higher values at increasing distances (Hoyt 1939). He used data from the federally sponsored Real Property Inventories that had been conducted during the 1930s (U.S. Department of Commerce 1934), and concluded that the principal variations in rent were in residential sectors that radiated from the city center, rather than in concentric zones (Figure 7.1). He explained this pattern as the result of early sectoral segregation by income near the city center that was perpetuated by builders who tailored new housing on the edge of the city to the kinds of households moving outward.

Hoyt's analysis entered the literatures of geography, planning, and real estate, and was widely used after World War II to locate suburban shopping centers. The sector concept entered the thinking of analysts, planners, developers, and builders, and it assumed a self-fulfilling quality as real-estate investment decisions based on it perpetuated geographical patterns that it was designed to describe and explain.

Hoyt used data from the 1960 census of population and housing to verify the trends he had identified in 1939 (Hoyt [1966]). Analysis of twenty metro areas after the 1970 census and fifty-three cities after the 1980 census disclosed a remarkable persistence of these trends (Abler and Adams 1976; Adams 1987). This chapter examines the sectoral structure of the

Minneapolis–St. Paul metropolitan region, and describes some of the market mechanisms that maintain it.

LOCAL HOUSING MARKETS

What does housing mean for an urban area? Urban housing provides shelter and a neighborhood setting, both of which supply a crucial basis for labor reproduction. The location of a house affects school choice and segregates children as a means of cultural reproduction. Housing choice can serve consumption style and social congregation and segregation. Housing is part of a city's capital assets. It can serve as a speculative investment vehicle that produces unearned capital appreciation for those enjoying preferential access to mortgage credit and preferential treatment under the tax laws. Housing represents wealth that can be taxed to support public services. Planners control the location of new housing to manage demands for services and transportation facilities.

It is customary to consider the U.S. housing stock as a whole and to examine how various subgroups of the nation's households use their share (Sternlieb and Hughes 1986), but this macro approach fails to illuminate the attributes of neighborhood settings. Moreover, it cannot evaluate the geographic structure of local housing markets that control demand, supply, real estate values, and ultimately the fate of each urban neighborhood within the submarkets that constitute the total metropolitan housing market (Adams 1987, 125; Palm 1978).

Over time, most residential neighborhoods of central cities decline in relative desirability compared with their suburban counterparts that offer newer houses, lower densities, easier movement, and more exclusive socioeconomic environments. Suburban developers anticipate that they can build high-priced new houses and sell them for a profit at a specific suburban location. If the development fails or is slow to succeed it is not repeated unless project scale or housing prices are adjusted.

The construction of new suburban housing draws people out of the central city and softens the inner segments of housing submarkets (Lansing, Clifton, and Morgan 1969; Adams 1987, 132). Over time, the income levels of central-city households and the market values of central-city houses fall behind the suburbs. Housing prices slide in the city, where housing stocks remain relatively unchanged while demand falls, and rise in the suburbs, where stocks are rising slowly but demand continues to be strong.

Certain portions of some central cities seem to resist housing market decline (Adams 1987, 133–40, 145–57). The normal life cycle of a housing unit, from new and expensive to old and cheap, is interrupted when it is maintained in ways that sustain its relative desirability. The deterioration process can be slowed or reversed if neighborhood attractiveness is improved

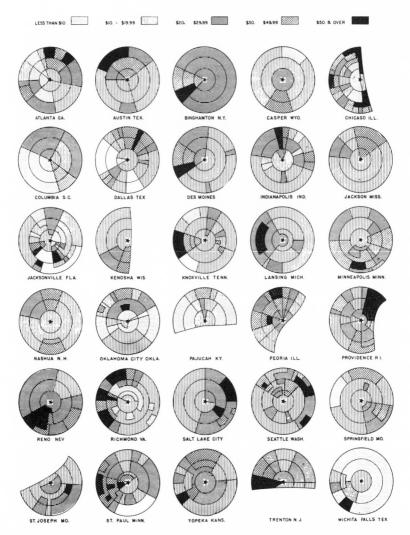

FIG. 7.1   Rental areas in American cities.

even though houses in the neighborhood continue to age. The value of a housing unit depends on the structure itself and on the lot on which it stands. The value of the lot depends on the attractiveness of the neighborhood and its location in the metropolitan system (Adams 1987, 132).

Housing Submarkets

Many midwestern metropolitan housing markets have become partitioned into well-defined submarkets that originated near downtowns. The basis for sectoral differentiation of housing submarkets was laid by the differential growth of downtown (Ward 1971; Abler, Adams, and Gould 1971, 381–82). During the late nineteenth and early twentieth centuries, most foreign immigrants settled near the sources of unskilled employment at the edges of the emerging central business districts (Ward 1968, 343). Workers walked to their downtown jobs.

Middle-class neighborhoods usually emerged on the side of downtown upwind (or at least not downwind) from heavy transport and manufacturing areas, on higher or rougher terrain that was inconvenient for goods movement and processing, and on sites close to white-collar downtown jobs. Salaried workers enjoyed stable incomes and access to mortgage credit. They were able to upgrade their housing faster than workers in other sectors, and they moved outward to better housing at a brisk rate. This outward movement encouraged the expansion of the white-collar employment areas of downtown toward the middle-class sectors, and promoted the eccentric expansion of the city toward its middle- and upper-middle-class sectors (Krakover and Casetti 1988).

Socioeconomic Class and Housing Demand

Midwestern urban households can be stratified into five socioeconomic classes distinguished by their wealth, their annual income, and the stability of their annual income. The proportions of a city's households in each class determine its demand for new housing (Adams 1989). Middle- and upper-middle-class households normally enjoy continuing real increases in annual income and wealth, and superior access to mortgage credit. They often move to better housing as soon as they can afford it, so middle- and upper-middle-class housing sectors expand outward more vigorously than other sectors (Binford 1985; Monkkonen 1988).

Builders set numerous vacancy chains in motion at the suburban edges of the most active housing sectors. When a household occupies a new housing unit it creates a vacancy at its former address. The vacancy is filled at the second address by a household moving from a third address, and the vacancy moves from unit to unit through a housing sector. Households move in one direction; vacancies move in the opposite direction.

In middle- and upper-middle-class housing sectors long vacancy chains extend from the zone of new construction at the suburban edge to the old neighborhoods in the inner city. Housing prices drop as vacancies accumulate in the older inner areas. Low-income newcomers are attracted to the areas of surplus high-quality, low-priced housing. African Americans have been the largest group since the 1920s.

The upper class has little impact on the supply of vacancies because it is small and does not relocate much. Upper-class housing is often physically isolated from other sectors, and its principal influence on housing markets is in setting styles and tastes.

During the electric streetcar era, new housing was built near streetcar lines. After World War II, it was built at suburban locations that enjoyed automobile access. Urban infrastructure (water, sewer, roads, bridges, parks, schools, police and fire protection) generally has been a consequence of new housing construction instead of being part of a capital improvements master plan.

Working-Class Housing Sectors

Before World War I, working-class households concentrated near their principal employment areas in sectors bypassed by the middle and upper classes. They were often low lying, near heavy transportation facilities, and relatively isolated from the central business district by poor transit and by rail movements at grade level. Traditional working-class housing has been shelter rather than a symbol of consumptive display, and ownership has been a major goal. Ties in the neighborhood have been strong to family, church, labor unions, and the local Democratic party. Most residents are descended from immigrants and earn their livelihoods as wage workers.

New housing at the edge of working-class sectors traditionally has been built to accommodate population growth. American working-class households reach their peak earnings potential at relatively young ages, and their annual income trajectory flattens out early in life, whereas middle-class income normally continues to rise steadily until retirement. Surplus housing was rare in working-class housing sectors after World War II because there was little speculative construction. Vacancy chains are shorter in working-class sectors than in middle-class sectors.

HOUSING SUBMARKETS IN THE TWIN CITIES

The Twin Cities of Minneapolis and St. Paul provide a case study of housing submarket structure and operation in a midwestern metropolis. The Twin Cities have fourteen sectoral submarkets for housing (Figure 7.2). Their existence is confirmed by studies of residential mobility, and by planners, developers, builders, financiers, and transportation and marketing specialists who know the region. Each sector has its unique history, character, demography, housing market conditions, and retailing tastes.

Cedar/Riverside–Hiawatha–Lake Nokomis–Minnehaha Park

This sector started before 1900 at Seven Corners, where Washington Avenue crosses Cedar Avenue, around a core of Scandinavian immigrant settlement. It extended southeast along the Chicago, Milwaukee, St. Paul and

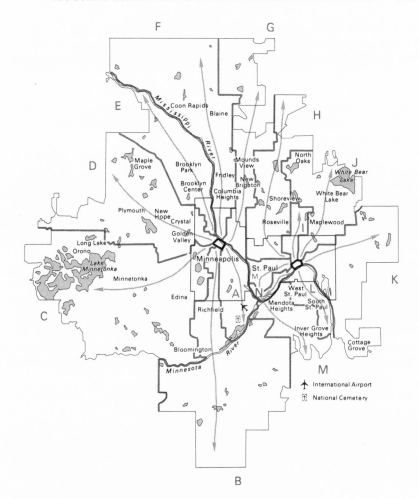

FIG. 7.2   Sectoral housing submarkets in Minneapolis–St. Paul.

Pacific Railroad yards and the adjacent industrial corridor paralleling Hiawatha and Minnehaha avenues to the city's edge at Minnehaha Park. The sector forms a cul-de-sac terminating at river valleys, the airport, and the national cemetery. It lacks adjacent suburban development and an immediate rural area source of immigrants, so outmovement and housing turnover traditionally have been minimal.

South Minneapolis–Richfield–East Bloomington

This middle-class sector expanded southward along the Nicollet Avenue streetcar line. It enjoyed unimpeded access to downtown. Minneapolis south of downtown has had most of the city's housing. It is the part of the city closest to the most populated part of rural and small-town Minnesota. For more than a century, South Minneapolis between the Lake District and the Hiawatha-Minnehaha corridor has absorbed a lion's share of the city's newcomers. The strong market for housing in this sector attracted developers by the score. The vacancy chains started by sustained southside development softened housing markets just south of downtown, and enabled a succession of newcomer groups to enter the city. White Anglo-Saxon Protestant business leaders, professionals, and clerks were followed by Irish, Germans, and Scandina-vians of the second wave, then Romanian Jews and African Americans after 1900, and finally in our own time by American Indians and Southeast Asians.

Southwest Lake District–Edina–Minnetonka

The southwest sector is home to the out-of-sight rich and captains of local industry who initially settled just south of downtown, then around Lake of the Isles, and eventually near eastern Lake Minnetonka. More recently they have found retreats in Orono and around Long Lake. The southern flank of this sector is home to the newly affluent of Edina, West Bloomington, Eden Prairie, and Minnetonka. This sector has grown more slowly than South Minneapolis, because the financially secure have less reason to continue "moving up by moving out" than those who mark their progress by frequent changes of address.

Near North Minneapolis–Golden Valley–Crystal–New Hope–Plymouth–Maple Grove

The northside sector is a smaller version of the South Minneapolis sector, enclosed largely by West Broadway on the north and Olson Memorial High-way (State Highway 55) on the south. A prosperous wedge of Scandinavian and German settlement extended northwestward from the central business district. Steady development of new housing at the outer edges of the sector after 1920 meant large numbers of vacancies in the sector's inner neighbor-hoods, leading to the emergence along Plymouth Avenue from the river to Penn Avenue of the city's major concentration of Jewish immigrants from eastern and southeastern Europe and Russia. With the prosperity that fol-lowed World War II, this group relocated to the west and southwest, and their former housing was occupied by African Americans moving up the social and economic ladder.

North Minneapolis–Brooklyn Center–Brooklyn Park

This sector is aligned with the industrial corridor between West Broad-way and the Mississippi River. It originated in the railroads and industrial activity upriver from St. Anthony Falls. A mixture of working-class and lower-middle-class tastes persists into the suburbs. Some of the riverfront of this sector has parks, open space, and high-quality residences, but much of it is squandered on run-down houses, industry, and low-budget commercial activity, reflecting neighborhood tastes and preferences.

Northeast–Columbia Heights–Fridley–Coon Rapids

To the extent that Minneapolis features a genuine blue-collar, working-class, immigrant, ethnic-flavored neighborhood resembling those of the industrial cities of the northeastern United States, it is probably lower Northeast, east of the river and north of St. Anthony Falls. Crisscrossing railroads, small factories and machine shops, Democratic-Farmer-Labor (DFL) ward clubs, Roman Catholic, Eastern Rite Catholic, and Orthodox churches all testify to the eastern, southeastern, and southern European origins of the families who entered here after 1900, when the original Scandinavian and German laborers and tradesmen prospered and moved northward to higher land and nicer houses in upper Northeast.

Southeast–New Brighton–Mounds View–Blaine

Southeast Minneapolis (east of the river and St. Anthony Falls) was a cul-de-sac surrounding the University of Minnesota and bounded by St. Paul, Northeast, and the river until the construction of Interstate Highway 35W opened it up to the suburbs and attracted developers. Today it thrives as a mixture of middle-class and working-class tastes and styles.

Como Park–St. Anthony Park–Roseville–Shoreview

St. Paul's elite established their homes west of downtown in Ramsey Hill and on Summit Avenue. Their admiring middle-class imitators flanked them in sectors northwest and southwest of downtown. Although houses for workers were built near industrial areas along the rail corridors through the Midway district, the dominant atmosphere was middle-class and upwardly mobile. Roseville developed after World War II at the northwest edge of St. Paul. It absorbed St. Paul households moving up and out, extending outward the flavor of the tasteful and well-tended neighborhoods left behind.

North End

St. Paul's North End developed around Rice Street as a tightly knit white, Catholic, working-class area. Its expansion northward was thwarted first by the tendency of working-class areas to expand outward slowly when they moved at all, and secondly by the upper-middle-class North Oaks community at the northern end of Rice Street. Working-class sectors do not expand into elite and quasi-elite areas. Not only will the lower classes not be admitted (walls and fences are sometimes erected to document the social separation), but developers and merchant builders shy away from zones where the nature of the prospective market is unproved or ambiguous.

Lake Phalen–Maplewood–White Bear Lake

Several historic thoroughfares run northeast from St. Paul's east side Lake Phalen neighborhood to the south shore of White Bear Lake, which developed early as a public recreation area and summer place for several of the city's first families. The elite recreational cachet added luster to this sector, but the small east-side population base kept post–World War II suburbanization low. Moreover, the sparsely populated areas northeast of the Twin Cities provide a steady yet small migration flow into this sector.

East Side–Battle Creek Park–Hudson Road–Cottage Grove

This small middle-class area on the East Side faced east when the main thrust of St. Paul and the metro area was to the west. The steady growth of 3M's (Minnesota Mining and Manufacturing, Inc.) corporate offices and facilities on Hudson Road (U.S. Highway 12) just east of the city has been a major stimulus to east-side developments, along with a recent boom in small hobby and horse farms. This sector has been relatively quiet and undeveloped despite its proximity to both cities, whose growth has been oriented in other directions.

West Side–West St. Paul–South St. Paul–Inver Grove Heights

St. Paul's West Side always had a distinctive lower-middle- and working-class personality. This character was maintained and extended when the neighborhood grew south and southeast to the meatpacking plants and industrial areas of South St. Paul. The Jewish immigrant population began relocating from the floodplain and low-lying areas to the neighborhood west of downtown after World War I. Their places were taken by Mexican migrants who had worked their way north to St. Paul and then stayed. The growth of the sector is slow.

Summit Avenue–Macalester Park–Highland Park–Mendota Heights

St. Paul's best addresses were along Summit Avenue, and for those who failed to achieve that big prize, there were vast expanses of high-quality, upper-middle-class areas throughout the western and southwestern part of the city. When expansion to the southwest was blocked by Minneapolis and the river valleys, this sector made a sharp left turn, leaped over the Mississippi River, and continued southwest of the city. When Interstate Highway 35E opened in the 1980s, it tied the sector together more snugly and promoted development of its highly favored suburban housing areas.

West Seventh Street

This street originally developed along a path connecting downtown St. Paul with Fort Snelling at the confluence of the Minnesota and Mississippi rivers. It has become the commercial backbone of a low-income, working-class neighborhood. Despite some pockets of historically significant homes, its mixed industrial, commercial, and residential landscape lacks the amenities that might attract and retain the middle class, but it does offer satisfactory low-cost housing to a large and vital fraction of St. Paul's lower-income working households. Like the North End, it is a cul-de-sac and does not project its character outward into nearby suburbs.

VARIATIONS WITHIN HOUSING SUBMARKETS

Vacancy Chains and the Market Rank of Neighborhoods

Vacancy chains can be used to delimit the geographical extent of sectoral submarkets. If high-priced new houses are built at the suburban edge of a sector (Sector B, Figure 7.3), then the relative market value of neighborhoods in the sector must drop. Neighborhood ranks are adjusted in stable sectors with little new construction (Sector A, Figure 7.3) by removing obsolete stocks or by upgrading existing stocks. Older neighborhoods maintain or even improve their relative desirability in exclusive sectors of high-priced houses if new construction is at middle as well as high prices (Sector C, Figure 7.3). Rank shifts in stable submarkets are modest compared with shifts in the quickly expanding middle- and upper-middle-class submarkets (Sectors B, D, M, and K, Figure 7.3).

Average Neighborhood Housing Value

Stable working-class and lower-middle-class housing submarkets contain a more limited range of median housing values than middle- and upper-middle-class sectors. New construction is at present prices. Vacancy chains are short, neighborhood ranks are stable, and housing diversity within the submarkets changes little (Sectors A, E, F, I, K, and L, Figure 7.4). The greatest market flux and price variation among neighborhoods is in middle- and upper-middle-class submarkets, where vigorous construction of expensive new houses leaves large numbers of low-priced units (Sectors B, D, H, and M, Figure 7.4). In the elite sector (Sector C, Figure 7.4) new construction responds to demand, but oversupply is atypical. Old neighborhoods do not

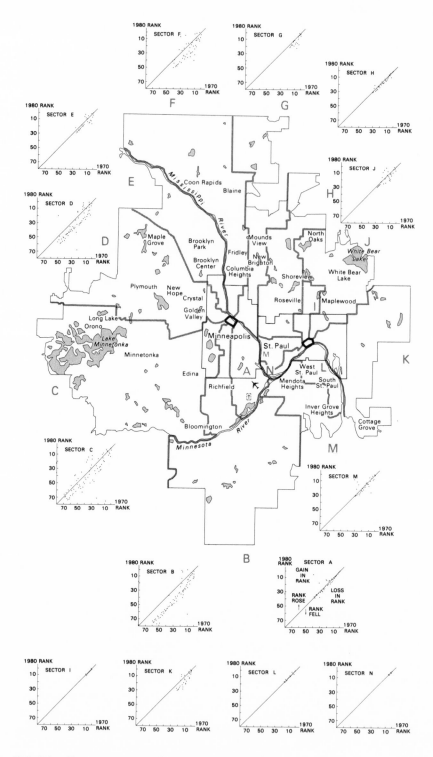

FIG. 7.3   Changes in tract ranks in housing submarkets.

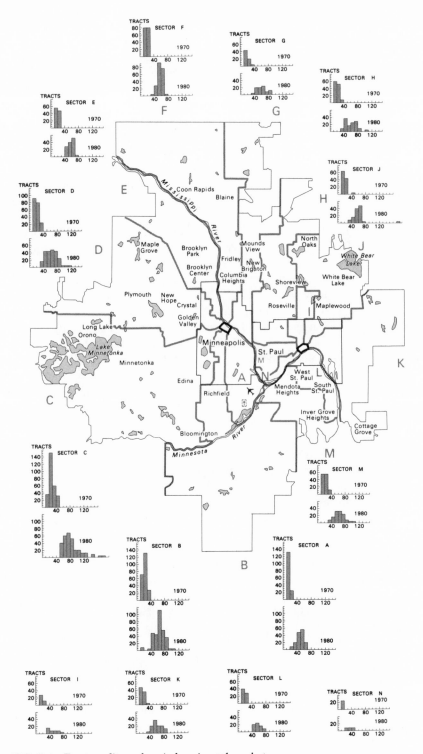

FIG. 7.4   Tract median values in housing submarkets.

necessarily lose their relative rankings, vacancy chains may be short, and significant housing demand can be traced to natural change within the sector.

House Price Inflation

In general, because population and effective housing demand steadily move outward, the prices of existing houses in real terms deflate in the inner areas of a submarket and inflate in the outer segments, depending on new construction in the submarket and changes in the number of households.

New construction at market prices is mainly at the suburban edge of the submarket. It is usually priced above the prices of nearby units, and normally enhances their value by improving their environment. Profit margins for builders are greater on more expensive housing units, so they build the most expensive units they can expect to sell promptly.

New construction in the innermost portions of submarkets usually has public assistance in the form of parcel acquisition and consolidation, low-interest loans, direct grants, and indirect subventions through property tax relief. The new units are almost always substantially more valuable than those they replace or those that remain. Replacing cheap old units with expensive new ones can stabilize the real value of existing housing by improving its environment.

A third form of new construction takes place when adjacent properties are cleared and replacement housing is built. Such construction usually requires public assistance under present tax laws and high interest rates unless the parcels enjoy exceptionally attractive physical environments (lakes or rivers), social environments (wealthy neighborhoods), or accessibility to attractive shopping or employment centers.

The addition or removal of housing units from tracts in a submarket, when combined with changes in the number of households in the submarket, changes the median value of the housing in each tract. To illustrate these value changes I drew a traverse through each sector, from the tract nearest downtown to the tract farthest out, intersecting as many tracts as possible with approximately straight lines (Figure 7.2). For each tract I divided the 1980 median value of owner-occupied housing by the 1970 median value, adjusted to 1980 prices using the consumer price index for housing. In the 1970s the total number of housing units in the Twin City region rose by 27 percent to almost 800,000. The median value of owner-occupied housing rose from $21,986 (or $48,094 in 1980 dollars) to $64,100, an average metropolitan increase of 33 percent in real terms. Any tract with a ratio of 1.33 or more gained in average value and relative attractiveness compared with the metropolitan average, and tracts with ratios below 1.33 lost (Figure 7.5).

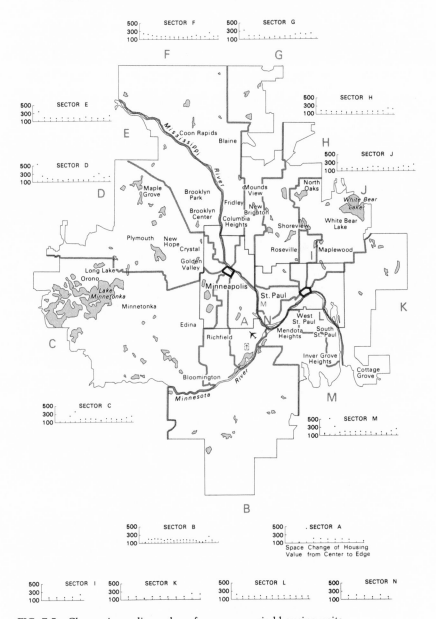

FIG. 7.5   Change in median value of owner-occupied housing units.

Within each sectoral submarket, the typical ratio was higher than 1.33 in tracts at the edge of the central business district, near or below 1.33 in the intermediate tracts with little new housing, and well above 1.33 in the developing suburban margins of submarkets that were not cul-de-sacs.

Real Estate Wealth Shifts

Another way to assess the consequences of housing submarket operation is to estimate the change in aggregate value of all the owner-occupied housing, in real terms, by tract, during the 1970s (Figure 7.6). Real estate amounts to 42 percent of total privately held wealth, of which 27 percent is net equity in principal residences (Ioannides 1988). Major capital gains accrue to home-

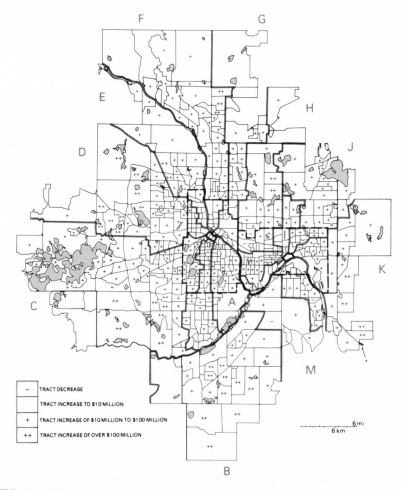

FIG. 7.6   Change in aggregate value of owner-occupied housing units.

owners in some tracts of some submarkets, and counterpart capital losses accrue to homeowners in certain inner-city neighborhoods.

A secondary set of derived gains and losses accrue to the commercial property owners and businesses in these areas. Capital gains encourage households to overspend their incomes, to the benefit of nearby retailers, but households in central-city neighborhoods incur negative wealth and curtail their spending.

Problems and Responses

The market value of housing units is what households will pay for them. The entry of the baby-boom generation into its house-buying years increased real housing prices in the 1970s, but the baby-bust generation is entering its house-buying years in the late 1980s. Housing demand will grow more slowly in the 1990s than at any time in the past forty years, and real housing prices will fall substantially (Mankiw and Weil 1988). These macrotrends play out differently in each metropolitan housing submarket.

Local housing officials use a variety of tactics to counteract the effects of adverse events within submarkets. They increase housing demand in targeted areas and among selected household groups by vouchers, loan and grant programs, and tax relief. They promote physical improvements of housing units by bribing builders to rehabilitate or rebuild. They acquire dilapidated properties, clear them, consolidate lots, and sell the properties to builders at low or negative prices to foster rebuilding. They enforce housing codes to maintain the housing stock and its environment. They may step up law enforcement and upgrade schools to enhance neighborhood attractiveness and maintain demand for housing. They may upgrade physical infrastructure by repairing streets, curbs, and gutters, replacing trees, and remodeling parks. They may improve transportation by modifying roads, transit, and parking facilities.

Structural responses can also change the rules about housing. The Depository Institutions Deregulation and Monetary Control Acts of 1980 and 1982 removed the protected status of housing finance and forced housing to compete with business and industry for capital, thereby raising significantly the cost of mortgage money. The U.S. Internal Revenue Act of 1986 eliminated tax breaks for owners of rental housing, forcing them to raise rents, lower outlays for maintenance, or abandon the rental business for other investment. The new tax law permits homeowners to deduct mortgage interest from their taxable incomes, but the elimination of deductability for other consumer interest encourages homeowners to use their housing equities to support other consumption. Second mortgages accounted for 10.8 percent of outstanding mortgage debt at the end of 1987, up from 3.6 percent at the beginning of the 1980s (Manchester and Poterba 1988).

Tax laws permitting the deduction of real estate taxes from taxable incomes of households and landlords and the deduction of mortgage interest are significant tax breaks for upper-income Americans, and encourage them to consume more housing than they otherwise would. This break for the rich is a penalty for lower-income households who get expensive housing while the rich get housing that is cheap and sometimes even free. Central-city governments subsidize new community development initiatives, often giving tax breaks on expensive business property while raising taxes on depreciating residential properties. The maldistribution of property wealth is further exacerbated. And so it goes.

In 1939 Hoyt described the sectoral residential structure of American cities, with sectors differentiated by housing value. A half century later the patterns identified by Hoyt appear to remain, but they may be slowly dissolving. The post–World War II construction boom in Minneapolis and St. Paul developed areas that had been platted earlier but lain unused during the years of depression and war. These areas were already served by transit and other city infrastructure. Early postwar building conformed to radial sectoral patterns.

The second tier of suburbs boomed in the 1950s and early 1960s. They were almost exclusively automobile oriented. Radial transit routes were increasingly irrelevant to development, but high speed radial highways enhanced sectoral housing submarkets. Their greatest impact was in sectors where housing demand was already strong.

From the late 1960s to the 1980s a third tier of suburbs developed on land opened up by circumferential highways. Radial sectoral influences waned as a century of radial transit influence continued to give way to a highway-based transport field that lacked any sharply defined directional bias. Variations in the outer segments of housing sectors increased steadily, but traditional variations between sectors, with few exceptions, were harder and harder to document. The effect of rail transit on the sectoral structuring of housing submarkets can now be seen as profoundly significant, yet temporary. Before 1890 a worker's home and workplace were close together, and the two bounded much of his daily activity. In the twentieth century, home and work were separated in space and linked by transit in ways that promoted the evolution of a sectoral structure of urban housing submarkets and their daily household activity. Today's suburban households, the typical metropolitan residents, have fewer and fewer ties with the central cities. A legacy of socioeconomic status, religion, race, and ethnicity can still be identified in each sector and used to distinguish one outer suburban zone from another, but these zones appear more alike and increasingly independent of their inner areas.

Each metropolitan region is a mosaic of sectoral housing submarkets. The Twin Cities region has fourteen. The interactions of housing demand and supply in each submarket have profound consequences for each neighborhood. Tactical responses aimed at modifying demand and supply can have short-term effects, but the legal, financial, and behavioral structures that have produced the housing submarkets in a metropolitan region will have to change before their consequences can take significantly different forms.

ACKNOWLEDGMENTS

I gratefully acknowledge research assistance by Jian Yi Liu and financial support from the Center for Urban and Regional Affairs, University of Minnesota.

REFERENCES

Abler, Ronald F., and John S. Adams. 1976. *A comparative atlas of America's great cities: Twenty metropolitan regions.* Minneapolis: University of Minnesota Press.

Abler, Ronald F., John S. Adams, and Peter R. Gould. 1971. *Spatial organization.* Englewood Cliffs, N.J.: Prentice Hall.

Adams, John S. 1987. *Housing America in the 1980s.* New York: Russell Sage Foundation.

———. 1989. The sectoral dynamics of housing markets within midwestern cities of the United States. In *The geographic evolution of the United States urban system.* Edited by John S. Adams. Moscow: Institute of Geography. Academy of Sciences of the USSR.

Binford, Henry. 1985. *The first suburbs: Residential communities on the Boston periphery, 1815–1860.* Chicago: University of Chicago Press.

Hoyt, Homer. 1939 [1966]. *The structure and growth of residential neighborhoods in American cities.* Washington, D.C.: Federal Housing Administration. Reprinted 1966 by the author with analysis of 1960 census tract data.

Ioannides, Yannis M. 1988. Housing, other real estate, and wealth portfolios. Paper read at NBER conference on residential real estate and capital formation, October 7–8, Newport, R.I.

Krakover, Shaul, and Emilio Casetti. 1988. Directionally biased metropolitan growth: A model and a case study. *Economic Geography* 64: 17–28.

Lansing, John B., Charles W. Clifton, and James N. Morgan. 1969. *New homes and poor people: A study of chains of moves.* Ann Arbor: Institute for Social Research, University of Michigan.

Manchester, Joyce, and James M. Poterba. 1988. Second mortgages, home equity borrowing, and household saving. Paper read at NBER conference on residential real estate and capital formation, October 7–8, Newport, R.I.

Mankiw, N. Gregory, and David N. Weil. 1988. *The baby boom, the baby bust, and the housing market.* Working Paper, No. 2794. Cambridge, Mass.: National Bureau of Economic Research.

Monkkonen, Eric H. 1988. *America becomes urban: The development of U.S. cities and towns, 1780–1980.* Berkeley: University of California Press.

Palm, Risa. 1978. Spatial segmentation of the urban housing market. *Economic Geography.* 54: 210–21.

Sternlieb, George, and James W. Hughes. 1986. *Demographics and housing in Amer-*

ica. Population Bulletin 41: 1. Washington, D.C.: Population Reference Bureau, Inc.

U.S. Department of Commerce. 1934. *Real property inventories.* Washington, D.C.: U.S. Government Printing Office.

Ward, David. 1968. The emergence of central immigrant ghettoes in American cities: 1840–1920. *Annals of the Association of American Geographers* 58: 343–59.

———. 1971. *Cities and immigrants.* New York: Oxford University Press.

Warner, Sam Bass, Jr. 1962. *Streetcar suburbs: The process of growth in Boston, 1870–1900.* Cambridge, Mass.: Harvard University Press.

Works Progress Administration. 1938. *Urban housing: A summary of real property inventories.* Washington, D.C.

EIGHT

Problems of Integrating
an Urban Society

W. A. V. Clark

The issues I address in this chapter have their origin in the urban mosaic, specifically the continuing separation of races, ethnic groups, and socioeconomic classes. Although a large literature focuses on the meaning of the varying levels of separation and their implications for the future of the American city, very little of that literature has considered the specific interventions that have attempted to modify or change the levels of separation. In contrast, this chapter examines attempts to reduce this separation. I address squarely the liberals' dilemma—we have committed substantial resources, considerable political capital, and thirty years to overcoming separation of the races to find that many steps have been counterproductive at the school and neighborhood level.

This chapter grows out of a decade of experience in litigation over school integration and school busing. Others have commented on the general nature of social science presentations related to litigation (Wolf 1981), but far fewer have discussed the influence of spatial structure on litigation and the resulting decisions. By focusing on the role, or the lack of a role, of spatial structure in litigation, the chapter points to a fundamental flaw in attempts to overcome segregation. Specifically, I ask if the litigation of social problems without appropriate recognition of the spatial arrangement of an urban society will substantially improve its well-being. The problems that have prevented the success of integration strategies have a common spatial thread. By ignoring space (in school busing programs), by focusing on boundary problems (in voting rights decisions), and by attempting to reorganize relative location (in subsidized housing), the litigants and judges have failed to recognize spatial primacy. This chapter parallels Gordon Clark's (1985) focus on local autonomy in judicial decision making, but I emphasize the context more than the decision-making processes. I briefly review the legal history of the civil rights movement, of school desegregation, open housing, and voting rights. I then discuss the context within which legal decision making has taken place, and conclude by evaluating the quest for an integrated society.

THE LEGAL CONTEXT

The last three and a half decades have seen an unprecedented struggle over the organization of society and, increasingly, over its spatial arrangement. This struggle for a just society intensified in 1954 when the Supreme Court made the historic landmark decision of *Brown v. Board of Education*. That decision, which culminated several decades of struggle over the rights of blacks for equal opportunities in education, is one of the most important pieces of social legislation of the twentieth century. In a short four-page decision in 1954, followed by an additional interpretation of the decision in 1955 (called *Brown II*), the Supreme Court swept away the *Plessy* (separate but equal) ruling of 1896 and opened elementary school systems to black and white students alike. Although the case is usually referred to as *Brown v. Board of Education*, and the primary case was in Topeka, Kansas, the decision actually amalgamated four separate cases. Henceforth, children were to go to their "neighborhood" schools, and these neighborhood schools were to provide equal opportunities for black and white students. Of course, *Brown v. Board of Education* did not sweep away decades of separate school systems, nor did it immediately guarantee all children an equal education, but it set in motion a series of events that included the Civil Rights Act of 1964, the Voting Rights Act of 1965, and the Open Housing Legislation of 1968.

Two points must be made about this process of legal intervention. First, there was no implicit, let alone explicit, reference to the spatial context of the legal decision. The only regional discussion was of the dual school system in the South, and at least initially *Brown* was perceived as applicable only to the South. (In the North—in most instances—there was not a pattern of de jure separate schools.) The second point is that legal intervention is not part of a process of ongoing policy evaluation. The decision by a court may or may not bring about the results desired by the plaintiffs, but it is only evaluated when additional cases are brought. If no cases are brought, then the original order stands as the legal precedent, and the rule of precedent is exceedingly powerful. For example, *Plessy v. Ferguson* (which authorized the separate but equal doctrine) was decided in 1896 and not overturned until *Brown v. Board of Education* in 1954. The Supreme Court had had many chances to question the correctness of *Plessy*, but failed to overturn it (Wolters 1984).

DECISIONS AND OUTCOMES

School Desegregation

Brown quickly won general acceptance because it appealed (and still appeals) to the notion that there should not be discrimination on the basis of race (Table 8.1). That notion, of course, has been extended to color and religious preference, and to jobs and other affirmative-action contexts. Certainly most Americans in the North opposed school assignments and legal distinctions based on race, and they thought it unfair to enforce the separation of any group from the mainstream of society. To some extent, the Civil Rights Act of 1964 was a broad-scale attempt to sweep away distinctions based on race, but it is important to recognize that the *Brown* ruling was originally a ruling on discrimination, not integration. The "Briggs dictum" (*Briggs v. Elliott*, 1955) aptly stated the difference (Wolters 1984, 60):

> a state may not deny to any person on account of race the right to attend any school that it maintains . . . but if the schools . . . are open to children of all races no violation of the Constitution is involved even though the children of different races voluntarily attend different schools (as they attend different churches). Nothing in the Constitution or in the decision of the Supreme Court takes away from the people the freedom to choose the schools they attend. The Constitution, in other words, does not require integration. It merely forbids discrimination. It does not forbid such segregation as occurs as the result of voluntary action. It merely forbids the use of government power to enforce segregation.

If the Supreme Court and district courts had followed the Briggs dictum, we would still have a large amount of racial separation—even racial isolation—in our schools, but it is unlikely that we would have had the turmoil, the white flight, and the resegregation of the past three decades. In 1968, however, the Supreme Court, in *Green v. New Kent County*, held that "School districts in the southern and border states must achieve as much racial mixing as possible" (Wolters 1984, 7), and that districts that have discriminated in the past must take affirmative action to achieve balanced racial enrollments. The 1968 decision provided the basis of the activism of the courts through the 1970s and into the 1980s. In 1971 the Court in *Swan v. Charlotte Mecklenberg Board of Education* established the principle of school busing; in 1973 in *Keyes v. School District No. 1* it said that school desegregation can be ordered in northern school districts, even when there had been no statutory separation of the races; in 1977 in *Dayton Board of Education v. Brinkman* the remedy was to match the amount of segregation; in 1979 in *Columbus Board of Education v. Penick* a violation in part of the school district can require that the whole district adopt desegregation reme-

TABLE 8.1 Supreme Court Decisions

Date		Site
	SCHOOL DESEGREGATION	
1954	*Brown v. Board of Education*	Topeka, Kansas
	School of desegregation unconstitutional	
1968	*Green v. County School Board of New Kent County*	Virginia
	Required affirmative action to overcome past effects	
1971	*Swann v. Charlotte Mecklenberg Board of Education*	North Carolina
	Established busing for school desegregation	
1974	*Milliken v. Bradley*	Detroit
	Desegregation across city-county lines not required	
	OPEN HOUSING	
1948	*Shelley v. Kraemer*	St. Louis
	Racially restricted covenants declared a violation of the Fourteenth Amendment	
1968	*Jones v. Alfred H. Mayer Co.*	St. Louis
	Right of minorities to buy and lease property	
1972	*Southern Burlington County NAACP v. Township of Mt. Laurel*	New Jersey
	Struck down exclusionary zoning	
1977	*Metropolitan Housing Development Corp. v. Village of Arlington Heights*	Chicago
	Differentiate intent and effect in exclusionary zoning	
	VOTING RIGHTS	
1969	*Allen v. State Board of Elections*	Mississippi
	Right of minority voters to cast ballots of equal value to whites	
1973	*White v. Regester*	Texas
	Held that multimember districts violated the Fourteenth Amendment	
1986	*Thornburg v. Gingles*	North Carolina
	Endorsed a simple three-part test of vote dilution	

dies; and in a host of other cases through the 1970s the Supreme and District Courts expanded their interventionist approach into school systems throughout the country—in the North and in the South. In addition, the Department of Health, Education and Welfare investigated the extent to which specific school districts were meeting the requirements of *Brown*.

Not all decisions favored the proponents of school desegregation. In

1974 the Supreme Court in *Millikin v. Bradley* refused to extend the desegregation program from a central-city school to suburban districts. In 1980, in *Armour v. Nix*, the Supreme Court reiterated this decision. In Indianapolis and in Wilmington specific actions of suburban or metropolitan districts required desegregation programs to cross school district boundaries, but in general the decision has been to avoid what are called metropolitan desegregation remedies (perhaps the only recognition of the role of spatial structure in school desegregation). This refusal to cross district boundaries in all but a few cases has been criticized widely as a retreat from the bold pattern of desegregation undertaken with *Brown* and continued with *Green v. New Kent County*.

The cases cited here are paralleled by desegregation litigation in more than one hundred school districts in the United States and perhaps as many as one hundred different remedies designed by the courts, local school districts, and the Department of Health, Education and Welfare. At least forty-two cities have court-ordered plans, another two dozen have plans designed by the Department of Health, Education and Welfare, and at least another dozen have Board-approved plans (for example, Seattle).

The most obvious spatially related decision of the school desegregation cases was the decision to implement busing to achieve integration (and racial balancing of schools), which led to a great deal of turmoil and has been identified as a major reason for white flight, both to suburban districts and to private schools. The refusal to support a system that integrates schools across political boundaries (either among several school systems or more usually between cities and suburbs) further emphasized the central city/suburban dichotomy. In some districts (particularly in the South, which had county school districts) the court rulings were in fact metropolitan plans, but even in such metropolitan plans, as in Charlotte Mecklenberg (Lord 1977), there is evidence of the "spatial effects" of white population losses from migration to surrounding districts.

Housing and Neighborhoods

The litigation over integrating public housing parallels the litigation in school desegregation (Table 8.1). The Fair Housing Act of 1968 (Title VIII of the Civil Rights Act) prohibited refusals to sell and rent that were racially motivated (Calmore 1985, 78):

> to undo the results of officially-approved housing discrimination between the years of 1930 and 1962. This goal includes achievement of residential integration of the metropolitan areas of the nation thereby co-joining the 1949 goal of a decent home and a suitable living environment for every American family with the 1968 goal of removing racial barriers to home acquisition.

As in school desegregation, some significant cases have set the bounds of debate over housing segregation. The central issues revolve around the role and placing of subsidized housing and exclusionary zoning, although the first important cases (*Shelley v. Kraemer* and *Jones v. Mayer*) were concerned with removing racially restrictive covenants and the freedom "to buy whatever a white can buy, the right to live wherever a white can live" (*Jones v. Mayer*, 392 U.S. 409, 1968).

The primary decisions of the 1970s are still Mt. Laurel and Arlington Heights. The Mt. Laurel litigation focused on a claim that a zoning ordinance precluded the development of low and moderate cost housing. The remedy was to insist that every developing municipality has an obligation to provide a "fair share" of the regional need for housing of persons of low and moderate income. This decision is now state law in California and an integral part of the debates over slow and managed growth. The court implicitly raised spatial questions. What is the appropriate region, and what mechanisms of allocation are appropriate?

In *Village of Arlington Heights v. Metropolitan Housing Development Corp.* in 1977 (known as *Arlington Heights I*), the Supreme Court held that even though the ultimate effect of a town's zoning decision might be racially discriminatory, this was inadequate to establish a constitutional equal protection claim. In other words, a constitutional challenge to exclusionary zoning must be premised upon a demonstrated discriminatory purpose (Kmiec 1985, 129). This decision set the grounds for debate about whether effect or intent is important in deciding a discriminatory case. On remand, the Seventh Circuit Court of Appeals, in *Arlington Heights II*, held that a violation can be established by showing discriminatory effect without a showing of discriminatory intent, and thus it created further confusion about intent versus effect. A considerable literature examines the effects and intents standards in terms of legal issues and housing discrimination, but most of it is of interest only to attorneys.

In general, residential integration has been even less successful than school integration. For example, the Gautreaux litigation in Chicago was designed specifically to improve subsidized housing in white areas in Chicago. It failed initially and has had little success later. Similarly, the Mt. Laurel litigation in New Jersey attempted to overcome restraints on subsidized housing and to improve integration in white neighborhoods. The notion is that subsidized housing enables low-income people to move into higher-income communities and towns. Neither the Mt. Laurel nor the Gautreaux litigation has had a significant impact on residential integration in either community. Recent legal rulings in Yonkers (Stille 1986) indicate that scattered-site subsidized housing is still a contentious issue, and opposition is substantial. White residents objected to scattered-site public housing in Garfield Ridge in 1972 and in Yonkers in 1988. Opposition to scattered-site public housing can be interpreted as white antipathy to racial integration, or as a desire to maintain neighborhood homogeneity and values. In some cases, this competition (particularly when there is a pent-up black demand in nearby neighborhoods) can be interpreted as a competition for territory. It is inherently spatial.

Berry (1979) identifies a number of factors in addition to strong preferences by whites and blacks as to why it has been difficult to integrate neighborhoods. The South Shore Commission was not successful in integrating the South Shore community, not only because it was not one of the more desirable areas of the city for whites, but because there was a predominance of apartment buildings as opposed to single-family residences (Berry 1979, 301), and the housing stock was older than in suburban communities. At the same time, the actions of the South Shore Commission made the area attractive to blacks, and the higher rates of turnover in apartment buildings made racial transition easy. He also notes the impact of specific demographic factors, including higher proportions of elderly residents, or families with young children. Finally, even normal mobility makes neighborhood transition certain when blacks continuously constitute the bulk of those who move into vacancies (Berry 1979, 175).

Voting Rights

The litigation over voting rights has been equally contentious, although the process has been much less tortuous than in education or housing. Voting rights litigation originated in the Federal Voting Rights Act, the 1965 Civil Rights Law that prohibited election procedures that discriminated against blacks and other minorities. This act has emerged in the 1980s as the basis of litigation over voting rights, as civil rights activists argue for overturning electoral systems that give white voters an unfair advantage. Beginning in 1969 in *Allen v. State Board of Elections* (393 U.S. 544), the Supreme Court established the right of minority voters to cast ballots of equal value to those of whites in areas where race still dominates the political process (Table 8.1). The decision that minority voters should cast ballots of equal value to those of whites is immediately a spatial problem, a problem of numbers of voters and areas within which they live and vote. Districting, redistricting, and gerrymandering are all geographical questions that have dominated the political process for as long as there have been elections. Indeed, politicians are acutely aware of the geography of metropolitan areas as they organize their districts to keep a majority of their party. This issue is increasingly the racial structure of districts rather than simply maintaining a winning margin for particular candidates.

In 1973 in *Zimmer v. McKeithen*, the Fifth Circuit devised a nine-point test for vote dilution that included a community's past attitudes, racially polarized voting trends, and the electoral success or failure of minority candidates. Although in 1980 in *Bolden v. City of Mobile* (446 U.S. 55), the

Supreme Court held that the minority plaintiffs had not proved that the electoral system was intentionally discriminatory (using language that had been used in housing and a number of other equal protection legal cases), the decision resulted in a change in the language of the 1982 Voting Rights Act. The test designed in *Zimmer v. McKeithen* was reestablished, but any right of minorities to be elected in numbers equal to their proportion in the population was disclaimed. Montague (1988) noted that the pace of litigation has accelerated under the Voting Rights Act since 1982. It seems to have been strengthened by *Gingles v. Thornburg* (1986), when the Supreme Court endorsed a simplified three-part test for the existence of racial polarization as the key factor in proving a vote dilution claim (Montague 1988).

Expert witnesses and statistical analyses have been used to bolster cases that presented data on vote dilution. The issue from a litigant's perspective is how to organize districts that will elect minorities. The current trend in voting rights actions is focused on identifying minority districts in which minorities can be elected, but guaranteeing minority election may in fact create a separate and possibly not equal representation. The creation of black majority districts may well boost the power of conservative white suburban districts where black influence has been eliminated (Cooper 1987), and it clearly raises additional spatial questions.

Interpretation

A common theme in all of these legal situations is the continuing attempt by a variety of litigants to undo separation of the races, to overcome the tendency (whatever the underlying cause) for racial and ethnic separation. The underlying assumption is that ethnic groups and races should be comingled in the future city. The focus has shifted from equal access to redressing past wrongs with affirmative positive actions. The legal process originated in attempt to open access within the urban structure to all races, but it has moved from overcoming past discrimination to a situation (through affirmative-action guidelines) in which each group will reflect some national average in occupation and education and representation (Glazer 1988). The debate now focuses on the role of quotas (or goals), and timetables, and in voting rights it emphasizes that separate districts for blacks and Hispanics are appropriate (that is, it is not discriminatory to draw boundaries around spatially separate residential areas).

There is, at the least, an irony between the attempt to integrate housing and to define racially separate voting districts. In school desegregation cases, segregation (although it originally meant state-ordered or city-ordered segregation of races) has come to mean black concentration in schools regardless of the cause, even if it is residential concentration or parental choice. (Newby [1982] has an insightful discussion of the varying meanings of segregation.)

The emphasis has shifted from the declaration of segregation as unconstitutional to court-ordered racial numerical requirements in schools, quotas in jobs, and (perhaps in the extreme) the attempt to determine how many members of a particular ethnic group should get certain jobs or promotions, attend particular schools, or live in designated areas. Glazer (1988) notes that this approach encounters consideration opposition. Why does it encounter opposition, and what are the problems with it? The difficulties, I believe, arise out of spatial demographic change, individual behaviors, and urban structure. Removing the lingering effects of private discrimination will not do much to change the levels of separation, but that is a separate debate.

UNDERSTANDING THE FAILURE

Demographic Change

Even though the rate of mobility may have declined in the late 1970s and 1980s from perhaps 20 percent to 17 percent, almost one-fifth of the population still changes residences every year, and more than half of the population has moved in a five-year period (Long 1988). Renters move more often than owners, and younger people move more often than older people, so half of the population has not actually moved. We are a restless society, however, and people move frequently: for jobs, to improve their housing, to escape crime in inner-city neighborhoods, and for a myriad of other reasons (Clark 1986a). The rich and persuasive literature on this mobility process implies a conflict between a restless society of individuals hoping to improve their well-being and their desire for neighborhood stability. The amount of movement is substantial. Some cities have had several hundred thousand household exchanges over a seven-year period (Figure 8.1). In some tracts, particularly those in rapid racial transition, 70 or 80 percent of the population has moved in a five-year period. The amount of movement is high, and the pattern of movement is quite structured.

A substantial fraction of the moves have been to the suburbs. Although whites have been moving to the suburbs for at least three decades (Frey 1985 and 1987; Berry and Silverman 1980), there is additional evidence of white relocation specifically related to court decisions. White flight in response to mandatory integration programs incorporates the loss of white students from public to private schools, the movement of white students out of the district, and the failure of students to enter the district. White flight is still primarily a phenomenon of large northern cities with a core city of minority residents surrounded by a ring of white suburbs. Desegregation decrees exacerbate segregation because the number of white students in the city schools declines, perhaps leading to an even more segregated condition than before desegregation was initiated. Whites have moved to the suburbs, and there is increasing evidence that affluent blacks are also doing so, if only to spillover tracts contiguous to the black concentrated central city (Clark 1987a, 1987b, 1987c). Hispanics in Southern California who moved to Orange County are clearly paralleling the earlier suburban movement of whites.

We live in a mobile—even restless—society, and demographic change is a basic element against which interventionist litigation has occurred. Demographic change produced a declining white student body in our schools just when the legal process was enforcing racial balance. As children graduated, there were fewer white children to fulfill this legal mandate. In many school districts integration has not failed because of massive resistance, but because there were not enough white students for a realistically integrated school system (Armor 1978; Clark 1984 and 1986b). The aggregate white losses are in the thousands, and the loss has decimated some schools (Figure 8.2). Norfolk, Virginia, lost almost seven thousand students more than the expected demographic loss. Court-ordered busing plans were responsible for at least 50 percent of the total enrollment loss in Boston (30,179), Denver (23,615), Detroit (50,328), Dallas (47,880), Oklahoma City (27,627), and Houston (56,014).

Demographic change affected the location as well as the total number of students available for school integration. The relocation of large numbers of whites and the increased numbers of blacks with a higher birth rate in central areas meant that inner-city schools were likely to be black and suburban schools were more likely to be white. White flight also deprived inner-city schools of the highly motivated pupils who arguably set a tone of order and relative respect for schools (Magnet, 1988).

Preferences and Prejudices

Economists first offered an economic interpretation of the role of preferences in generating residential separation. If whites have a greater aversion to living among blacks than do other blacks, then whites will offer more than will blacks for housing in predominantly white neighborhoods, and the residential areas of the two groups will be separated (Decker 1957; Muth 1969). These economists explained separation of the races in terms of the social preference of consumers. Schelling (1971; 1978) also focused on the role of preferences in generating separations in residential areas as well as in groups and clubs. He pointed out that even mild racial preferences can produce extreme separation in some hypothetical cases. Evidence gathered in national surveys and individual case studies documents white preferences for 80/20 and black preferences for 50/50 (Figure 8.3). Whites prefer neighborhoods with 80 percent white and less than 20 percent black, while blacks prefer neighborhoods that have equal numbers of blacks and whites. The white own-race preference is a strong element of the underlying dynamic in white residential behavior. Whites clearly do not choose neighborhoods that are much more than 20 percent minority. If we combine a high level of mobility with a

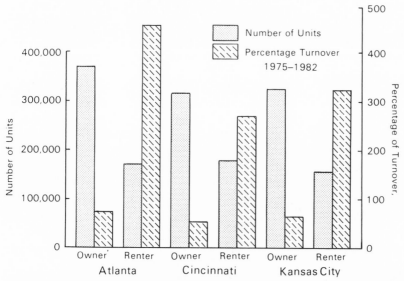

FIG. 8.1   Residential turnover, 1975–1982, in Atlanta, Cincinnati, and Kansas City.

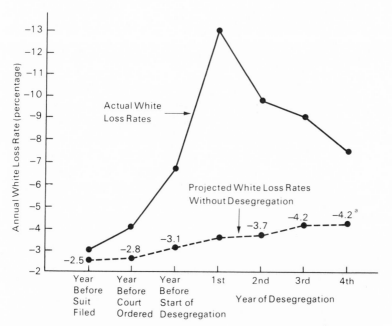

FIG. 8.2   Actual and projected white loss rates for northern school districts with court-ordered mandatory desegregation. Used with permission from D. J. Armor and D. S. Schwarzbach, *White Flight, Demographic Transition, and the Future of School Desegregation.* P-5931. Santa Monica: The RAND Corporation, 1978.

desire for social (perhaps racial) homogeneity, integrated neighborhoods are likely to be the exception and not the rule (Schnare 1977). Whether or not these preferences will break down in the long run is a subject for speculation rather than research.

Preferences are also at least partly behind the increase in private school enrollment. For a long time, private school enrollment in the United States has been stable in the range of 6–10 percent, but it has changed fundamentally during school desegregation in particular cities and in particular districts within cities (Figure 8.4). An increasing number of affluent white children are now educated in private schools rather than in the public educational system. Proponents of desegregation charge racism, proponents of private schools charge failing school standards and inadequate supervision, but neither claim invalidates the fact that the number of white pupils in the public school system has decreased.

Urban Structure

The uneven distribution of population by wealth and race is obvious in the increasingly black central cities and suburban white rings. This uneven distribution is reflected in differences in housing, in the electoral process, and, not least, in the racial composition of public schools. In general, central cities are poorer than white suburban areas, and the households, black and white, who relocate into central cities are poorer (Figure 8.5). The differences between central cities and suburbs have a broad association with racial concentration (Table 8.2). Despite the argument that housing is available in the suburbs for minorities, the differences in income are so great that these suburban neighborhoods cannot be easily integrated without substantial additional intervention. The combination of variations in individual wealth (Figure 8.6) and distinct spatial patterns in its distribution is a major barrier to the integration of metropolitan areas. Even within the black areas of cities there is significant spatial variation in socioeconomic status. Newer more suburban-like areas are more like suburban white areas in their socioeconomic status, whatever their racial composition (Figure 8.7).

In addition, metropolitan areas are a mosaic of political units. Central cities may be almost as large as counties, but suburbs consist of many individual cities and school districts, each with its own spatial basis. These competing political structures allow shifts between communities to avoid legal and social planning by courts and legislatures. Given the uneven distributions of wealth and race, and given the political mosaic, it is not surprising that this urban structure allows for considerable individual behavior.

Central cities have higher crime rates, more deteriorated housing, lower-cost housing, and larger concentrations of minorities in contrast to suburban rings that are still largely white and the recipients of substantial shifts from central cities (Katzman 1980). These differences are so substantial that the

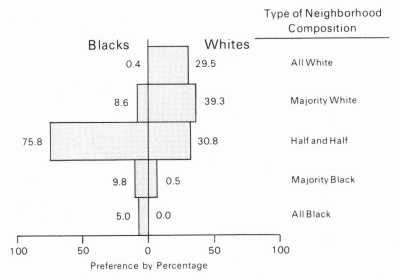

FIG. 8.3 Average preferences for neighborhood composition of blacks and whites.

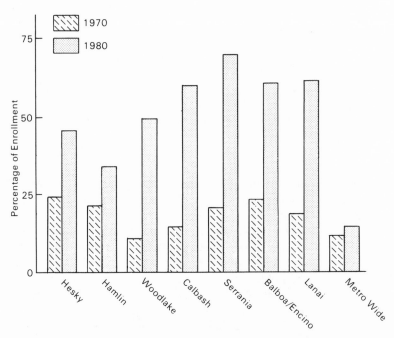

FIG. 8.4 Private school enrollment change in selected San Fernando Valley schools.

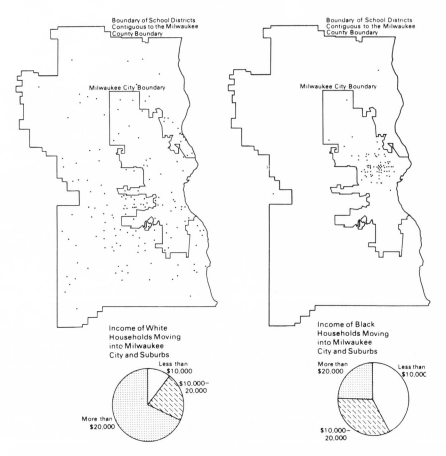

FIG. 8.5 Current residence of white (a) and black (b) respondents who moved into Milwaukee between 1981 and 1985.

demographic processes are unlikely to create metropolitan-wide racial integration in the foreseeable future, even if there were no racial residential preferences (Frey 1979; 1985; and 1987).

These urban structure implications are compounded by ongoing changes in metropolitan areas, which are changing both from deconcentration (Frey 1987) and from urban restructuring (Storper and Walker 1984). Employment opportunities in metropolitan centers have increased commuting fields and an extended urban system (Mitchellson and Fisher 1987a and 1987b). The ability of jobs and households to migrate over increasingly large areas further changes the separation of groups, classes, and races. The long-term effects of such changes are far from clear. The diffusion of the urban region is yet another spatial dynamic within which litigants attempt to integrate society.

TABLE 8.2   Number of Census Tracts in Milwaukee, 1980, by Percentage Black, Median Rent, and Value of Housing Units

		Percentage Black		
		0–30	30–70	70–100
Low Rent	1	14	7	34
	2	44	4	6
	3	51	7	1
	4	51	0	0
	5	58	0	0
High rent	6	56	0	0
Low value	1	14	6	33
	2	38	9	6
	3	51	3	0
	4	56	0	0
	5	54	0	0
High value	6	52	0	0

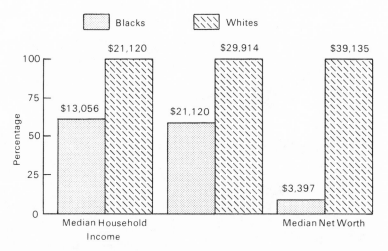

FIG. 8.6   Black household assets and equity as a percentage of white household assets and equity. Data source: U.S. Bureau of the Census. 1986. Household Wealth and Asset Ownership. *Current population reports*, ser. P-70, no. 7.

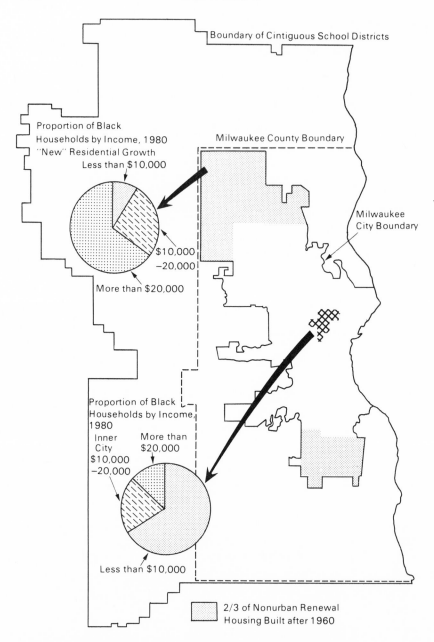

FIG. 8.7 Income of black households in two parts of Milwaukee, 1980.

WHAT ARE THE ALTERNATIVES?

This chapter has provided no direct views about the future of integration in an urban society. It is the liberals' dilemma that attempts hitherto have not overcome the separation in our cities—indeed, they may have exacerbated the distinction between inner cities and suburbs. Moreover, the view that all society's problems can be solved with litigation if not policy is certainly misplaced in the arena of these large-scale social/spatial problems. Whether or not schools, housing, and the ballot box can be used to change society is an open question. If discriminatory acts are vigorously prosecuted, should we go beyond that and manage integration? It is critical that nongeographers recognize the implications of spatial primacy and that the focus return to the more fundamental issues of quality education, affordable housing, and equal income distribution rather than racial balance per se, especially since recent research shows no real gains for learning from integration (Cook et al. 1984).

Even though academics seldom make policy, the information provided by research on the link between legal decision making and spatial processes is critical background for what will undoubtedly occur—further litigation. Legal interventions have ignored spatial structure, and problems have arisen as a consequence. Recognition of the spatial structure may not solve the errors, but it will prevent some of the excesses of the past. Informed research on the effects of spatial structure is critical in understanding how legal decisions will be made in the spatial and social arenas. The comments in *Swan* and *Millikin* contrast with the reality of spatial and social processes. In *Swan*, Chief Justice Burger wrote:

> People gravitate toward school facilities just as schools are located in response to the needs of people. The location of schools may thus influence the patterns of residential segregation of a metropolitan area and have an important impact on the composition of inner-city neighborhoods. In the past, choices in this respect have been used as a potent weapon for creating or maintaining a state-segregated school system. It may well promote segregated residential patterns which, when combined with neighborhood zoning further lock the school system into a mold of separation of the races.

There is no direct evidence that schools influence residential separation; at most schools affect residential patterns only indirectly.

In *Milliken v. Bradley* the court went further in the now-famous "unknown and perhaps unknowable forces in residential decision-making." There is already evidence to allow us to take issue with the pronouncement by the courts of unknowable forces, but the courts can make such pronouncements because presentation of known material is inadequate and attention to the spatial scale is insufficient. Social scientists clearly differ in worldview and in interpretation, as illustrated in a recent exchange between Clark (1986b) and Galster (1988), but the area of common ground is increasing. Informed analysis of the spatial basis of residential separation should guide any attempt to move forward to an integrated society.

REFERENCES

Armor, D. J. 1978. *White flight, demographic transition and the future of school desegregation.* Santa Monica, Calif.: Rand Corporation.

Berry, B. J. L. 1979. *The open housing question: Race and housing in Chicago, 1966– 1976.* Cambridge, Mass.: Ballinger.

Berry, B. J. L., and L. Silverman, eds. 1980. *Population redistribution and public policy.* Washington, D.C.: National Academy of Sciences.

Calmore, J. O. 1985. Proving housing discrimination: Intent versus effect and the continuing search for the proper touchstone. *Issues in Housing Discrimination* 1: 77–93.

Clark, G. 1985. *The judges and the cities.* Chicago: University of Chicago Press.

Clark, W. A. V. 1984. Judicial intervention, busing and local residential change. In *Geography and the urban environment: Progress in research and applications.* Edited by D. T. Herbert and R. J. Johnston. New York: Wiley.

———. 1986a. *Human migration.* Beverly Hills, Calif.: Sage Publications.

———. 1986b. Residential segregation in American cities: A review and interpretation. *Population Research and Policy Review* 5: 95–127.

———. 1987a. Demographic change, attendance area adjustment and school system impact. *Population Research and Policy Review* 6: 199–222.

———. 1987b. School desegregation and white flight: A reexamination and case study. *Social Science Research* 16: 211–28.

———. 1987c. Urban restructuring from a demographic perspective. *Economic Geography* 63: 103–25.

Cook, T., D. Armor, R. Crain, N. Miller, W. Stephen, and H. Wahlberg. 1984. *School desegregation and black achievement.* Washington, D.C.: National Institute of Education.

Cooper, M. 1987. Beware of Republicans bearing voting rights suits. *Washington Monthly.* February, 11–15.

Decker, G. S. 1957. *The economics of discrimination.* Chicago: University of Chicago Press.

Frey, W. H. 1979. Central city white flight, racial and nonracial causes. *American Sociological Review* 44: 425–48.

———. 1985. Mover destination selectivity and the changing suburbanization of metropolitan whites and blacks. *Demography* 22: 223–43.

———. 1987. Migration and depopulation of the metropolis: Regional restructuring or rural renaissance. *American Sociological Review* 52: 240–57.

Galster, G. 1988. Residential segregation in American cities: A contrary review. *Population Research and Policy Review* 7: 93–112.

Glazer, N. 1988. The affirmative action stalemate. *The Public Interest* 90 (Winter): 99–114.

Katzman, M. 1980. Implications of population redistribution for education. In *Popula-*

tion redistribution and public policy. Edited by B. J. L. Berry and L. Silverman. Washington, D.C.: National Academy of Science.

Kmiec, D. 1985. Exclusionary zoning and purposeful racial segregation in housing: Two wrongs deserving separate remedies. In *Issues in housing discrimination.* Washington, D.C.: U.S. Commission on Civil Rights.

Long, L. 1988. *Migration and residential mobility in the United States.* New York: Russell Sage Foundation.

Lord, J. D. 1977. *Spatial perspectives on school desegregation and busing.* Resource Paper, No. 77.3. Washington, D.C.: Association of American Geographers.

Magnet, Myron. 1988. How to smarten up the schools. *Fortune,* 1 February 1988, 86–94.

Mitchellson, R. L., and J. S. Fisher. 1987a. Long-distance commuting and population change in Georgia, 1960–1980. *Growth and Change* 18: 44–65.

———. 1987b. Long-distance commuting and population change in New York State. *Urban Geography* 8: 193–211.

Montague, B. 1988. The voting rights act today. *American Bar Association Journal* August: 52–57.

Muth, R. 1969. *Studies in housing.* Chicago: University of Chicago Press.

Newby, R. 1982. Segregation, desegregation, and racial balance: Status implications of these concepts. *The Urban Review* 14(1): 17–24.

Schelling, T. 1971. The ecology of micro-motives. *The Public Interest* 2: 61–69.

———. 1978. *Micro-motives and macro-behavior.* New York: W. W. Norton.

Schnare, A. 1977. *Residential segregation by race in U.S. metropolitan areas: An analysis across cities and over time.* Washington, D.C.: The Urban Institute.

Stille, A. 1986. Lawyers shape a city's future. *The National Law Journal* 8(35): 33–36.

Storper, M., and R. Walker. 1984. The spatial division of labor: Labor and the location of industries. In *Sunbelt, urban development and regional restructuring.* Edited by L. Sawyer and W. Tabb. Oxford: Oxford University Press.

Wolf, E. 1981. *Trial and error.* Detroit, Mich.: Wayne State University Press.

Wolters, R. 1984. *The burden of Brown: Thirty years of school desegregation.* Knoxville: University of Tennessee Press.

NINE

Special Populations in Contemporary Urban Areas

Reginald G. Golledge

The extension of science and technology into space, on the one hand, and into genetic codes and the neurochemistry of the brain, on the other, are examples of how new knowledge acquisition dramatically increases the complexity of the world in which we live. Although traditionally viewed as a mundane subject, geography has extended its interest in spatial structure, spatial relationships, and spatial interactions into these same new frontiers, these same uncharted areas. Today's geography is as complex as the world in which we live. Geographers have strayed far from the traditional disciplinary boundaries, and in my view this makes the discipline one of the most interesting and satisfying pursuits of knowledge. All this is possible because of the insights and adventures that attracted the attention of innovative researchers in current and past generations of geographers.

In keeping with what I see as a discipline of ever increasing depth and complexity, I would like to offer several variations on a single theme rather than address a single problem at length. In this chapter I develop a number of different scenarios, each tied to a common theme of urban problems, and each developed by a behavioral approach. I plan to venture beyond the bounds of normal populations interacting in normal spaces into the problems of special populations such as the mentally retarded, the mentally ill, and the blind. I plan to examine these populations not in the rarified institutional settings to which we so often confine them, but in what to us is a normal everyday environment. To my chosen population subgroups, however, such an environment represents a hostile and unconstrained world of extraordinary complexity (Table 9.1).

TABLE 9.1   Geographic Realities

Normalcy	Mentally Retarded	Blind or Vision Impaired
Spatial Occurrences		
Identify	Conceptually limited	Lacks many conventional modifiers (adjectives and adverbs)
Location	Unstable	Fuzzy
Magnitude	Broad monotonic classes	Few two-dimensional referents
Time	Task specific not generic	Time dominates space
Spatial Distribution		
Density	Low frequencies only	Limited to tactually sensed classes
Pattern or shape	Simple shapes/limited concepts of repetition	Comprehension limited by sensory deprivation
Scatter	Limited understanding of variance	Constrained by scale
Spatial Process		
Decision making/ choice	Severely constrained	Constrained by spatial knowledge
Spatial problem solving	Limited to one dimension	Restricted by ability to perform mental geometry and trigonometry
Movement habits	Limited and few	Mostly limited to select learned routes between known places
Other spatial interactions	Often controlled by supervision	Usually micro-scale small-group behavior—often dependent on others

THE MENTALLY RETARDED

The ways in which mildly and moderately retarded individuals differ from "normal" populations in the acquisition, storage, and use of spatial knowledge include: (1) impaired information processing and sensing abilities; (2) inability to comprehend large-scale macrospaces, functionally complex environments, or two-dimensional abstract representations of large-scale environments; (3) selective physiological impairment, including localized brain damage and rotation or reflection problems such as might be found in those suffering from dyslexia; and (4) limited problem-solving ability.

Given these limitations, it is almost inevitable that members of this population would have difficulty understanding the many dimensions and nuances of today's urban systems. For example, they may not easily understand the functional differentiation of buildings at various locations, or that different buses passing the same location may have quite different destinations. Place identity can become clouded by multiple agents for single locations; location may be unstable depending on point of view; magnitude may have little meaning beyond a small number of broad monotonically ordered classes; and time may be recognized in a task-specific context but not generically. Activity patterns may be few and uncomplicated. Even simple patterns or shapes of distributions may be unrecognized. Fundamental geographic concepts of scatter, dispersion, or spatial variance may not reach a threshold level of understanding. Movement problems may be solved only in one dimension, with concepts of network and connectivity being poorly understood. To avoid complex and continuous decision making, habitual movements may become dominant, and search and exploration may be limited. Depending on the degree of retardation, personal and spatial interactions may be controlled through a process of supervision.

Given this severely constrained ability to comprehend even elementary components of a complex built environment, it is no wonder that the deinstitutionalized mildly and moderately retarded population contributes significantly to some of today's major urban problems. Two of these problems are of increasing concern nationwide, whether the urban place be small or large.

The first problem relates to the burden placed on community life and institutions by the deinstitutionalized retarded populations who are inadequately prepared to live in a complex urban setting. Since the late 1960s, following wholesale deinstitutionalization pioneered by the then governor of California, Ronald Reagan, deinstitutionalization has spread nationally in an attempt to economize on state expenditures and to make family, friends, and communities more responsible for the supervision and support of retarded populations. In many cases, however, the alternative of returning to the familial bosom was not available, thus loosing on communities a subpopulation ill-prepared to integrate into their daily life and customs. Many individuals were deemed ready to be turned loose in society after they had satisfactorily completed a series of psychological and social tests that showed, among other things, that they could lace their own shoes, walk up and down stairs one at a time, use bathrooms without supervision, prepare some necessary food items, and behave in an acceptable manner in small group situations.

There is no evidence that urban specialists such as geographers, planners, and designers have ever been consulted in the development of criteria that might indicate ability to handle the complexities of real-world environments. When confronted with the masses of people in bustling, busy cities, the richness of an environment studded with both known and unusual urban functions, and a scale of location and interaction that requires integration of different transport modes between unseen origins and destinations, it is little wonder that problems arise. Although many serious community attempts have been made to intervene in this process by establishing halfway houses, group homes, and other friendly institutions that help the deinstitutionalized individual accommodate to new environments, they were unable to guarantee that individuals would cope and survive. It should not be surprising, therefore, that the deinstitutionalized retarded contribute significantly to two of today's most severe urban problems: homelessness and the overcrowding of penal institutions.

Without the security of a group home, and without the potential for bringing in income at much beyond the level of absolute poverty, the deinstitutionalized retarded individual has become a significant member of today's homeless populations in virtually all urban environments. Although most attention is given to normal healthy individuals (particularly families with small children) who have suffered such economic disaster that they are no longer able to participate in even the lowest cost housing markets and are forced into homelessness, the homelessness of equally as many if not more individuals is the direct result of deinstitutionalization policies.

The second major problem area for the retarded population involves institutional change. Individuals not well prepared to cope with complex urban environments may violate community social, moral, and legal codes, often within a short time of deinstitutionalization. Sometimes the result is arrest and imprisonment. When released, further violation of community codes results in new arrest, and recidivism soon becomes a way of life. The penalty to the community is overcrowding in penal institutions and additional drains against community and state finances for support and upkeep of such individuals; secondary impacts include the moral and personal decay resulting from this way of life.

In addition to these two major problems, the deinstitutionalized individual often becomes an easy target for a wide variety of criminal acts, ranging from robbery to rape and murder. The number of such individuals who become yet another statistic on the daily crime clock of urban areas far outweighs the number who are integrated into the community and succeed in coping and living.

Although on the surface the contribution of the retarded to today's urban problems may seem more social, legal, and moral than geographical, I contend that the ill-preparedness of these individuals to cope with the exigencies of everyday living in urban systems inevitably leads to code violations and an inability to cope. Geographers have a responsibility to use their expertise on behalf of this special group. We must begin by trying to understand the spatial abilities and performance levels various retarded populations are able to achieve. It makes little sense to walk into institutions prepared to give lectures and training on today's cities if the potential student population is unaware of even the most primitive spatial concepts.

About a decade ago, I joined geographer John Rayner and social worker psychologist Joseph Parnicky at Ohio State University in a multiyear project to attempt to find what retarded individuals could learn about urban environments (Golledge, Rayner, and Parnicky 1979). We designed experiments to test fundamental spatial concepts associated with location, interaction, movement, and place recognition. I will describe two experiments with mentally retarded (moderately and mildly) and normal populations in two quite different environments (Columbus, Ohio, and Santa Barbara, California) and then draw some inferences from the findings. We devised levels of tasks to provide data on declarative, procedural, and configurational knowledge structures. We also examined actual spatial behavioral problems.

We conducted the experiments in two separate locations with two different subject sets. In Columbus, an experimental group of fifteen recently deinstitutionalized mildly and moderately retarded individuals living in two group homes in the center of the task environment were compared with a contrast group of thirty-one "normal" adults living in the same neighborhood. Most of the contrast group were socioeconomically deprived. In Santa Barbara, an experimental group of six recently deinstitutionalized mildly and moderately retarded individuals living in two group homes in the study area were compared with a contrast group of fourteen "normal" adults living in the same area. The Santa Barbara contrast group had no socioeconomically deprived adults.

The level-one experiment examined each subject's declarative knowledge base of the task environment. Each individual was asked to list the features, characteristics, and places they knew best in the study area. Sets of common well-recognized environmental cues were established from these lists. As a check on familiarity of these cue sets all subjects were asked to identify photographs of the cues (a scene recognition task). This procedure allowed us to define a set of common cues rated as highly familiar and recognizable by all members of the subject population. Sixteen such cues were identified in each area. Both cue sets were scattered throughout the task environment, although they were slightly concentrated near the group homes. At the end of the experiment we were satisfied that each subject group was equally familiar with the location and identity of all members of the experimental cue set. This result indicated that even subjects of moderate retardation acquired a declarative knowledge structure of the large-scale complex environment in which they lived. We did not, however, try to identify how complete neighborhood knowledge was for the retarded subgroups, largely because the standard procedures used to elicit such information (i.e., extended verbal lists, sketch mapping, and so on) appeared to be beyond the capabilities of many members of this subgroup.

The level-two experiment involved sequencing and distancing of cues along routes. In this experiment route definition was restricted to those cues commonly used by the retarded subgroup. All routes had a common origin, the location of the larger of the two group homes in Columbus and the location of the most central group home in Santa Barbara. Destinations included sheltered workshops (the prime place of employment for most of the retarded), supermarkets, discount stores, department stores, and theaters.

The task required subjects to reconstruct the order and relative distance apart of a small set (n = 6) of highly recognizable cues along each route. In addition to the origin and destination, at least four other cues were selected on each route. Each cue was at a major choice or decision point along the route. Although the routes were commonly traveled by retarded subgroups, contrast group subjects were not always familiar with the routes. Thus, all subjects (i.e., both experimental and contrast groups) walked over each route with an experimenter a number of times. The final task was undertaken in a laboratory setting. The initial task was simply to arrange markers representing the cues along a straight line representing the learned routes. Here only the order of the cues was examined. In a second experiment subjects were asked to place the cues at their relative locations, thus giving an indication of their distance apart. We hypothesized that each subject group would handle the sequencing task with little difficulty, but that the contrast groups would be better able to perform the relative distance task. Although selected individuals in both retarded subgroups performed the sequencing experiment correctly, a greater proportion of the contrast groups in each area ordered cues correctly. Both contrast and experimental groups in each area, however, consistently produced significant correlations, indicating a common ability to recognize fundamental order and sequencing properties of cues along routes.

The distancing component of this task provided the first indication of differences in spatial comprehension between contrast and experimental groups. Many members of the retarded subgroups performed poorly on the distancing task. A significantly greater proportion of contrast group members in each area successfully performed this task. We concluded that metric relations might not be well understood by members of our retarded subgroups, even when those metric relations were confined to a one-dimensional problem.

A third level experiment attempted to assess the configurational knowledge in each subgroup. The task environment, again constructed in a laboratory setting, consisted of a map board representing the experimental neighborhoods. Tapes placed along the edges of the board were identified as the major streets bounding the neighborhood. Additional tapes representing the main north-south and east-west streets within the experimental neighborhood were also indicated on the board and named. The location of the largest, or most central, group home (respectively) for each area was also indicated on the map board and identified by a photograph. Photographs three inches by

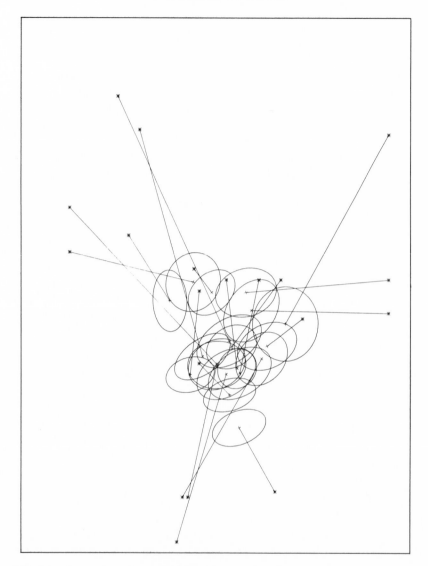

FIG. 9.1   Composite error map, Columbus experimental group.

two and a half inches were mounted on small napkin holders. Each subject in turn was shown similarly mounted photographs of other cues used in the declarative knowledge experiment. Scene recognition ability was again checked, ensuring that each cue was easily recognized by all subjects. Instructions were then given to place each photograph at the location on the map that best represented its real location. Subjects were allowed to alter locations at will until they were satisfied with a final configuration. This experiment

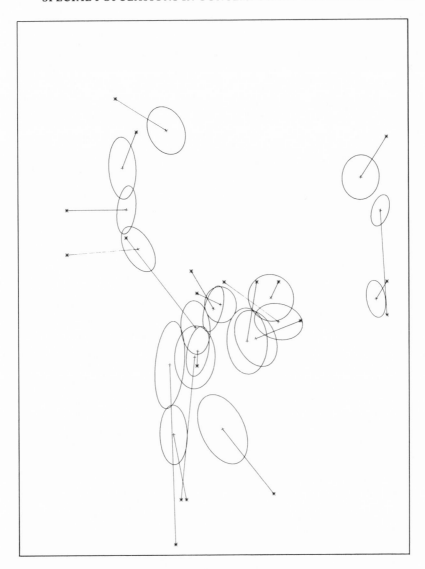

FIG. 9.2   Composite error map, Columbus contrast group.

was designed to test each subject's ability to re-create a two-dimensional arrangement of well-known cues at a reduced scale. To complete the experiment successfully a subject would be required to translate the various distance and directional components of the fundamental declarative knowledge structure into a two-dimensional format, thus reconstructing a metric representation of cue locations scaled to represent proportionally the actual physical configuration of cues in the task area. An "error ellipse" summarizes the distribution of the subjective locations of each cue that were defined by the subject population, and a straight line joining the actual location of each cue with the center of its error ellipse indicates the displacement of the cue from its true objective location (Figures 9.1–9.4). The size of each error ellipse represents the range of locational estimates made by the members of each group, and its shape indicates whether the subjective locations are randomly distributed (circular) or directionally biased (elongated). The distortion distance and the size of each ellipse are greater for both experimental groups. The small error ellipses of the Santa Barbara contrast group illustrate the comparative locational accuracy of the contrast groups particularly well (Figure 9.4).

Despite the substantial range of performance levels of members of the

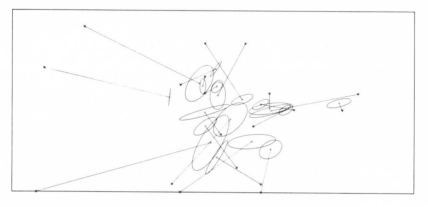

FIG. 9.3   Composite error map, Santa Barbara experimental group.

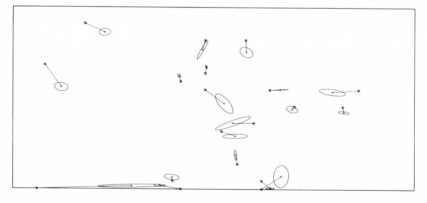

FIG. 9.4   Composite error map, Santa Barbara contrast group.

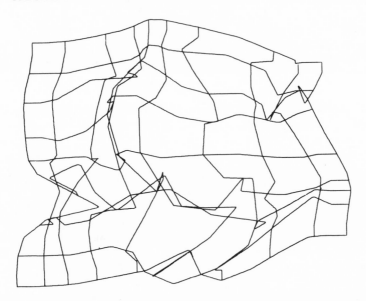

FIG. 9.5   Subjective configuration produced by a member of the experimental group.

FIG. 9.6   Subjective configuration produced by a member of the contrast group.

contrast group in each area, most of them could perform this experiment with a statistically significant degree of correlation between subjective and objective configurations, but few members of the experimental group in either location were able to perform at this level. The experimental group appeared unable to handle the scaling, abstraction, and spatial component of the set tasks. Standard regular grids were warped to fit the subjective configurations produced by the subject populations. The contrast group representations show some distortion, but they clearly retain most of the geometric properties of the regular grid (Figure 9.5). The grids for the experimental group (the retarded subjects), however, are warped, distorted, and folded in such a way as to preclude comparison with a standard grid (Figure 9.6). The dislocation of cues was much greater among the experimental group. Asterisks show the original location of each cue and letters show the subjective location chosen by one Goleta subject (Figure 9.7); the lines connecting asterisks and letters show the direction and distance of displacement. Vectors join the original and subjective locations for a member of the Goleta contrast group (Figure 9.8); the arrowhead ends at the subjective location, and the vector shows the direction and distance of displacement. The bidimensional correlation coefficients for subjective and objective configurations showed that several members of the Santa Barbara experimental group performed relatively successfully. Each was at the higher end of the mildly retarded scale. Only one individual in the Columbus experimental sample had an equivalent status.

A number of inferences can be drawn from these three-level experiments. Even low/moderately retarded individuals develop a satisfactory declarative knowledge base about the area in which they live and interact. Likewise, all members of each population showed a satisfactory ability to recognize spatial properties of order or sequencing, implying that all were capable of developing a procedural knowledge structure that would enable

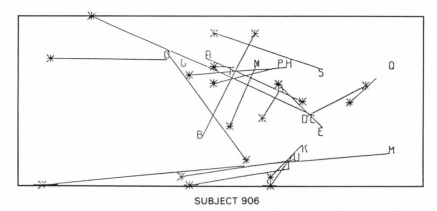

SUBJECT 906

FIG. 9.7   Difference between images for a member of the experimental group.

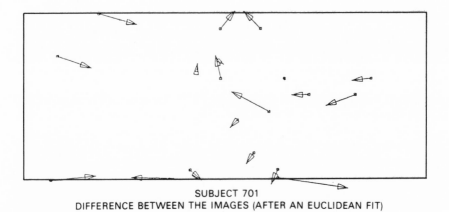

SUBJECT 701
DIFFERENCE BETWEEN THE IMAGES (AFTER AN EUCLIDEAN FIT)

FIG. 9.8   Difference between images for a member of the contrast group.

them to learn routes and absorb and retain relevant information that would allow them to make the correct decisions to navigate a route successfully. When we began examining higher level metric properties of routes and configurations, however, performance of the moderately and mildly retarded subjects dropped below levels that could be expected by chance alone. In contrast, virtually all members of the contrast group in each area were able to perform the abstract reasoning required of both the procedural and configurational experiments with a reasonable degree of competence.

The direct implication of these studies is that the geographer can offer as much as any other social or behavioral scientist to assessing the competence of retarded persons to live successfully in real-world environments. It is of critical importance to be able to know and evaluate the spatial competence of such populations before decisions are made to deinstitutionalize them, to locate them in self-sustaining environments such as group homes, or to expect them to be able to cope by themselves with the complexities of living in real-world environments.

COMMUNITY HOMES FOR THE MENTALLY ILL

Location theory has traditionally occupied a significant place in geographic research. Originally developed as a formal paradigm for locating heavy industry and rationalizing the large-scale movement of raw materials, labor, energy, and manufactured products, successive modifications of theory and the development of robust locational models have drastically expanded the range of practical problems that can be addressed by such theory and the models developed to represent it. Typical problems may range from locating new industries in developing economies to the location of hazardous waste disposal centers, branch banks, or child-care centers. Such models are used to locate shopping centers, to recommend which educational facilities should be closed, and to determine head office location for multinational corporations.

As location theory widened in scope, it incorporated more and more nontraditional variables. Such variables began playing significant parts in decision-making processes where the facility or institution had considerable negative externalities. Whereas the externalities associated with locating a hazardous waste dump are usually quite obvious, externalities are also important in more subtle decision-making situations. As an example of the latter, this section focuses on the problem of locating group homes or halfway houses for mentally disturbed persons.

Deinstitutionalization of mental patients as a way to cut public expenditures gained momentum in the early 1970s and has proceeded actively up to this time. As a result, new demands have been placed on communities that have acted as hosts to what heretofore had been considered a "socially undesirable group." This group, the mentally disturbed, had traditionally been confined to large centralized institutions (Dear and Taylor 1982). Reaction of communities to rumors about or site selection for small community-based facilities serving such deinstitutionalized populations has generally been less than effusive. Despite the legal backing of antidiscrimination laws, negative local attitudes have frequently prevailed in decisions on site selection for such facilities.

Geographers have been interested in the location of mental health facilities for some time (Wolpert et al. 1975; Dear 1977; Smith and Hanham 1981a, 1981b; Dear and Taylor 1982; Hall and Taylor 1983; Taylor et al. 1982). Many of these approaches, however, seek solutions to this awkward problem in the context of normal geographic space. This is a problem where affect (i.e., emotions, feelings, attitudes, and preferences) is at least as important as objective environmental features (e.g., neighborhood density, income and social class) in decision making. Categorical (yes/no) judgments may in such circumstances have such fuzzy boundaries that they erode the potential for using deterministic solutions based on optimizing, maximizing, or minimizing principles. To solve location problems, therefore, we need a geography that allows different attribute characteristics to be combined in multiple ways. We also need to be able to show how trade-offs of different levels of affective involvement are made with different spatial properties (e.g., locational centrality in a neighborhood, street accessibility, distance from other community activities such as elementary schools, preschools, and so on). Wolpert et al. (1975) have argued that locational decisions degenerate into siting conflicts when some divergence of opinion exists between two or more parties interested in the appropriateness of a particular outcome. Conflict is likely to occur when differential utility is attached to the outcome of a decision process, or where such utility is perceived markedly differently by disparate groups.

Halfway houses for the mentally ill fall into the general class of "public facilities with negative externalities." A negative externality exists when the actions of one agent negatively affect the welfare of another. Examples of negative externalities associated with community homes for the mentally ill include: an inability to sell nearby property at a reasonable price; loss of rental income in nearby units because of fear and suspicion; higher taxes because of the increased local government costs associated with the facility; increased competition for housing among householders, as specific units are withdrawn from the market by government legislation; and changes in relative accessibility of homes to neighborhood and community facilities because of fear and suspicion associated with the location of the facility.

Neighborhood cognitive maps undergo drastic transformation when any of these externalities are perceived to be associated with a facility siting (Figure 9.9). New travel patterns might emerge for pedestrians; some pedestrian traffic will be changed to vehicular; and the cognitive map of the neighborhood may be rubbersheeted to provide folded and distorted feature relationships, with such distortions being caused by the facility site.

A telephone survey of community attitudes about the location of public facilities with negative externalities in the Santa Barbara area indicates that the type of clientele (i.e., be it mentally ill, retarded, alcohol or drug abuse, or child care, and so on) has a significant effect on the degree of neighborhood acceptability. For each type of clientele one can define the degree of acceptance with respect to changing distance from the proposed site facility. Some facilities (e.g., child care) are relatively distance invariant; others (e.g., location of a freeway exchange) might obtain some degree of local acceptance; others, such as a drug or alcohol abuse center, might conform to the maxim "distance makes the heart grow fonder," with greatest rates of rejection in the immediate vicinity of the proposed site; and finally, for others (e.g., the mentally retarded and the mentally ill), a "too close for comfort" syndrome might be exhibited with rejection of the concept of nearby location and more confident acceptance if it is "not on our street" (Dear and Taylor 1982). In comparison of the objectively measurable and perceived factors that have traditionally been used in the literature, Hedden (1984) showed that subjective evaluation of the type of facility, cognized distance of the site, and perceived need for staffing and supervision were the most critical values influencing facility acceptability. Equally important, however, was an ability to articulate these feelings and perceptions. Hedden found that the composition of the local power structure was an important ingredient in facility siting by showing the negative relationship between median household income and the number of noxious public facilities by census tract in Santa Barbara county. In effect, she argued that community facilities for disadvantaged populations are ghettoized.

This scenario has suggested that noxious public facility siting be examined in the context of transformed geographic space rather than in the Eucli-

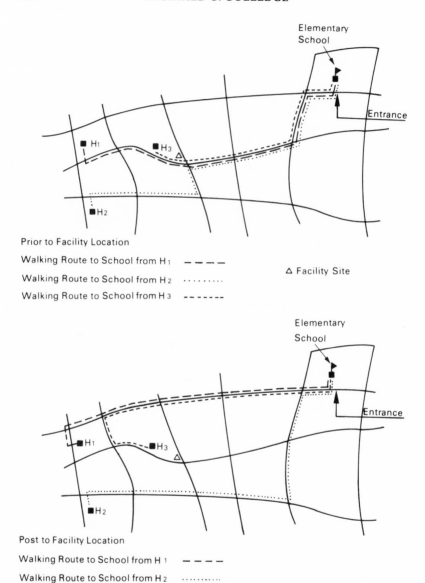

FIG. 9.9   Changed neighborhood space after facility location.

dean context in which locational phenomena are usually represented. Perceptions, feelings, attitudes, and preferences distort the Euclidean space of conventional locational models. Spatial terms such as close, near, and distant become tied to emotional norms and to individual householder conceptions of proximity. Until the geographer is prepared to venture into these different realities, his/her ability to solve what nowadays are often regarded as "intractable problems," because of the dominance of subjective variables, will lag far behind her/his other problem-solving abilities.

SPATIAL COMPETENCE OF THE VISUALLY IMPAIRED

It is sometimes suggested that individuals who have been blind since birth (congenitally blind) cannot be expected to have the same degree of spatial competence and the same type of spatial knowledge structures as those developed by people with vision. Because of the absence of vision, it is tacitly assumed that visually impaired individuals would have difficulty in understanding two- and three-dimensional spatial concepts, that the spatial domain will often be replaced by a temporal domain, that ability to comprehend the nature of macro spaces will be reduced, and that there will be a resultant lowered ability to perform the acts of mental geometry and trigonometry that are essential parts of procedural and configurational knowledge.

Familiarity with the nature, contents, and structure of any external environment depends on the amount of interaction with such environments. It also depends on the ability to access other information sources about the environment. Our experiments examining spatial competence of the visually handicapped (Golledge et al. 1988; Loomis et al. 1986; 1988) start with the assumption that an appropriate declarative knowledge base *can* be constructed. Although such a base probably will be more closely defined by the location of learned routes than by the richer general background information that could be compiled by those visually experiencing the same environment, there is no evidence to suggest that such a knowledge base cannot be developed by the visually handicapped. Some evidence (Golledge et al. 1988) suggests that the contents of such a knowledge structure will differ significantly between sighted and nonsighted groups. The declarative knowledge of the sighted person would have macrospatial information including visual frames of reference (e.g., heights of buildings or trees, background mountains or other topographic features, distinct colors, shapes of environmental features, and so on). The equivalent structure for the visually handicapped person might include more surface features (e.g., pavement textures, curbs, vegetative cover, overhanging branches, other obstacles or barriers to movement, and so on). Many of the dominant cues for the visually handicapped group would be incidental components in the knowledge structure of a sighted individual, and vice versa (Table 9.2).

TABLE 9.2   UCSB Campus Cues in Navigation Process by Blind and Sighted Subjects

---

Blind Subject

1. Mat near door of Ellison Hall
2. Steps
3. Cemented walls and planters
4. Ivy growth and plants
5. Texture difference between ivy and cemented path
6. Ivy and pillar
7. Shape of the Kerr Center steps
8. Ivy on the right
9. Lamppost
10. Bike path
11. Long breezeway through South Hall
12. Planters
13. Pillar
14. Pillar
15. Ivy
16. Auditory cues of bikes
    bike path
    bike racks

17. Shape of music building
18. Auditory cue (music being played)
19. Pillars and doors
20. Wall ends
21. Sharp turn (follow the shape of the building)
22. Walk past Lotte Lehman Hall
23. Obstruction (bulletin board)
24. Shadows
25. Steps
26. Driveway
27. Bike path
28. Bike stand
29. Shape of UCEN
30. Auditory cues
31. Olfactory cues (UCEN restaurant)
32. Door to UCEN

Sighted Subject

1. South wing of Ellison Hall
2. North Hall
3. Library
4. Bike paths
5. Arbor take-out
6. Kerr Hall/Learning Resources
7. Statuary in front of library
8. Flame trees
9. Storke Tower
10. Bike racks

11. Bike paths
12. Psychology/library parking area
13. Lotte Lehman Hall
14. Student high-rise dorms
15. Postal kiosk
16. UCEN parking
17. Side view of Lotte Lehman Hall
18. Bike paths
19. Storke Plaza
20. Steps to UCEN door

In this scenario we pay little attention to the declarative knowledge structure itself. Instead, we focus on procedural and configurational knowledge, with the greatest emphasis on the former. I report briefly on some recent results obtained from experiments designed to understand the levels of spatial competence that can be expected in visually handicapped populations and in those with normal vision. Consider the following tasks: (1) estimating spatial properties of distance and direction subsequent to carrying out spatial behavior (production and estimation tasks); (2) finding the degrees of success achieved when translating cognized spatial manipulations such as mental geometry or trigonometry (e.g., closing figures, taking shortcuts, undertaking search and exploration) indicative of a configurational knowledge structure. In these experiments we identify two levels of tasks; level one tasks focus on essential spatial characteristics required to navigate a route (components of route or procedural knowledge), and level two tasks require integration of declarative and procedural characteristics to perform complex high-level navigational tasks.

Level one tasks are defined both as stand-alone tasks and compounded tasks. Stand-alone tasks include: (1) learning an arbitrary distance unit, then estimating different distance lengths expressed in terms of this measure; (2) walking a constant distance while maintaining a constant directional heading; (3) estimating turn angles; (4) reproducing by spatial movement distance lengths learned on earlier trials; and (5) reproducing learned turn angles within the learned environment.

These experiments were carried out in a carefully controlled environment. The environment was a forty-five-meter by twenty-five-meter university gymnasium. All light sources were eliminated from the gymnasium. Sighted subjects were blindfolded before entering the gymnasium and performed all tasks while blindfolded. Subjects were tracked by an integrated video camera and computer system developed by Loomis. Two cameras were set up at the midpoint of adjacent sides of the fifteen-by-fifteen-meter-square work area. They were connected to and driven from the computer keyboard. Wide-angle lenses attached to the cameras comfortably encompassed the entire work area. The two cameras allowed triangulation techniques. Each subject wore a head-mounted light source. To remove possible auditory interference during experiments, subjects also wore a stereophonic headset. Initial experiments were undertaken by broadcasting a sound to a specific location in the study area and testing the ability of the subject to move to the location of the sound while being continuously tracked by the video cameras. Tracking was dynamically recorded on the television monitor and was stored for later examination and output as a hard copy of the location of the sound source and the subject's tracking movements. Having validated the usefulness of the technical device for recording spatial movement, specially developed software was used to calculate all distances and turns made by each subject in level one and level two experiments.

Data from the level one experiments provide the following inferences. The first concerns the distance estimates of sample subjects over a range of lengths from four to twelve meters. Subjects learned these lengths by performing multiple trials involving walking a distance guided by a rope stretched between two stanchions. Results paralleled some of those found in cognitive distance studies. Larger distances were underestimated and shorter distances were overestimated. These experiments were undertaken initially at three different walking speeds (slow, normal, and fast), with subjects defining their own speed rates. Errors were greatest at the slowest walking speeds, and walking speed was more critical in the estimation than in the reproduction tasks (Figures 9.10 and 9.11). In later movement experiments, the fast speed was eliminated as an experimental factor.

For an angle-of-rotation task, blindfolded subjects were placed inside a hulahoop supported on stanchions. Both hands grasped the hoop at a line clearly marked zero degrees north. A marker was placed on the hoop to represent a preselected angle of rotation. Subjects rotated their hands and bodies from the zero line to the marker several times in order to learn the turn angle. The marker was then removed and the subjects were asked to reproduce the angle they had just learned by moving their hands and rotating their

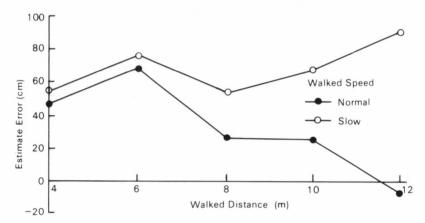

FIG. 9.10   Errors in estimating distance as a function of walked distance for normal and slow walking speeds.

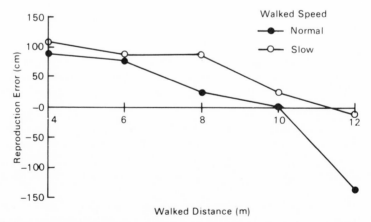

FIG. 9.11   Errors in reproducing distance as a function of walked distance for normal and slow walking speeds.

bodies until they felt they had duplicated the learned angle. The position where their hands came to rest was recorded as their estimate of the turn angle. Seven angles, ranging from sixty to three hundred degrees, were used as base angles, and each subject undertook three trials. Subjects showed some learning effects over trials, but more important, they showed consistently good angular estimation (Table 9.3). A small error of about five degrees was constant regardless of angle size. This might imply a general ability correctly to sense, implement, and learn the multitude of angles experienced in normal pedestrian traffic.

A different picture emerges when angle estimation is part of a movement task. Subjects were guided over two legs of a triangle. The angle between the legs varied from sixty to three hundred degrees. After several repetitions of this process of walking, turning, and walking, subjects were placed in front of a table top on which was mounted a moving indicator similar to the hand on a clock. Subjects were asked to estimate the angle they had just turned by placing the indicator at the appropriate angle. The reproduction task followed the estimation task. The subjects were led to a starting point, instructed to move forward in a straight line, then turn a specified angle, and continue in a straight line until they were told to halt. The turn angle of reproduction was measured as the significant data unit (Table 9.4). Reproduction produces much smaller errors than estimation. Angles of ninety degrees or less are underestimated, and larger angles are increasingly overestimated. Embedding the estimation task in a movement process apparently taps a different type of information processing than the stationary body rotation task of the

TABLE 9.3 Subject's Reproduction of Turn Angles: Stationary Rotation (Hulahoop Task)

Subject	Angle to Be Reproduced						
	60°	90°	135°	180°	225°	270°	300°
MFL (Trial 1)	50	90	115	192	245	150	305
(Trial 2)	45	85	135	175	237	265	310
(Trial 3)	57	85	135	205	255	280	315
RSP (Trial 1)	60	70	115	195	210	250	310
(Trial 2)	75	95	135	142	215	245	270
(Trial 3)	55	61	127	170	170	275	265
JDC (Trial 1)	50	90	135	165	215	265	315
(Trial 2)	50	110	135	170	190	275	335
(Trial 3)	60	90	162	175	245	290	302
Average	55.8	86.2	132.7	176.6	220.2	266.1	303.0
s.d.	8.3	13.3	13.1	17.7	26.5	14.5	20.9

TABLE 9.4   Average Errors (Degrees) for Estimates
and Reproductions as a Function of Turn Angle

Angle	Estimate	Reproduction
60	−5.76	1.16
90	−1.60	3.50
135	1.02	1.57
180	6.78	3.57
225	10.57	5.67
270	21.31	2.86
300	20.42	−3.02

hulahoop experiment. Angle estimation error apparently increases with angle size when turns are part of a general movement pattern. The route memory required for all but extremely regular journeys (as with ninety-degree turns) is probably highly error prone—a point to be remembered by planners seeking aesthetic reasons to move away from regular street grids.

Level two tasks examine simple components of navigational behavior, but required integration of distance and turn-angle knowledge capabilities. Experiments at this level include: (1) walking with the experimenter over a standard distance, rotating 180 degrees and returning unaided to the origin; (2) learning an angle from a large jointed compass, then unaided walking three meters, turning the learned angle and walking another three meters; (3) learning the distances and turn angle comprising two segments of a triangle, then performing both angular rotation and distance production required to return unaided to the origin; (4) learning the distances and turn angles for three sides of a quadrilateral, then performing the required rotation and distance production task to complete the quadrilateral; (5) learning figure completion tasks when the figure involves zigzags and segment crossovers; and (6) while blindfolded, performing mapboard tasks to locate nodes and simple geometrical figures, then estimating all possible interpoint distance pairs from the learned locations.

Most of these level two experiments are underway. They compare the performance of congenitally blind, early and late blinded, and blindfolded sighted subjects on all facets of the experiment. We have graphic summaries of performance on the constant heading and return task, triangle completion task, and quadrilateral completion task from the initial group of twelve blindfolded sighted subjects at the Santa Barbara site (Klatzky et al. 1989). Pilot subjects tested on the more complex zigzag and intersecting segment tasks were uniformly unable to complete them.

While we await comparative data from our blind subjects, the results with the twelve blindfolded sighted subjects do indicate that all can perform noncomplex tasks such as learning a length of distance or learning a rotation angle with a high degree of competence. Procedural knowledge is based on these premises, but some identifiable errors creep in once integration of declarative and route components is required. For example, most individuals veer consistently either to the left or to the right when asked to traverse a distance along a constant heading. Similarly, in tasks involving walking a distance and turning an angle, errors in angular estimation increase with the size of the angle. Principles of surveying or orienteering suggest that such errors accumulate during more complex tasks involving many different length route segments and different directional changes. If a person consistently veers to the left or to the right, some compensation may occur on a route with equal numbers of left or right turns, or with more turns in the nonveer direction. As yet we have no evidence as to the exact way in which this error accumulates, but we hope that ongoing experiments will provide some information. It also appears that tasks tied to bodily movement, such as locomotion, are better performed than those requiring only cognitive manipulation (e.g., segment or configuration estimation). It appears to be quite difficult to perform mental geometric or mental trigonometric tasks (such as figure closure). Until we know more about the errors built into the most fundamental level of spatial behavior and spatial knowledge, we cannot readily interpret more complex actions such as learning and reproducing characteristics of multisegment routes. It is obvious that the geographer has as much to contribute as any other scientist to the discovery of the feasible components in a complex spatial knowledge structure, regardless of the nature of the populations studied.

The different scenarios I have examined in this chapter illustrate ways that geographers have reacted to changes in the state of knowledge, scientific and technological breakthroughs, humanist and societal concerns, and the change from the description of geographic phenomena to the inquisitive theoretical and empirical speculations in the logic and analytical methods of science. Not all geography has followed a scientific or technical bent, and to this extent the discipline is as wide-ranging and well-balanced as ever, but geographers today are faced with an increasingly complex set of relationships between humans and the various environments in which they live. It is necessary to break the bonds that have in the past confined them to specific realities and specific narrow problems, and limited their contributions to societal well-being and to the accumulation of knowledge. Geographers today are discarding many prior constraints. They know that most human activities have an important and elemental spatial component. Having accepted this, they can dispense with the second-class citizen neurosis that has plagued the discipline throughout much of recent history and can rightly take positions at the forefront of the fraternity of knowledge seekers.

The different scenarios I have examined in this chapter illustrate ways that geographers have reacted to changes in the state of knowledge, scientific and technological breakthroughs, humanist and societal concerns, and the change from the description of geographic phenomena to the inquisitive theoretical and empirical speculations in the logic and analytical methods of science. Not all geography has followed a scientific or technical bent, and to this extent the discipline is as wide-ranging and well-balanced as ever, but geographers today are faced with an increasingly complex set of relationships between humans and the various environments in which they live. It is necessary to break the bonds that have in the past confined them to specific realities and specific narrow problems, and limited their contributions to societal well-being and to the accumulation of knowledge. Geographers today are discarding many prior constraints. They know that most human activities have an important and elemental spatial component. Having accepted this, they can dispense with the second-class citizen neurosis that has plagued the discipline throughout much of recent history and can rightly take positions at the forefront of the fraternity of knowledge seekers.

What remains is to speculate about the future and roles that geographers might play therein. Geographers have not realized their capabilities or potential for extending their knowledge base. Until they do, their role in the future (e.g., in the urban context) will remain stereotyped and limited. To expand their knowledge structures they must actively explore beyond the boundaries of conventional disciplinary limits. They must acknowledge that space and its dimensions are not limited to known geometries. They must explore, and if necessary, be prepared to create their own spaces in terms of suitable and relevant concepts, precepts, events, and processes. They may need to invent new languages, new reasoning processes, new methods, or new theories to help understand the realities into which they may venture. They should not feel constrained by the existing state of other disciplines; for example, I do not believe that there exists a mathematics suitable for use in most geographic situations. To explore future problems in innovative ways, geographers may need new languages and new knowledge structures, or at least an ability to extend their existing structures and skills into all spatial domains regardless of scale or complexity. This is the challenge of the future.

REFERENCES

Dear, M., et al. 1977. Psychiatric patients and the inner city. *Annals of the Association of American Geographers* 67: 588–94.

Dear, M., and S. Taylor. 1982. *Not on our street*. London: Pion Limited.

Golledge, R., J. Loomis, R. Klatzky, J. Pellegrino, S. Doherty, and J. Cicinelli. 1988. Environmental cognition and assessment: Spatial cognition of the blind and visually impaired. Paper presented at the Environmental Cognition and Assessment Conference, June 28–July 3, Umeå, Sweden.

Golledge, R., J. Rayner, and J. Parnicky. 1979. *The spatial competence of selected populations*. National Science Foundation final report. Santa Barbara: Department of Geography, University of California at Santa Barbara.

Hall, G., and S. Taylor. 1983. A causal model of attitudes toward mental health facilities. *Environment and Planning A* 15: 525–42.

Hedden, S. 1984. Spatial dimensions of perceived noxious externality fields. Master's Thesis, University of California at Santa Barbara.

Klatzky, R., J. Loomis, R. Golledge, J. Cicinelli, S. Doherty, and J. Pellegrino. 1989. Acquisition of route and survey knowledge in the absence of vision. *Journal of Motor Behavior* 22 (1): 19–43.

Loomis, J., R. Klatzky, R. Golledge, J. Pellegrino, and S. Doherty. 1986. *Analysis of navigation without sight*. National Institute of Health grant PHS EY07022-01. Santa Barbara: University of California at Santa Barbara.

———. 1988. *Analysis of navigation without sight*. National Institute of Health grant PHS EY07022-02. Santa Barbara: University of California at Santa Barbara.

Smith, C., and R. Hanham. 1981a. Proximity and the formation of public attitudes towards mental illness. *Environment and Planning A* 13: 147–66.

———. 1981b. Any place but here! Mental health facilities as noxious neighbors. *Professional Geographer* 33: 326–34.

Taylor, M., B. Hughes, M. Dear, and B. Hall. 1982. Predicting community reactions to mental health facilities. Paper presented at the annual meeting of the Association of American Geographers, April 26, San Antonio, Texas.

Wolpert, J., M. Dear, and R. Crawford. 1975. Satellite mental health facilities. *Annals of the Association of American Geographers* 65: 24–35.

TEN

The Costs of Regional Growth

Julian Wolpert

Theory can be tested and developed most reliably when a manageable portion of the real world is thoroughly and intimately understood. The immense variety of challenging issues relating to local and state government offer promise of new theory development and opportunities for remedying real problems. My laboratory is the New York metropolitan region and its hundreds of fragmented jurisdictional units. My focus is the mixed blessings of rapid growth.

The New York region (including the New Jersey and Connecticut suburbs) has grown exceedingly rapidly in the past six or seven years. The economic growth has been expressed in a boom of office and retail construction, new high-tech industry, and new jobs. The office space equivalent of a Dallas–Fort Worth has already been added to the metropolitan area. With the completion of construction now underway and committed in the next ten years, a Chicago will have been added. The contrast is stark compared to the stagnation and pessimism in the 1970s, yet growth has brought mixed blessings—greater disparities between jurisdictions, gridlock on many highways, frequent breakdowns and delays in mass transit, greater costs in providing public services, a labor shortage, an absence of affordable housing, and a significant loss of irreplaceable open space—all factors that are now threatening to end the boom. Does this erosion of locational advantages simply reflect the workings of the familiar equilibrium tendency, or can additional lessons be learned from the process of regional growth and decline?

REGIONAL GROWTH STRATEGIES

Rapid spurts of regional growth in the United States are commonly followed in rapid succession by severe decline or stagnation. The resultant regional growth strategies are conceived and implemented in a fragmented way during these stressful periods of decline. The accommodations and trade-offs that are made in state and local strategies to stimulate development and combat recessions differ fundamentally from the long-term policies prevalent in more stable periods and the programs that follow rapid growth (Brower 1976; Gleeson 1977). The growth strategies include economic development loans and grants, targeted infrastructure projects, tax abatements, and other inducements to stimulate private market activity. The stated long-term policies, on the other hand, are to conserve open space, minimize exposure to environmental hazards, redevelop older cities, and rationalize existing infrastructure (Gleeson 1977).

The major problems that accompany economic decline (e.g., depopulation, unemployment, inadequate revenues for state and local services, and declining value of investments in land, homes, and commercial establishments) inevitably overwhelm consideration of the potential negative spillovers of growth policies. States and localities are also less able than are the national government or a firm to discount the future rounds of benefits and disbenefits resulting from their growth programs and to make midcourse adjustments (Rafuse 1965).

Regional growth strategies generally assume that state and local development programs can be effective in creating new output and not merely shifting activity from one place to another. They also assume that public investments in creating locational incentives will be appropriately multiplied and the benefits will be absorbed locally. Growth strategies admittedly require unevenly distributed costs and provide, initially at least, uneven benefits as well, but the crises prompting diversions from the agendas of normal times are expected to be only temporary.

These primary assumptions, which underlie most local and regional growth strategies (Molotch 1976), pervade the policies and programs of states and localities competing with one another for the benefits of growth. Some strategies are more successful than others in capturing short- or long-term benefits for their regions. It is questionable, however, whether separate regional efforts yield aggregate benefits for the country as a whole or whether local efforts bring net returns to their regions. The focus of this chapter is another questionable assumption, that is, whether regional strategies do more good or harm to the economy and quality of life in the localities and states where they are implemented.

My objective here is to examine some of the fundamental assumptions that underlie subnational growth strategies and to trace their costs and other consequences, at least in a limited way. My thesis is that the net long-term benefits of state and local growth strategies are likely to be quite modest. Such growth programs typically fail to anticipate the distinctive and often conflicting agendas of the fragmented jurisdictional units that comprise our economic regions (Danielson and Doig 1982). The programs also fail to anticipate or properly discount a wide range of environmental and other costs. They are also maldistributive and difficult to adjust, modify, or reverse when their negative effects become apparent. The policy prescription is not to try to reduce regional boom and bust spurts, which probably cannot be manipulated at state or local levels anyway. Instead, the policy thesis argues for long-term development programs and policy instruments that allow for potential downturns and that can be adjusted in midcourse at a regional level to correct for the side effects of rapid growth or decline.

THEORETICAL BACKGROUND

The theoretical literature has some useful insights on regional growth strategies in the American context of fragmented political jurisdictions. The most prominent example of this context is the metropolitan region comprised of a center city and a diverse set of suburban municipalities (typically including high-status residential communities, industrial suburbs, townships with considerable developable land, and so on). The units are linked functionally in the agglomeration, but are fragmented in their fiscal management and land-use control. The units are also nested in more inclusive county and state tiers that each have distinctive and instrumental parts to play in development, as well as in growth, control programs.

THE ALLOCATION OF ECONOMIC GROWTH

The theory applied to the structure of these fragmented units and tiers is derived from the economics of the firm, location theory, and the political economy concepts of public choice (predominantly the analyses of Tiebout [1956], Mills and Oates [1975], Henderson [1979], Inman [1979], Downs [1957], and Peterson [1981]). The formal theory pertains more to the optimal provision of local public goods across communities and the assignment of households among them, but the same structure would also appear to apply to the siting decisions of firms and to the succession from growth to decline in the metropolitan economy. The theory base provides a normative framework for our expectations of how the growth mechanisms should be expected to operate in metropolitan regions and sets the parameters for the empirical analysis. The basic concepts and efforts at logical deduction may not qualify as theory, but the review of the literature should indicate why rigorous theory and formal model development on this issue are so severely constrained. This chapter uses a public choice argument that largely ignores the rich institutional and behavioral literature on the politics of state and local government that is reviewed adequately elsewhere (e.g., Peterson 1981; Logan and Molotch 1988; Danielson and Doig 1982).

POLITICAL FRAGMENTATION AS AN ASSET

Our neoclassical theories of the location of economic activity have been put to a severe test in the growth surge of the past decade. Economic growth has been most rapid and concentrated in selected suburbs of western and northeastern metropolitan areas (e.g., Boston, New York, Los Angeles). These suburbs are in metropolitan areas with the highest factor prices—the greatest labor shortages, the highest wages and housing costs, the most congested journeys-to-work, high property and business taxes, and the toughest environmental restrictions (Mieszkowski 1979).

This novel localization pattern of recent economic growth after the severe declines in the mid-1970s raises some significant questions about the locational behavior of firms and the instrumental role of local and state government as agents or partners in fostering economic growth. A major research question concerns the locational advantages of these regions despite their high-factor prices. The explanation has not been analyzed rigorously, but earlier studies point to the resurging importance of access to the major metropolitan agglomerations of commerce, finance, and industry serving domestic and international markets (Engerman 1965). These exogenous factors, which affect the demand for a region's goods and services, are important, but a sound argument can be made that diversity in the range of residential and work-site opportunities facilitates development in the largest metropolitan areas.

The rapidly growing agglomerations are comprised of diversified suburban communities. Is the diversity of the suburbs and their differentiation from the inner city an added locational asset for a metropolitan area, not only to residents but to firms as well? Tiebout (1956), Henderson (1979), and Mills (1979) have shown, for example, that fragmented local governments can provide efficient resource allocation for provision of public services for residents, at least for those services achieving scale economies in the autonomous jurisdictions.

The extended Tiebout argument would suggest that firms in large, fragmented agglomerations can select from among a wide choice of sites that balance trade-offs for local accessibility, land prices, and tax packages, and still benefit from their presence in the agglomeration. Firms can be sited in one community, with their executives and professionals residing in another, and can draw their lower-wage workers from elsewhere in the metropolitan area. These opportunities for firms are facilitated by the fragmentation of jurisdictions in metropolitan areas and their diverse patterns of managing

their responsibilities for land-use control, provision of services, and generation of revenue. The greater the fragmentation into different types of communities and the dependency on property tax for revenue, the more competition between local jurisdictions to attract firms and developers. The more
limited also is the need to internalize negative spillovers from firms' operations beyond the jurisdiction's boundaries. The Tiebout argument for the
locational behavior of firms must be qualified, of course, for different types
and sizes of firms, the number and mix of firms in any given jurisdiction, and
the degree of correspondence between residents' and firms' preferences for
government activities, programs, and tax packages (Epple and Zelenitz 1981;
Inman 1979).

If diversity is an asset, recent growth should be most rapid (holding other
factors constant) where the Tiebout framework of diverse and internally
homogeneous jurisdictions and home rule traditions are most prevalent. Evidence of the spatial distribution of recent economic growth should establish
that both the continued decentralization of the service sector from center city
to suburb and the formation of new service firms in suburban areas are
facilitated by a Tiebout-type pattern of suburban settlements, a framework
that would support a public-choice thesis of market activity and argue for
policy instruments that facilitate private market choices for siting development activity. A reasonable case can be made that the political economy of
Tiebout-type jurisdictions affects the locational incentives for residents and
firms both through their contributions to the competitiveness of the agglomeration and through their fostering of redistribution of economic activity
within the agglomeration.

Would a Tiebout-type pattern of fragmented jurisdictions that is optimal
for residents also provide the most efficient conditions for firms? This difficult
and complex question can only be answered by knowing how firms participate (or how their preferences are reflected) in municipal decisions on fiscal
and land-use issues. The diversity of an agglomeration's suburban areas could
not by itself, of course, be credited for stimulating growth when the other
locational factors are negative, but the heterogeneity of such areas should
contribute to the competitive advantage of the agglomeration.

LAND USE AND FISCAL AUTONOMY

The Tiebout process leads in the simplest case, where jurisdictions are
largely autonomous and local property taxes are the major source of revenue
for providing services, to a continuum of distinctive community units. The
suburban communities in a metropolitan area are differentiated by distinctive agendas for land-use control, expenditures for services, and revenue
generation, and generally also by the socioeconomic composition of their
residents (Logan and Schneider 1981). At one extreme are those communities with the highest capacity to tax for local services, but opting for

either a high- or low-service mix depending on their exercise of exclusionary zoning. At the opposite extreme are those towns and townships most eager for the services but least able to generate local tax revenues. Where autonomy over land-use management and taxing powers for schools and other local services is less concentrated at local levels, differentiation between jurisdictions should be less pronounced (Mills 1979).

A simplified public choice framework (assuming internal homogeneity) would predict a preference by the more well-off communities to retain authority over land use and over a localized tax base system. The needier places, on the other hand, would prefer that land management and revenue generation for service provision be shifted to higher jurisdictional levels (e.g., counties and states). The same framework would predict that the more well-off communities would be more successful at fiscal zoning in competing for new commercial and residential development than would the needier places. Developers and commercial firms would still compete for sites based upon factor prices and access to markets, but within single metropolitan areas they could opt for locations providing the greatest free-rider opportunities relative to regionwide disparities and service needs. In the allocation of growth opportunities, the exclusive communities would gain the desirable ratables and the residual places would achieve smaller marginal gains by being forced to be less selective.

THE LIFE CYCLE OF GOVERNMENTAL FUNCTIONS

Peterson (1981) and others distinguish between the development, allocation, and redistribution policies that government units exercise. The redistribution function would (according to both theory and practice) be the responsibility of the most inclusive tiers of government (e.g., at the federal and state level) to offset the ability of residents and firms to evade transfer payments by migration. The local jurisdictions in this framework specialize in the allocation responsibilities through their provision of local public services. The development functions are scattered among the tiers with distinctive programs carried out at federal, state, county, and municipal levels.

The local jurisdictions are likely to have a greater role in redistribution than implied by the Peterson schema, although the process is latent in the exercise of fiscal zoning and generally works in a regressive direction. Peterson also does not examine the dynamic aspects of these three types of programs and their changing emphases in periods of rapid economic growth as opposed to steep decline. Development programs, for example, would be emphasized by the local units in recessions, as would be the tendency to shift even a greater share of redistribution activities to the more inclusive units. Furthermore, if the growth-to-decline successions show some regularity, a life cycle of sequential priorities would probably evolve at all tiers of government, linking a development emphasis to downturns and an allocation focus to transition periods of stability or modest growth, and concentrating on redistribution activities and comprehensive long-range planning after periods of rapid growth.

PERVASIVE DECLINE

Under conditions of pervasive decline in the demand for the region's goods and services, distinctive development policies emerge in localities, counties, and states. State units would initially develop growth strategies to remedy a regionwide problem, such as unemployment, which would reduce state revenues and raise the costs for welfare and other transfer payments. Typical state growth policies include economic development grants and loans and a targeting of investments in highway and other infrastructure capital projects (Mieszkowski 1979). State policies prompted by the need to compete with other states can be expected to relax long-standing objectives in favor of offering the best possible package of incentives to prospective firms. Highway improvements can, for example, be shifted to the network sites preferred by developers. Development authority loans would follow the siting decisions of investors rather than maintain the longer-term objectives for spatial targeting of development. The incentive programs, by lowering the entry costs, permit greater choice by firms in selecting an efficient site from the portfolio of community options.

Local municipalities would be inclined to compete more strongly with one another for ratables to maintain revenues for local services and to be even less redistributive. During the period of decline in demand for sites, communities that have something with which to bargain (e.g., developable land, low property tax rates, and so on) have an advantage over their more built-up neighbors with higher costs for local services. In a large agglomeration with many diverse suburban communities, it is more difficult to make a case in a decline than in a growth phase that any single place has unique locational advantages or a monopoly position in bargaining for development.

Typical municipal growth programs involve partial remission of property and business taxes and favorable land management and zoning treatment (Baldassare 1986). Such policy initiatives should improve the opportunities of firms to bargain successfully for those sites within the region that satisfy their own market objectives in this Tiebout-type portfolio of differentiated communities. In the development phase, the more well-off communities would benefit from their autonomy and fragmentation and have little incentive to cooperate with one another or to coordinate efforts with the more inclusive county or state units.

Municipalities, in their pursuit of growth, often assume, however, that commercial ratables generate fewer costs than does residential development, and that taxes on commercial property are shifted to nonresident owners who will not participate politically in local affairs (Logan and Molotch 1988).

Rapidly developing communities tend to defer housing construction, especially for low and moderate income wage earners. Municipalities also have an incentive to ignore or to underestimate the loss of their irreplaceable open-space resources, the neighborhood spillovers of their development on adjoining communities, or the additional regional infrastructure needed to service the added congestion.

EXTENDED AND RAPID GROWTH

After a period of extended and rapid growth in the metropolitan region as a whole, incentives are stronger at municipality, county and state levels to manage growth and to deal with such redistribution issues as equity in taxes and service provision and environmental protection. Anxieties about preserving home rule should not be as prominent during such periods. In fact, most efforts originating at these stages erode home rule powers of local jurisdictions, for example, in promoting statewide land use and transportation planning, income-based state tax programs, and environmental controls (Gleeson 1977).

Concessions both at state and at local levels are difficult to withdraw or to reverse once rapid growth occurs, however, because government needs extended time to alter its programs. Depending on the duration, magnitude, and sector emphasis of the growth surge, the prior disparities between communities in the ability to attract development have probably increased. If the growth surge is highly concentrated and persists long enough, however, the net benefits that accrue for the most rapidly growing communities and for the region as a whole will probably begin to erode.

The preferences of the population in the growing communities may have changed as a function of the changing composition of residents, the growing congestion, the loss of open space, and other side effects of growth. At the height of the growth period, communities experiencing congestion and the loss of open space, and which are affected by the negative spillovers of development in neighboring jurisdictions, will be more motivated to surrender some of their home-rule autonomy in favor of land-use controls at more inclusive levels of government.

The central city and the industrial suburbs, which would benefit from more centralized targeting of development, probably would join the same coalition. The state unit also has an incentive to centralize development and revenue control in order to economize on new infrastructure in growth areas while existing highways and other facilities in slow growth zones have underused capacity. The laggards are those communities preferring, and anticipating, further growth. The delay in achieving sufficient consensus to adopt comprehensive and redistributive statewide programs can persist until the rapid growth phase has concluded and the preoccupation of policy shifts again to economic development issues. Meanwhile, rapid growth under a fragmented regime leaves in its wake an increase in disparities, a loss of irreplaceable open and accessible space, a level of congestion that inhibits further development, and costly infrastructure debts.

THE TEST OF ASSUMPTIONS

A host of untested assumptions underlying this extended Tiebout-Peterson framework require formal analysis and testing:

1. Diversity in locational opportunities is a consequence of the degree of jurisdictional fragmentation in a metropolitan area and its population size and territorial extent.
2. Diversity and fragmentation are locational assets for firms in a metropolitan area.
3. A welfare gain arises from the greater range of locational choices.
4. The fragmentation outcome reveals interdependent maximizing behavior by residents, firms, and jurisdictions.
5. The policy emphasis of jurisdictional units is a function of their tier level in the territorial hierarchy.
6. The policy emphasis of all units shifts as a function of stage in the decline-growth succession.
7. Development policies of local jurisdictions tend to amplify economic disparities between units.
8. Shifts to redistribution policies occur only at the end of growth periods but are vulnerable to the exigencies of the ensuing decline trend.
9. The outcome of repeated cycles is an erosion of the locational advantages of metropolitan regions through the loss of irreplaceable resources (e.g., developable land, accessible open space) and the high cost of redevelopment.

A BEHAVIORAL APPROACH TO LOCAL AND STATE STRATEGIES

The assumptions and implications of this extended Tiebout-Peterson framework would need to be examined through cross-sectional and longitudinal analyses of jurisdictional units at all tiers of regional hierarchies, and integrated with a study of the behavior of residents and firms. A model for municipal behavior, for example, could begin with a simplified public choice approach following the Peterson framework. Jurisdictions would maximize some candidate objective functions, including expected revenues from their property tax bases, or the ratio of revenues derived from firms relative to those paid by residents. The constraints could include controls of internal spillover effects and open-space conservation. The weighting of objectives and constraints is determined by the demand for sites in the municipality, weights employed in the recent past and their outcome, and the policies of neighboring communities and those in the more inclusive territorial units (i.e., counties and states).

A portfolio of feasible fiscal and land-use policy instruments is available to the jurisdiction that differs in expected net returns and consistency with the environmental concerns. The instruments include various concessions and exactions from developers, property tax and service allowances, and land-use controls.

The model then posits a selection of policy responses (with some lag) by municipalities, to an internal fiscal condition, and to a demand for sites and neighborhood spillovers that would vary across the diversity of communities and stages in the decline-growth sequence. At the same time that local policies are introduced to stimulate or control growth, county and state units are implementing their own programs in a sequence that can be characterized (at least in an abstracted way) using the same generalized type of model.

THE EMPIRICAL ANALYSIS

The issues are, of course, much more complex than described in the simplified model, which can provide only an initial framework for empirical study. Even this approach, however, would require a large body of comparative time-series data across a sample of metropolitan areas. The complexities of the issues and data demands restrict this chapter to preliminary tabular data; other issues and the regression tests will be examined later.

The empirical issue here is the relationship of fragmentation to the costs of regional growth that can be studied (through the variance between jurisdictions) in a single agglomeration:

1. *Metropolitan diversity*—an examination of the diversity between jurisdictions of a metropolitan area before the onset of the growth stage (the base line). A Tiebout framework would predict relative homogeneity in land use and population composition within fragmented jurisdictions and heterogeneity between the units. This phase probes the variance in local property taxes and service expenditures that can be associated with the land-use differences and socioeconomic composition of municipalities. How consistent is the differentiation of the units across a wide range of community characteristics?

2. *Changes in disparities with economic growth*—the relationship of economic growth to the diversity between jurisdictions. Theory would presume widening disparities between jurisdictions during rapid growth. This thesis is examined by assessing the effect of state development and transfer programs on ameliorating the disparities between the municipalities during the growth period.

3. *Relative changes in the costs of growth*—the relationship of economic growth in the jurisdictions to the changing cost of service provision and loss

of open space. The behavioral model of municipal development suggests that growth would be constrained by a preference to retain open space and to exercise fiscal control on the growth of expenditures for services. The test of this thesis will examine the changes in service costs and extent of open space that are related to the differential growth rates of the municipalities.

THE UNITS OF ANALYSIS

The units selected for analysis are 179 contiguous New Jersey municipalities in eight counties in the western quadrant of the New York agglomeration (Figure 10.1). The municipalities differ significantly in form of government (boroughs, cities, towns, and townships), per capita income, tax rates, and land devoted to housing, commerce, industry, and open space (Danielson and Doig 1982). Some of the urbanized municipalities (e.g., Newark, Trenton, and Jersey City) had considerable capital sunk in traditional industry, many abandoned commercial structures, few large sites available for new industry, and little prospect of attracting new economic development even with locational subsidies. The region also contains suburban residential towns as well as exurban and more rural municipalities that differ in the so-

FIG. 10.1   The study area in northern New Jersey.

cioeconomic composition of their population, level of service provision, and land-use distribution.

These jurisdictional units can all be described in terms of baseline conditions (i.e., in 1975) before and during the recent growth surge with respect to: economic and social characteristics of residents; employment; land-use distribution; building permits and housing starts; number and value of residential, commercial, industrial, farm, and vacant parcels; sources of revenue (i.e., from property taxes, wages, user fees, and federal and state transfers); expenditure patterns (e.g., schools, public safety, courts, public works, health and hospitals, debt payment); and indebtedness. In addition, data are available on development authority loans, urban development action grants (UDAGs), and infrastructure investments for highway improvements.

For the comparative analysis, the 179 municipalities were ranked according to mean per capita income in 1970 and grouped into five categories from lowest to highest income. Each of the five categories was divided into two groups according to population density (i.e., rural areas or towns). The resultant ten groups of eighteen communities (and one with seventeen) span the range from lowest income rural areas to highest income towns (Table 10.1).

THE ANALYSIS OF METROPOLITAN DIVERSITY

How can the diversity of the jurisdictions be understood? The Tiebout framework provides important insights as to how the fragmentation probably developed historically. The analysis in the study area should demonstrate general consistency across the ten groups of diverse municipalities between the allocation of land use, the socioeconomic composition of the population, the local property tax rate, and the level of public service provision.

Higher property tax rates were consistent with higher densities and a greater proportion of minority population in the 1975 base line period (Table 10.1). Rates would have been even higher if not for state revenue transfers, especially to the low-income cities and towns. Tax rates for residents were moderated by industrial, commercial, and farm ratables. Per capita public service expenditures (i.e., municipal revenues) were higher in the more rural and higher-income groups of communities. The residential tax base was the major determinant of service expenditures.

The data generally confirm our intuitive notions of these communities and the Tiebout effect at the base line period in the recession of 1975. Fragmentation and autonomy had created a wide range of diverse siting opportunities for development within the larger New York agglomeration. The older industrial towns had high property tax rates and relatively lower expenditure levels for services, despite the revenue transfers. The lower-density, higher-income residential suburbs were blessed with lower rates and higher

TABLE 10.1 Selected Characteristics of 179 Study-Area Municipalities, Grouped by per Capita Income and by Rural/Urban (Low/High) Population Density, 1975

	Per Capita Income										
	Lowest 1		2		Moderate 3		4		Highest 5		Total
Density	Low	High	Low	High	Low	High	Low	High	Low	High	
Means											
Per capita income (1970)	3060	3051	3476	3451	3830	3783	4307	4319	6415	5385	4101
Population	6030	56167	17188	32372	18487	24306	8867	15192	9276	18771	20676
Percent minority (1970)	2	21	4	10	3	13	4	6	1	6	7
Density	1293	11917	1087	10514	968	8502	564	5291	993	4495	4563
Employment	1381	17393	4622	9833	5121	8976	3223	7673	2824	4929	6607
Tax rate ($ per $100 valuation)	2.99	4.19	2.95	4.17	2.98	3.53	2.69	3.2	2.67	3.78	3.31
Revenue/capita $	596	552	569	512	609	553	730	550	815	665	583
Property tax/capita $	452	268	407	356	466	397	559	432	654	547	398
Residential/capita $	238	112	224	181	245	210	276	265	417	383	219
Business/capita $	74	54	69	73	78	86	113	81	77	68	70
Transfers/capita $	78	136	68	77	62	77	71	52	59	44	71
Other/capita $	96	73	77	55	84	68	97	62	100	61	74
n =	18	18	18	18	18	18	18	18	18	17	179

service levels thanks to their commercial and industrial properties. The lower-income rural areas had low tax rates but lower service levels as well due to the shortage of ratables, but they had an abundance of vacant and farm land zoned for development.

DISPARITIES AND ECONOMIC GROWTH

Did the disparities between the communities increase during the 1975 to 1985 period of rapid development? The study area as a whole increased its tax base by about 20 percent after allowance for inflation. Many of the poorer industrial towns, however, experienced continued disinvestment, while the more rural communities enhanced their tax base significantly (Table 10.2). As expected, employment from commercial and industrial development proceeded more rapidly than did residential construction, especially in the more affluent rural communities. Tax rates declined throughout the region, but more in the growing rural areas than in the towns. Revenue transfers were more evenly distributed. Revenues for services increased least in the needier towns. The state's economic development assistance also favored (on a per capita basis) the rapidly growing rural areas over the lower-income towns and cities. Highway extensions and improvements were also concentrated in the more rural communities where rapid growth was taking place.

The Tiebout-Peterson framework appears to be generally confirmed in this study. The increase in demand for accessible and relatively low-cost land for development was satisfied within the agglomeration. Proving that the diversity of development options contributed to the rate of growth would require comparative data across metropolitan areas. The limited data for the 179 municipalities show only that rapid growth favored the places that had developable land and were autonomous in land-use decisions. The data also show that investments in highway improvements, revenue transfers, and development assistance from the more inclusive state unit fostered or at least followed the locational preferences of firms and developers for sites in the lower-density places.

THE COSTS OF REGIONAL GROWTH

Does rapid economic and population growth in fragmented and autonomous jurisdictions (with development assistance from more inclusive territorial units) undermine the locational assets and advantages of the region? The ten groups of municipalities demonstrate diversity in property taxes and other revenues for providing public services at the base line period (Table 10.3). The widest disparities were in expenditures for schools. Twice as much was spent per resident (not per school child) in the most affluent lower-density communities as was spent per resident in the low-income cities. Other

TABLE 10.2 Percentage Changes in Population and Economic Growth, 1975–86

Density	Lowest 1		2		Per Capita Income Moderate 3		4		Highest 5	
	Low	High	Low	High	Low	High	Low	High	Low	High
Population Growth										
Population	13	−8	17	−8	24	−5	28	−2	3	−8
Residential Parcels	23	−2	23	4	23	5	19	8	11	6
Apartment Parcels	57	−23	−29	10	51	5	64	−2	153	−17
Economic Growth										
Per Capita Income	57	17	50	21	45	21	44	33	38	22
Employment	46	−7	46	4	87	3	81	10	47	31
Property Values/capita	123	136	126	127	137	147	182	161	186	183
Property Tax Rate	−22	−20	−24	−13	−24	−12	−26	−25	−29	−26
Transfer Revenue/capita	65	84	108	117	86	91	100	131	117	156
Economic Development Assistance ($ per capita)										
Total 1975–86	1062	711	2067	818	1927	861	1202	751	490	442
UDAG ($ per capita)	0	60	0	15	0	9	4	16	0	2
Highways										
Interstates (%)	39	28	61	33	89	22	78	39	56	0
State routes (%)	50	44	61	67	78	56	44	56	56	24

services were also more generously supported both in the lower- and higher-density richer communities.

The rapid growth surge was accompanied by a significant increase in municipal expenditure especially for general (i.e., administrative) and judicial and safety (i.e., police and fire) functions. Some costs rose faster in rural than in higher-density areas, and some increased more in lower- than in higher-income communities. To some extent, expenditures were driven by the increase in tax base, but costs also rose because of the added costs of local or spillover development or continued disinvestment. The pattern is too complex to be unraveled with my limited data. Disparities in provision of services increased with the growth spurt, but the diversity between jurisdictions lessened as a function of their added expenditures.

The same trend toward greater equalization and less heterogeneity can be observed from the density changes, a proxy for loss of open space and increased congestion (Table 10.4). Densities of population, employment, and commercial and industrial parcels rose much more rapidly in rural than in more urbanized jurisdictions and in the moderate-income zones. Population density declined in the most affluent communities, but the increase in internal and nearby employment and commercial and industrial development probably contributed to the added automobile congestion their residents are now experiencing.

According to the extended Tiebout-Peterson framework, a period of rapid regional growth should be followed by some surrender of fragmented autonomy in favor of greater control by more inclusive territorial units to remedy the market failures under home rule. Declining demand for goods and services in the private sector should prompt oligopolies to augment their diversity and autonomy (Dixit and Stiglitz 1977). A substantial increase in demand should lead more toward consolidation and monopoly to take advantage of industrywide efficiencies and economies. We should expect a similar process by units of government when they become aware that growth management must be delegated to more inclusive units to overcome spillovers from neighbors still eager to grow. At that stage, more centralized development efforts can target development to remedy disparities and reduce undesired spillovers on communities that have had their fill of growth.

In the case-study region, rapid growth in the more rural areas, greater separation of work and residence due to fiscal zoning, and an increase in multiple-worker households (necessary due to rising prices for accessible housing) have added to the growing congestion, traffic delays, and costs of transport for area firms. The growing labor shortage has pushed up wages. The increase in housing costs has discouraged in-migration of additional workers and has begun to affect the siting decisions of firms. The region's growth has only begun to trickle down to the older industrial towns and has done little thus far to reduce disparities.

TABLE 10.3 Municipal Expenditures

Density	Per Capita Income									
	Lowest 1		2		Moderate 3		4		Highest 5	
	Low	High	Low	High	Low	High	Low	High	Low	High
Per capita expenditures 1975										
General	31	33	28	25	31	30	34	28	37	23
Judicial	3	2	2	2	2	2	3	2	2	2
Safety	35	77	40	67	38	63	47	61	62	61
Public Works	42	46	44	42	52	41	58	45	51	48
Health/Welfare	2	11	4	6	4	5	4	3	3	5
Recreation	3	7	5	8	7	7	6	8	9	11
Schools	408	278	423	288	477	313	496	383	563	442
Total	596	503	621	489	695	516	736	597	826	670
Percentage changes in per capita expenditures 1975–86										
General	190	167	129	162	118	115	162	141	148	151
Judicial	140	166	162	176	121	185	123	193	134	164
Safety	141	97	126	103	125	99	133	108	118	95
Public Works	110	114	90	110	70	109	77	108	79	131
Health/Welfare	130	72	117	105	88	121	87	78	101	95
Recreation	63	37	64	53	98	62	78	19	32	52
Schools	65	61	69	88	69	92	95	88	92	97
Total	80	79	78	96	75	96	99	94	96	100
Percentage change 1975–86										
Per capita revenue	83	83	86	92	80	96	103	96	103	103
Revenue/Business	-11	-15	-8	-9	5	-3	8	-5	-2	-4
Transfers	65	84	108	117	86	91	100	131	117	156
Equalization tax rate	-26	-28	-28	-17	-28	-20	-30	-28	-33	-31

TABLE 10.4   Percentage Change in Municipal Density Measures, 1975–86

	\multicolumn{10}{c}{*Per Capita Income*}									
	\multicolumn{2}{c}{*Lowest* 1}		\multicolumn{4}{c}{*Moderate*}				\multicolumn{2}{c}{*Highest* 5}
	1		2		3		4		5	
Density	Low	High	Low	High	Low	High	Low	High	Low	High
Population Density	10	−8	2	−11	10	0	14	−9	−4	−9
Employment Density	93	−7	46	4	79	13	74	16	51	31
Commercial Parcels	15	−14	13	−2	2	2	26	8	17	4
Industrial Parcels	27	−11	51	10	32	9	16	7	25	10
Developable Parcels	17	11	−14	−15	−3	−8	18	8	1	−18
Total Parcels	22	−4	17	3	17	4	19	8	10	4

Predictably, sustained rapid growth has also been accompanied by a revival of interest in state land-use planning to reduce further sprawl and in-state fiscal reform to remedy disparities, especially in the financing of local schools. The chances of implementing these reforms, however, are likely to depend on the continuation of growth.

This preliminary examination of recent growth in the case-study region indicates that the extended Tiebout-Peterson approach may help to explain why this fragmented agglomeration has grown so rapidly and why further growth is now being assessed relative to environmental and equity concerns. The simplified determinism of this public-choice approach does not, of course, capture the complexities of the political process within and between the units of local and state government, but the close fit of the framework is encouraging enough to warrant further development of formal theory as well as comparative study to examine the assumptions more thoroughly.

REFERENCES

Baldassare, M. 1986. *Trouble in paradise: The suburban transformation in America.* New York: Columbia University Press.

Brower, D. 1976. *Urban growth management through development timing.* New York: Praeger Publishers.

Danielson, M. N., and J. W. Doig. 1982. *New York: The politics of urban regional development.* Berkeley: University of California Press.

Dixit, A. K., and J. E. Stiglitz. 1977. Monopolistic competition and optimal product diversity. *American Economic Review* 67: 297–308.

Downs, A. 1957. *An economic theory of democracy.* New York: Harper.

Ellickson, B. 1979. Local public goods and the market for neighborhoods. In *The economics of neighborhood.* Edited by D. Segal. New York: Academic Press.

Engerman, S. 1965. Regional aspects of stabilization policy. In *Essays in fiscal federalism*. Edited by R. A. Musgrave. Washington, D.C.: Brookings Institution.

Epple, D., and A. Zelenitz. 1981. The implications of competition among jurisdictions: Does Tiebout need politics? *Journal of Political Economy* 89: 1197–217.

Gleeson, M. E. 1977. *Urban growth management systems: An evaluation of policy related research*. Report no. 309. Chicago: American Society of Planning Officials, Planning Advisory Service.

Henderson, J. V. 1979. Theories of group, jurisdiction, and city size. In *Current issues in urban economics*. Edited by P. Mieszkowski and M. Straszheim. Baltimore: Johns Hopkins University Press.

Inman, R. P. 1979. The fiscal performance of local governments: An interpretive review. In *Current issues in urban economics*. Edited by P. Mieszkowski and M. Straszheim. Baltimore: Johns Hopkins University Press.

Logan, J. R., and M. Schneider. 1981. Stratification of metropolitan suburbs. *American Sociological Review* 46: 175–86.

Logan, J. R., and H. L. Molotch. 1988. *Urban fortunes: The political economy of place*. Berkeley: University of California Press.

Mieszkowski, P. 1979. Recent trends in urban and regional development. In *Current issues in urban economics*. Edited by P. Mieszkowski and M. Straszheim. Baltimore: Johns Hopkins University Press.

Mills, E. S. 1979. Economic analysis of urban land-use controls. In *Current issues in urban economics*. Edited by P. Mieszkowski and M. Straszheim. Baltimore: Johns Hopkins University Press.

Mills, E. S., and W. E. Oates. 1975. *Fiscal zoning and land use controls*. Lexington, Mass.: Lexington Books.

Molotch, H. 1976. The city as a growth machine: Toward a political economy of place. *American Journal of Sociology* 82: 309–32.

Peterson, P. E. 1981. *City limits*. Chicago: University of Chicago Press.

Rafuse, R. W., Jr. 1965. Cyclical behavior of state-local finances. In *Essays in fiscal federalism*. Edited by R. A. Musgrave. Washington, D.C.: Brookings Institution.

Tiebout, C. M. 1956. A pure theory of local expenditures. *Journal of Political Economy* 64: 416–24.

ELEVEN

Industrial Development in Southern California, 1970–1987

A. J. Scott and A. S. Paul

Southern California is defined here as the great conurbation stretching from Santa Barbara through Los Angeles to San Diego (Figure 11.1). The population of nearly 16 million in 1987 ranks second only to the New York metropolitan region in the United States, and its manufacturing labor force of 1.25 million workers exceeds the manufacturing labor force of any other area of comparable geographical extent in the country. Manufacturing activities in Southern California grew at an unusually fast pace during the 1970s and early 1980s, a period of massive deindustrialization and job loss in many metropolitan areas of the Frostbelt.

In this chapter we attempt simply to document the main contours of industrial development in Southern California, and to remark on the sources of its success and some of its problems. We begin by situating recent trends in the Southern Californian economy in the context of an apparent transition in the United States away from Fordist mass production and toward more flexible forms of organization (Harvey and Scott 1988). We describe patterns of change in the manufacturing system of Southern California since the early 1970s, emphasizing variations in employment by location, sector, and establishment size. We pay special attention to mass production, craft specialty production, and high-technology industry. We then discuss institutional structures and the roles of ethnicity, race, and gender in the manufacturing labor markets of the region. Finally, we attempt to pinpoint problems of the local manufacturing system and to indicate some possible policy responses. Our findings necessarily are highly preliminary, given the size of the task and the

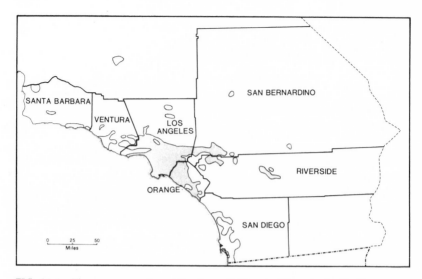

FIG. 11.1   The seven counties of Southern California. The principal built-up areas are shaded.

surprisingly meager literature. Our analysis is only a prelude to a more extensive research program.

THE SYSTEM IN CONTEXT

The Pathway to Industrialization

The manufacturing economy of Southern California seems to have evolved quite differently from the older and more traditional centers of the North and East. The main industrial development of Southern California came after the Second World War and, in contrast to many parts of the Manufacturing Belt, it has been based less on mass production than on a unique mix of specialty craft production and high-technology industry with considerable flexibility of organizational and local labor market structures. Southern California seems to be one of the paradigmatic cases of a new flexible model of industrial development that is starting to diffuse throughout North America and Western Europe (Soja, Morales, and Wolff 1983; Soja and Scott 1986).

Recent evidence suggests that mass production in the advanced capitalist economies has begun, in part at least, to give way to a new pattern of industrial organization. Economists of the so-called Regulationist School apply the descriptive label *Fordist* to the old industrial system, and they commonly discuss it in the larger context of a regime of Fordist accumulation (Aglietta 1976; Boyer 1986). The new (post-Fordist) pattern has flexible internal and external production relations, and we shall therefore refer to it as a system of flexible production organization. Storper and Scott (1989) argue that its distinctive features include:

1. a basis in sectors such as revivified craft specialty production and high-technology industry (as well as services) that produce variable, design-intensive, and small-batch outputs, as opposed to the standardized large-batch outputs of mass production industries.
2. a tendency to deepening social divisions of labor and a concomitant dependence on external economies, whereas classical mass production is marked by an insistent search for internal economies of scale and scope.
3. the substitution of external labor markets for internal labor markets, accompanied by rising instability of employment, as manifest in accelerated turnover and increasing part-time and temporary work.
4. the reagglomeration of production in urban settings far from older foci of Fordist industrialization, as in the new Sunbelt growth centers.

Piore and Sable (1984) have alluded to similar phenomena in their account of the emergence and consolidation of "flexible specialization" as a mode of industrialization.

Recent Growth

Regional growth based on flexible production organization and related industrial activity is highly developed in Southern California. This growth is part of a wider system of employment change both in the region and in the United States. Between 1970 and 1985, manufacturing employment in Southern California grew by 24.2 percent (Table 11.1), which is remarkably high compared with the rate of change (-1.7 percent) in the United States as a whole (Teitz 1984). Until the 1980s, manufacturing was the single most important employment group in Southern California. White-collar jobs (as represented by finance, insurance and real estate, and services) increased rapidly between 1970 and 1985, echoing a similar expansion nationally, and by 1985 services had displaced manufacturing as the most important employment group (Table 11.1). Even employment in agricultural services, forestry, and fishing grew apace, apparently as a result of the intensification of agricultural land use in the region.

Although the Southern Californian economy remains strongly focused on manufacturing, it is also, as in the U.S. economy at large, evolving steadily toward greatly increased white-collar employment, both absolutely and proportionately. This trend is not a sign of the imminent advent of some species of postindustrial society. On the contrary, the service economy and the manufacturing economy are intimately interdependent. Many service sectors are directly and indirectly related to manufacturing, either by providing managerial, financial, and commercial inputs, or, as in education and health in particular, by serving the labor force in an increasingly human- and capital-

TABLE 11.1 Employment in Major Industrial Groups in Southern California and the United States, 1970 and 1985

	Southern California			United States		
	1970	1985	Change (%)	1970	1985	Change (%)
Agricultural services, forestry, fisheries	14,524	35,678	145.6	189,026	381,632	101.9
Mining	22,834	18,166	−20.4	600,715	943,372	57.0
Construction	179,226	283,220	58.0	3,197,382	4,479,533	40.1
Manufacturing	1,121,359	1,392,666	24.2	19,761,548	19,433,606	−1.7
Transportation and other public utilities	221,096	314,456	42.2	3,837,876	4,815,535	25.5
Wholesale trade	240,729	402,746	67.3	4,035,995	5,625,007	39.4
Retail trade	690,987	1,094,166	58.3	11,071,289	16,851,827	52.2
Finance, insurance and real estate	225,461	445,867	97.8	3,674,899	6,004,136	63.4
Services	721,127	1,605,378	122.6	10,461,468	21,543,425	105.9
Not classified	16,048	81,816	409.8	435,094	1,041,184	139.3
Total	3,453,391	5,674,159	64.3	57,265,292	81,119,257	41.7

Source: U.S. Department of Commerce, Bureau of the Census, County Business Patterns.

intensive society (Noyelle and Stanback 1983). At the same time, services and manufacturing in Southern California are both more or less equal participants in the modern turn to flexibility as an operating principle of economic organization and production. From a purely structural perspective, indeed, there is often little to distinguish the one from the other in the modern (flexible) economy.

In fact, manufacturing in Southern California, far from representing an outdated and decaying production ensemble, is of continuing major importance in the overall "roundaboutness" of the production system, albeit in a much modified form compared to the classical pattern of American mass production (Cohen and Zysman 1987; Piore and Sable 1984). The absolute quantitative significance of manufacturing employment in Southern California remains remarkably high, notwithstanding the robust ascent of the service economy (Table 11.1). In fact, manufacturing employment in some counties of the region is growing at a rate that nearly matches the rate of growth of service employment.

DIMENSIONS OF GROWTH AND CHANGE

Manufacturing employment in Southern California grew fairly continuously from 1970 to 1985, with local downturns in 1971, 1975, and 1981 to 1983 (Figure 11.2). In order to make sense of this pattern, with its many crosscurrents, we need to examine (1) employment growth and change by county, (2) sectoral patterns of expansion and contraction, and (3) variations in the job generation process by establishment size.

Growth and Change by County

The seven counties of Southern California had widely varying rates of manufacturing growth between 1970 and 1985 (Table 11.2). Los Angeles County, the largest county, had the lowest rates of growth, 17.0 percent for establishments, and 4.2 percent for employment. This performance is impressive when compared with the large absolute declines in manufacturing in many Northeastern metropolitan areas during the same period. San Bernardino and Riverside counties had intermediate growth rates, and the other four counties had extremely high rates. Growth in employment exceeds growth in number of establishments in every county, and greatly so in most counties. Average establishment size is declining over time, which may indicate a deepening social division of labor and rising levels of flexibility in local production systems.

The aggregate rate of growth of manufacturing in any county appears to be inversely related to the vintage of its industrial plant. The growth rate is related to the degree to which the county was a center of older industrial activities focused on mass production and associated sectors. Los Angeles,

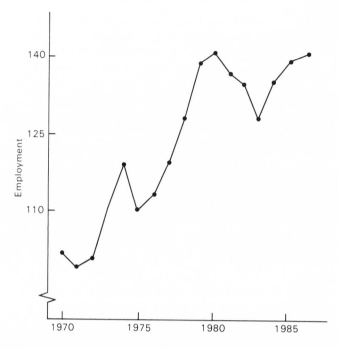

FIG. 11.2   Manufacturing employment in Southern California, 1970–1985.

TABLE 11.2   Manufacturing Establishments and Employment in Southern California, by County, 1970 and 1985

County	Establishments			Employment		
	1970	1985	Change (%)	1970	1985	Change (%)
Los Angeles	16,663	19,490	17.0	853,932	889,784	4.2
Orange	1,927	5,535	187.2	118,489	253,296	113.8
Riverside	402	819	103.7	20,333	31,036	52.6
San Bernardino	633	1,278	101.9	32,370	40,563	25.3
San Diego	1,043	2,674	156.4	73,302	121,178	65.3
Santa Barbara	241	517	114.5	11,701	22,444	91.8
Ventura	233	726	211.6	11,232	34,365	206.0
Total	21,142	31,039	46.8	1,121,359	1,392,666	24.2

Source: U.S. Department of Commerce, Bureau of the Census, *County Business Patterns.*

Riverside, and San Bernardino counties, unlike Orange, San Diego, Santa Barbara, and Ventura counties, were (and in some cases still are) the site of Fordist mass production in sectors such as petroleum, rubber tires, steel, cars, and other metallurgical and machinery industries. We compared manufacturing growth rates between 1970 and 1985 in each county against aggregate employment in 1970 in the four mass production industries and computed Spearman's rank correlation coefficient (r_s) for rates of change in (a) the total number of manufacturing establishments and (b) the total employment in manufacturing against (c) aggregate employment in mass production (as defined above) in 1970. The values of r_s are, respectively, -0.96 and -0.86, both significant at the 0.05 level or better. These results reflect the decline of mass production, but they also hint that one precondition for the growth of new flexible production activities (high-technology industry above all) is detachment from land uses and labor markets shaped by earlier industrialization based on Fordist and related sectors (Scott 1988b; Storper and Scott 1989). The new high-technology industrial complexes (or technopoles) in Orange, San Diego, Santa Barbara, and Ventura counties (as well as some of the more suburban parts of Los Angeles County, but not Riverside or San Bernardino counties) are prime examples of this phenomenon.

Sectoral Patterns

The five largest two-digit manufacturing sectors in Southern California in 1985 were SIC 36 (electric and electronic equipment), SIC 37 (transportation equipment), SIC 35 (machinery except electrical), SIC 34 (fabricated metals), and SIC 23 (apparel and other textile products) (Table 11.3). SIC 23 is a typical craft specialty industry; the other four are mainly (although not entirely) elements of the high-technology industrial complex of Southern California, either directly (as in the three- and four-digit subsectors producing computers, electronic equipment, or aerospace products) or indirectly (as in the subsectors producing aluminum moldings or specialized machines for the high-technology industries).

Three major ensembles of industrial sectors can be detected (Table 11.3). One is a declining ensemble of mass-production industries, and the other two are rapidly growing ensembles focused on flexible craft production and high-technology industry. Each of these ensembles has distinctive organizational, labor market, and locational features, but it is difficult to define them unambiguously on the basis of available statistics. A rough and ready definition combining two- and three-digit SIC categories identifies each ensemble by a selected core of symptomatic sectors with significant employment levels Table 11.4). The standard industrial classification is so crude that some industries that should be included in an ensemble are omitted, and some industries that should be omitted are included. We should treat the categories in Table

11.4 with considerable circumspection, but our main objective is not to be exhaustive, simply indicative. Grave definitional problems would still remain even if we were to attempt to identify the three ensembles by means of more finely grained four-digit SIC categories, and serious problems of non-disclosure of relevant information crop up at this level of disaggregation. We have included SIC 781 (motion picture production and services) in the craft industry ensemble. This sector is defined as a service in the standard industrial classification, but it is more akin to manufacturing industries such as apparel,

TABLE 11.3   Employment in Two-Digit Industries, Southern California, 1970 and 1985[a]

SIC	1970	1985
19 Ordnance and accessories[b]	103,145	—
20 Food and kindred products	65,836	63,909
21 Tobacco manufactures	0	0
22 Textile mill products	8,298	13,467
23 Apparel and other textile products	61,241	96,610
24 Lumber and wood products	11,053	23,340
25 Furniture and fixtures	31,265	54,541
26 Paper and allied products	21,291	24,125
27 Printing and publishing	56,706	89,261
28 Chemicals and allied products	30,580	36,984
29 Petroleum and coal products	10,073	9,342
30 Rubber and miscellaneous plastic products	35,531	57,976
31 Leather and leather products	5,091	8,337
32 Stone, clay, and glass products	28,784	30,639
33 Primary metal industries	37,807	27,161
34 Fabricated metal products	84,096	111,898
35 Machinery, except electrical	110,543	142,407
36 Electric and electronic equipment	143,822	235,796
37 Transportation equipment	184,658	234,074
38 Instruments and related products	29,903	57,666
39 Miscellaneous manufacturing industries	30,105	28,708
Not classified	31,533	46,425
Total	1,121,359	1,392,666

Source: U.S. Department of Commerce, Bureau of the Census, *County Business Patterns.*

[a]The employment data are computed from county totals; where county totals are not available, due to disclosure rules, employment has been estimated from the frequency distributions of industrial establishment size given in *County Business Patterns.*

[b]After 1972, SIC 19 was abolished and industrial activity formerly classified in this category was distributed over SICs 34, 36, 37, and 38. The 1970 and 1985 data for these SIC categories are not strictly comparable.

TABLE 11.4   Major Industrial Ensembles and Numbers of Employees
in Southern California, 1970 and 1985[a]

Industry	1970	1985	Change (%)
Mass production and related industries			
SIC 29 Petroleum and coal products	10,073	9,342	−7.5
SIC 301 Tires and inner tubes	6,393	206	−96.8
SIC 331 Blast furnaces and basic steel products	8,427	3,442	−59.2
SIC 371 Motor vehicles and equipment	21,340	25,829	21.0
Craft specialty production			
SIC 23 Apparel and other textile products	61,241	96,610	57.8
SIC 25 Furniture and fixtures	31,265	54,541	74.4
SIC 27 Printing and publishing	56,706	89,261	57.4
SIC 31 Leather and leather products	5,091	8,337	63.8
SIC 391 Jewelry, silverware, and plated ware	1,552	2,291	47.6
SIC 781 Motion picture production and services	24,637	76,269	209.6
High-technology industry			
SIC 357 Office and computing machines	31,002	44,044	42.1
SIC 366 Communications equipment	60,449	110,870	83.4
SIC 367 Electronic components and accessories	38,463	74,572	93.9
SIC 372 Aircraft and parts	136,556	118,732	−13.1
SIC 376 Guided missiles, space vehicles, and parts	68,500	72,836	6.3

Source: U.S. Department of Commerce, Bureau of the Census, *County Business Patterns.*
[a] Data are estimated where disclosure is withheld (see footnote a to Table 11.3); in 1970, SIC 376 was not yet defined and employment was estimated by extrapolation.

furniture, or printing and publishing (Storper and Chrisopherson 1987). For this reason, and because of its importance in the economy of Los Angeles, we have reclassified it with the latter industries.

In 1985, mass production, craft, and high-technology industries, as defined, accounted for 56.5 percent of all manufacturing employment in Southern California. The remaining industries of the region are for the most part either directly or indirectly connected to the three major ensembles, and especially to the high-technology industrial ensemble. The major exception is the food industry, which provides outputs for final consumption.

MAJOR ENSEMBLES

Mass Production Industry

Manufacturing in Southern California was never so focused on mass production as it was in the Manufacturing Belt. In their postwar heyday in the 1950s, mass production industries accounted for only 7 or 8 percent of all manufacturing employment in Southern California. These industries were concentrated in Los Angeles (petroleum products, automobile assembly, tires, and machinery industries), with smaller outlying industries in Riverside (metallurgy and machinery) and San Bernardino (steel). By 1970 employment in mass production industries in the region had fallen to 4.1 percent of the total, and by 1985 to only 2.8 percent.

Mass production industries in Southern California declined not only as a percentage of employment, but absolutely as well. Decentralization and intensified competition from Japan and the newly industrializing countries cost many jobs in mass production. Employment declined 16.1 percent between 1970 and 1985. Employment in SIC 371 (motor vehicles and equipment) increased during this period, but this increase was primarily in parts and accessories manufacture. Employment in assembly declined. Both Ford and General Motors closed down major facilities in Los Angeles. The rubber tire and inner tube industry in the region virtually disappeared during this period.

Specialty Craft Industries

Specialty craft industries are labor intensive, given to product differentiation, and fragmented into many flexibly specialized but interconnected establishments. Craft specialty industries are unusually well represented in Southern California. In 1985, the ensemble employed 327,309 workers, an increase of 81.3 percent between 1970 and 1985 (Table 11.4). The significance of craft production in the economy of Southern California is at first perhaps surprising, given both the supposed archaic character of these industries and the reputation of Southern California as a center of high-technology industry, but one of the features of the recent turn to flexible production organization both in North America and in Western Europe has been the active resurgence of such industries and their reemergence as significant foci of growth (Piore and Sable 1984; Scott 1988b).

The largest craft industries in the region are SIC 23 (apparel), SIC 27 (printing and publishing), and SIC 781 (motion picture production and services). SIC 781 is the most rapidly growing craft industry. Employment in it increased 209.6 percent between 1970 and 1985. Los Angeles County accounts for 81.2 percent of the region's employment in this ensemble. Most of these industries are in specialized "marshallian" industrial districts in or near downtown Los Angeles (Becattini 1987; Scott 1988a).

The centralized and agglomerated locational pattern of craft industries is exemplified by women's dress manufacturers in central Los Angeles (Figure 11.3). Clothing manufacturers cluster together along with associated trades: cutting and sewing contractors, button and thread suppliers, sewing machine repair shops, and so on (Scott 1988a). All of the major craft industries in Los Angeles have a similar social division of labor and locational agglomeration in specialized industrial districts. Around each individual district is typically a

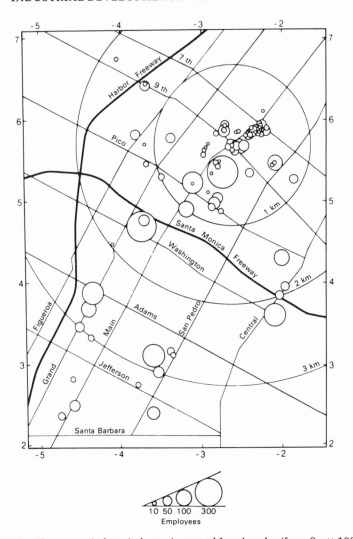

FIG. 11.3   The women's dress industry in central Los Angeles (from Scott 1988b).

residential zone that houses a high proportion of its workers. Except for the motion picture industry, where closed-shop hiring practices still prevail, most of the craft industries of Los Angeles depend largely on low-wage immigrant and female workers.

High-Technology Industry

The high-technology industrial establishments in Southern California range from large systems houses (R & D-intensive batch production factories, often employing many thousands of workers) to small sweatshops producing printed circuit boards or customized electronic assemblies. Employment in the high-technology industrial ensemble increased by 25.7 percent between 1970 and 1985 (Table 11.4), but the largest component, SIC 372 (aircraft and parts), actually lost employment. SIC 366 (communications equipment) and SIC 367 (electronic components and accessories) are two of the most rapidly expanding industries in the region (Table 11.4).

Many producers in the high-technology industrial ensemble in Southern California seek flexibility of process and product configurations, and hence the ability to shift rapidly from one market to another as opportunities change. This feature encourages vertical disintegration of functions and the formation of spatially agglomerated technopoles (Scott 1988a). Southern California has eighty-five high-technology industrial establishments that employ one thousand workers or more. Significant clusters are at Goleta, Chatsworth–Canoga Park, Van Nuys, the North Airport Area, El Segundo–Hawthorne, Torrance, Anaheim–Santa Ana, Irvine, the Golden Triangle of

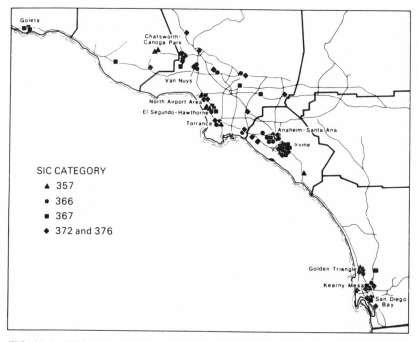

FIG. 11.4   High-technology manufacturing establishments employing at least one thousand workers, with county boundaries and selected freeways. The SIC codes are 357, office and computing machines; 366, communications equipment; 367, electronic components and accessories; 372, aircraft and parts; and 376, guided missiles, space vehicles, and parts. Data source: *California Manufacturers Register, 1987* and county directories.

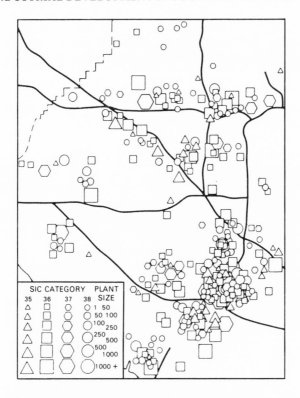

FIG. 11.5   The Orange County high-technology complex (from Scott 1988a).

TABLE 11.5   Department of Defense Prime Contract Awards in Southern California, by County, 1985

County	Award Value (Millions of Dollars)	Value as Percentage of Total Awards in California
Los Angeles	15,486	53.2
Orange	2,945	10.1
Riverside	59	0.2
San Bernardino	541	1.9
San Diego	2,220	7.6
Santa Barbara	795	2.7
Ventura	405	1.4
Total	22,451	77.2

Source: County Supervisors Association of California, *County Fact Book,* 1987.

San Diego, Kearny Mesa, and San Diego Bay (Figure 11.4). All of these clusters are interpenetrated by dense constellations of small- and medium-sized establishments, many providing specialized inputs and subcontract services. The largest and most dynamic technopole of the region is focused on Irvine in Orange County (Figure. 11.5). It has an extremely variegated internal structure and centripetal locational tendencies, which testify to the powerful external economies that come from institutional fragmentation and spatial agglomeration within flexible production complexes (Scott 1988a).

Much of the growth of high-technology industry in Southern California can be ascribed to federal defense and space spending (Markusen et al. 1985; Schiesl 1984). The seven counties of Southern California receive 77.2 percent of the value of all prime contract awards in the state (Table 11.5). We can be reasonably confident that the aggregate trend line for awards mirrors more or less faithfully the trend for Southern California (Figure. 11.6). Employment in the high-technology industrial ensemble depends intimately on the level of statewide prime contract awards. The impact of defense spending goes far beyond the high-technology ensemble, because it has been estimated that, for every job created in California by direct military spending, 2.79 are created indirectly in the state (State of California 1982). Los Angeles County, with its abundance of aerospace manufacturers, receives the preponderance of defense contracts in the region (and presumably the state), followed by Orange County and San Diego County (Table 11.5).

Job Generation and Establishment Size

Flexible production systems often multiply external economies by the proliferation of specialized small establishments and stimulate relatively rapid growth of employment in small establishments. This sort of growth has been extremely vigorous in Southern California over the last decade and a half (Table 11.2).

Manufacturing establishments in Southern California were divided into three size categories: small (1–99 employees), medium (100–499 employees), and large (500 and more employees). Rates of employment growth for each category are inversely related to establishment size (Appendix, Table 11.6, Figure 11.7). Total employment increased 43.3 percent in the smallest establishment size category between 1970 and 1985, and decreased 4.9 percent in the largest. We should be extremely cautious about these comparisons, however, because of an inherent bias in the estimating procedure (Appendix). Given these qualifications, our findings are consistent with results reported by Birch (1979), whose more broadly based study of job generation patterns in the United States as a whole from 1969 to 1976 showed that employment grew most rapidly in the small firm segment of the economy.

The employment growth paths (Figure 11.7) are probably biased in their vertical relationship, but we can be a little more confident about the individu-

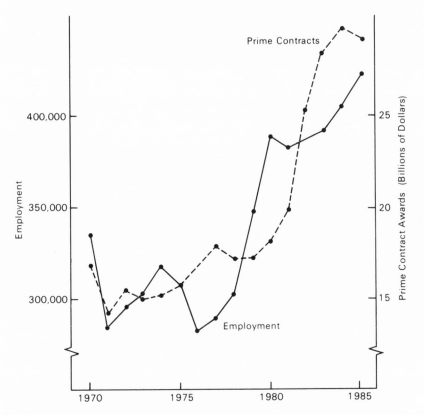

FIG. 11.6 Employment in the core high-technology industries of Southern California and Department of Defense prime contract awards in the state of California in constant 1985 dollars. Data source: *County Business Patterns* and Department of Defense, *Prime Contract Awards by State.*

al trends. The instability of employment levels rises as establishment size category increases. If we fit a simple time-series function to each trend line, the values of the standard error of the residuals increase significantly with increasing establishment size category. This finding runs counter to the common assumption that large (core) manufacturing establishments secure a niche facilitating comparatively stable growth of output (hence employment) levels, whereas small (peripheral) establishments are forced to accommodate to an extremely unstable pattern of output and employment growth (Berger and Piore 1980). In fact, the converse has been the case for Southern California manufacturing establishments in the recent past (Figure 11.7). The combined effects of differential employment cutbacks and expansions, including plant closures and openings, have had in aggregate a far greater periodic amplitude in the large establishment sector than in the small, but the notably stable employment expansion of the smallest establishment size category also is marked by high turnover rates both of establishments and of workers.

These results suggest a question for future investigation: to what degree does the comparatively vigorous growth of employment in small- and medium-sized manufacturing establishments in Southern California reflect increased uncertainty in final products markets and a consequent crisis for inflexible large and vertically integrated production units? The steadily expanding number of small- and medium-sized establishments in the region provides additional circumstantial evidence of the hypothesized intensification of flexible production in the local economy.

MANUFACTURING LABOR MARKETS

As manufacturing systems in the United States evolve away from Fordism, they are also associated with a restructuring of labor relations and labor markets (Kochan, Katz, and McKersie 1986). These changes present a number of difficult and largely unresolved questions. There are many indications that the current restructuring of labor relations and labor markets itself is part of the wider turn to flexibility, as marked by such phenomena as the increasing substitution of external for internal labor markets, declining rates of worker participation in labor unions, the increased incidence of short-term (as opposed to long-term) labor contracting, intensified job mobility even among skilled and highly paid workers, rising levels of part-time and temporary work, accelerating incursions of immigrant workers into unskilled occupations (thereby accentuating segmentation of labor markets), and so on.

Published data on most of these matters are not available for manufacturing labor markets in Southern California, but casual observations lend credibility to the speculation that manufacturing labor markets in the region are indeed shifting to flexible post-Fordist production arrangements. Two

TABLE 11.6   Manufacturing Employment Growth in Southern California by Establishment Size

Establishment Size Category	Total Employment		Change (%)
	1970	1985	
1–99	359,120	514,907	43.3
100–499	350,579	486,219	38.7
500+	411,661	391,540	−4.9

Source: Calculated from data in U.S. Department of Commerce, Bureau of the Census, County Business Patterns.

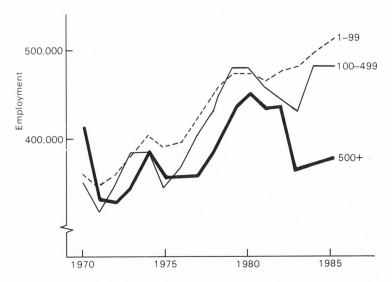

FIG. 11.7   Employment in Southern California manufacturing by establishment size, 1970–1985.

main groups of issues concern contractual features of the labor market and the social differentiation of workers.

Hours Worked, Wages, and Unionization

Available data do not allow us to consider turnover, job mobility, part-time work, and temporary work in the manufacturing labor markets of Southern California, but published statistical sources do enable us to examine three important variables.

First, the average annual number of hours worked per production worker in manufacturing has declined steadily since the early 1970s (Figure 11.8). Manufacturing production workers in the region worked 1,980 hours on average in 1970 and 1,919 hours in 1982, a drop of 3.1 percent. This trend is consistent with a similar trend in the U.S. economy. It may reflect a shortening of the normal working day or the normal working week, but it may also be due to increased labor turnover with more part-time and temporary work as permanent features of employment.

Second, average wage and salary levels (in constant dollars) of manufacturing employees in Southern California have fallen steadily since the early 1970s (Figure 11.9). Average constant-dollar remuneration fell 10.4 percent per production worker and 6.8 percent per nonproduction worker between 1970 and 1982. Declines of 2.9 percent and 1.3 percent were recorded in the United States for the same period. Manufacturing workers in Southern

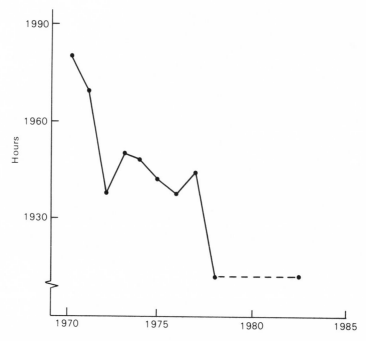

FIG. 11.8   Average annual number of hours worked by production workers in manufacturing in Southern California, 1970–1985. Data are not available for 1979, 1980, and 1981. Data source: *Annual Survey of Manufactures.*

California are increasingly unable to maintain the standard of living that they enjoyed ten or fifteen years ago, and their standard of living is falling more rapidly than among manufacturing workers in the country as a whole.

Third, manufacturing worker unionization rates in Southern California have declined dramatically over the last decade and a half in both absolute and relative terms. Data are available only for Los Angeles, Orange, and San Diego counties (Table 11.7). These counties contain the lion's share of manufacturing employment in the region, however, and they are representative of regional trends. Southern California again reflects a broad national trend, although more intensely. In Los Angeles, Orange, and San Diego counties, rates of union membership among manufacturing workers declined by 35.5 percent, 51.1 percent, and 50.8 percent, respectively, between 1970 and 1983, whereas the decline was 37.2 percent in the United States as a whole. Orange County, with its high-technology industrial complex dating only from the late 1950s and early 1960s, has by far the lowest rate of unionization of the three counties.

These data on labor hours, wages, and unionization rates, limited and

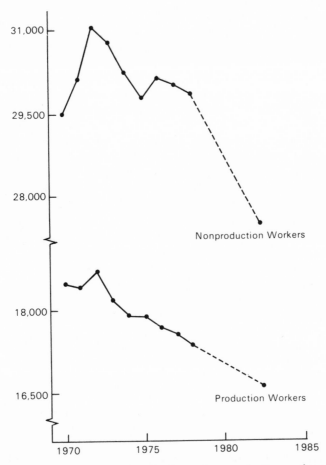

FIG. 11.9   Average annual pay of production and nonproduction workers in manufacturing in Southern California, 1970–1985, in constant 1982 dollars. Data are not available for 1979, 1980, and 1981. Data source: *Annual Survey of Manufactures*.

imperfect as they may be, suggest that manufacturing labor markets in Southern California have been restructured during the 1970s and early 1980s. This restructuring has involved a diminution of stable relatively high-wage forms of labor contracting underpinned to some degree by union agreements, and a corresponding expansion of unstable, low-wage, nonunionized jobs. These remarks are tentative, and more empirical research is necessary before they can be firmly advanced, but they are reinforced by data on the social structure of manufacturing labor markets.

Ethnicity, Race, and Gender

Labor markets in Southern California are dualistic and becoming more so. Especially in high-technology industrial sectors one occupational segment consists of high-wage managers and skilled technical workers, and the other consists of unskilled, low-wage workers. Workers in the lower segment face relatively high turnover rates and prolonged bouts of unemployment, although employment instability in the upper segment has also been increasing (Noyelle 1987). The lower segment is increasingly composed of immigrant and female workers, large numbers of whom, perhaps the majority, have no legal resident status in the United States (Maram, Long, and Berg 1980; Morales 1983; Muller and Espenshade 1985). The impact of the Immigration Reform and Control Act of 1986 is as yet unclear, but so far enforcement procedures apparently have been applied with less than full vigor.

In 1970, 219,314 manufacturing workers with Spanish surnames or Spanish as a first language comprised 19.8 percent of the total manufacturing labor force in Southern California, and 63,865 blacks comprised 5.8 percent. In 1980, 424,482 manufacturing workers of Spanish/Hispanic origin comprised 29.7 percent of the total manufacturing labor force, 81,297 Asians and Pacific Islanders comprised 5.7 percent, and 84,088 blacks comprised 5.9 percent. Changes in census definitions make comparisons difficult, but the number of immigrants (Hispanics and Asians especially) in the manufacturing labor force has certainly had a large absolute and proportional increase. The proportion of blacks has remained static. The number of female workers increased from 27.9 percent in 1970 to 32.5 percent in 1980. How are these different fractions accommodated within the manufacturing system? What are their interrelations on local manufacturing labor markets? To what degree do they complement or compete with one another?

We compiled data from the Public Use Microdata Sample census tapes for 1980 for selected social characteristics of the manufacturing labor force. Five variables were defined for nineteen industrial sectors: H_i (persons of Spanish/Hispanic origin), A_i (Asians and Pacific Islanders), B_i (blacks), I_i (persons who immigrated into the United States between 1975 and 1980), and F_i (females). Each is measured as a proportion of the labor force in the ith SIC category. With the exception of A_i and B_i these variables overlap to some degree, and their sum for any value of i is always greater than unity. We added a sixth variable, M_i, which stands for mean establishment size in the ith SIC category.

The correlation coefficients for every possible pair of these variables (Table 11.8) are summarized in a simple cluster analysis (Figure 11.10). The lines indicate positive correlations with a significance of 0.05 or better. The basic structure of intercorrelation clearly identifies two major dimensions. One cluster of four variables indicates strong positive relationships between Hispanics, Asians, immigrants, and females. A simple two-variable cluster

TABLE 11.8   Correlation Matrix of Manufacturing Labor Force Characteristics[a]

	H_i	A_i	B_i	I_i	F_i
A_i	−0.02				
B_i	−0.51*	−0.95			
I_i	0.94*	0.21	−0.62*		
F_i	0.43*	0.73*	−0.44*	0.63*	
M_i	−0.33*	−0.01	0.59*	−0.33	0.21

[a] H_i = Spanish/Hispanic origin; A_i = Asians and Pacific Islanders; B_i = blacks; I_i = immigrants 1975–80; F_i = females; M_i = mean establishment size; n = 19.
*significance of 0.05 or better.

indicates significant covariation between blacks and establishment size. Manufacturing labor markets in Southern California are split between recent immigrants, concentrated in small manufacturing establishments, and blacks, who are underrepresented in all manufacturing sectors, but are more likely to be employed in large establishments.

Hispanics, Asians, immigrants, and females are associated with textiles, apparel, furniture, leather, electrical/electronic equipment, and instruments (Table 11.9). Blacks are more clearly associated with petroleum products, primary metals, and transportation equipment (with a fairly even split between the automobile and aircraft sectors). The first group had two distinctive subsets: Hispanics and immigrants were associated with furniture and leather industries, and Asians and females were associated with the electrical/electronic equipment and instruments industries. The textile and apparel industries are equally associated with Hispanics and Asians.

These extremely preliminary results obviously call for more rigorous empirical research, but three broad conclusions may be cautiously advanced. First, many small-scale labor-intensive craft specialty sectors (spilling over into the high-technology industrial ensemble) seem to prefer recent immigrants or women as employees. Second, Hispanics dominate the labor force in certain low-technology sectors, whereas Asians dominate some high-technology sectors. This division may be a result of differential skills and cultural attributes, or it may simply reflect locations of particular kinds of workplaces relative to particular kinds of neighborhoods. Third, blacks are employed in manufacturing predominantly in sectors that are dominated by large establishments or that are closely allied to the mass production ensemble. The relatively greater incidence of labor unions and affirmative action programs in such establishments has helped to shield blacks from competition as a result of the immigration of large numbers of low-wage unskilled workers.

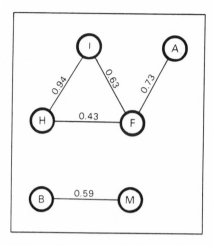

FIG. 11.10   Cluster analysis of minority groups in the manufacturing labor force
(see Table 11.8). The lines represent positive correlation coefficients with
significance of 0.05 or better. I = immigrants 1975–1980, A = Asians and Pacific
Islanders, H = Spanish/Hispanic origin, F = females, B = blacks, and M = mean
establishment size.

Bailey (1987) and Muller and Espenshade (1985) have claimed that
blacks and recent immigrants do not compete with each other in labor markets in the United States. Initially this notion might seem to apply in Southern
California, where the total manufacturing labor force increased by 29.9 percent between 1970 and 1980 and the total number of blacks in the labor force
increased by 31.7 percent. Furthermore, recent immigrants and blacks do
work in different industrial sectors, which might suggest that each group is
active on different labor markets. Nevertheless, we interpret the sectoral split
in employment patterns as a direct expression of competition between the
two groups. We suggest that the employment of blacks in manufacturing
would have been much greater than it currently is in the absence of Hispanic
and Asian immigration, but it would have been significantly diminished even
here in the absence of institutional restraints on the operation of labor markets in certain large establishment sectors.

A simple logistic regression analysis of B_i against I_i shows that

$$B_i = 1/[1 + 11.534exp(3.340I_i)]$$
$$R^2 = 0.44; F = 13.34; d.f. = 1,17;$$

with an overall level of statistical significance greater than 0.01. This equation
has no direct causal meaning, but it suggests that blacks are underrepresented
in sectors that immigrants have successfully invaded. Blacks constitute a
legally legitimate fraction of the citizenry of the United States and, given their

TABLE 11.9   Dominant Social Characteristics of Two-Digit Manufacturing Sectors, Southern California, 1980[a]

Standard Industrial Classification	Spanish/ Hispanic Origin	Asians and Pacific Islanders	Blacks	Immigrants 1975–80	Females
20 Food and kindred products	*	*	*	*	*
22 Textile mill products	*	*		*	
23 Apparel and other textile products	*	**		**	**
25 Furniture and fixtures	*			*	
29 Petroleum and coal products			*		
31 Leather and leather products	**			**	*
33 Primary metal industries			*		
36 Electric and electronic equipment		*			*
37 Transportation equipment			*		
38 Instruments and related products		*			*

Note: SICs 21, 24, 26, 27, 28, 30, 32, 34, 35, and 39 have been omitted from this table because they have no significantly dominant social group.

Source: Computed from *Census of Population,* Public-Use Microdata Sample Tapes, 1980.

[a] The table is derived as follows: Calculate for the ith SIC category the proportion (x_{ij}) of its workers in the jth social group; one asterisk indicates that $x_{ij} = m_j + 0.75U_j$, and two asterisks indicate that $x_{ij} = m_j + 1.50U_j$, where (a) m_j is the mean of the jth column vector $(x_{1j}, x_{2j} \ldots x_{nj})$, and (b) U_j is the standard deviation of the same vector.

recent history, both individually and collectively they have a developed consciousness of their civil rights. Recent immigrants, however (especially the large proportion that is undocumented), have little such consciousness and they are marginalized politically both in society at large and in the workplace. They are thus (in practice and in the perception of employers) more likely than blacks to tolerate inferior working conditions, authoritarian labor relations, and low wages (including wages below the legal minimum). Thus, even where immigrants and blacks are equally unskilled, employers are more likely to select immigrants in preference to blacks unless institutional restraints interfere. Immigrants are concentrated in labor-intensive small establishment sectors, where such restraints are presumably least developed, and blacks, in contrast, are most frequently employed in large establishment sectors where such restraints are best developed. Blacks represented only 5.8 percent of the manufacturing labor force in 1970, and still only 5.9 percent in 1980, despite persistently high levels of unemployment among the black population. Orange County, which is one of the most intensely industrialized and rapidly growing counties of the region, had a population in 1980 that was 14.8 percent Hispanic and 4.5 percent Asian and Pacific Islander, but only 1.3

percent black. Our reasoning suggests why blacks are the only one of these three social groups to have been excluded to a significant degree from participation in Orange County's growth.

POLICY ISSUES

A series of problems has developed in Southern California as the craft specialty and high-technology manufacturing systems have grown. These problems threaten the viability of manufacturing in the region, and they call urgently for evaluation and remedial action. Four clusters of policy issues seem especially significant: technological innovation, local labor markets, dependence on federal defense contracts, and problems of governance and regulation.

Technological Innovation

Technological innovation frequently demands large developmental expenses for outcomes that are extremely uncertain. Large firms are typically able to absorb such risky expenses, but small firms often fail to pursue innovative possibilities that could be highly profitable. This problem is an exacerbated case of market failure due to impacted information; only by making a certain investment can a firm find out what it needs to know in order to assess the costs and benefits of that investment. The net result is that pure market mechanisms alone may produce suboptimal rates of technological (and commercial) innovation, even within flourishing industrial districts. The problem is compounded where firms are tempted to adopt the (self-defeating) stance of a free rider, and thus to postpone action indefinitely.

Firms sometimes form strategic alliances or research and development cartels in order to spread the costs of risky investments. Even this type of response, however, is often less than socially optimal, especially where many small firms predominate and where their capability for prealliance scanning and information-gathering activities is limited. Because of these predicaments, governmental authorities in many parts of the world have instituted agencies for technology information exchange and innovation. The activities of MITI in Japan and the newly inaugurated program of regional centers for innovation and technology transfer (CRITTs) in France are exemplary (Johnson 1982; OECD 1986).

The manufacturing economy of Southern California would benefit enormously from similar institutional arrangements. Such arrangements could assist in the promotion of innovative ideas, and in mediating information exchanges among groups of firms, as well as between firms and university researchers. The capital market imperfections that impede innovative activity must also be corrected. Such markets have structural biases against small firms. The risks unique to these firms impede their participation in debt and equity markets (in which innovation is treated like any other business investment) and even venture capital markets (which are biased in favor of larger firms) (Daniels 1982; U.S. Department of Commerce 1979). A number of states now provide equity financing to small innovators, as exemplified by the Connecticut Product Development Corporation or the New York Corporation for Innovative Development (Schwandt and Wilson 1987). Southern California needs similar programs.

Local Labor Markets

Craft specialty production and high-technology industry in Southern California rely to an increasing degree on flexible external labor markets, which suggests that labor skills are becoming less firm-specific and more sector- and agglomeration-specific. The formation of labor skills is almost certainly, as a corollary, becoming more socialized; it is being detached from employment experiences in any specific firm. The result is greater opportunities and the need for educational institutions and programs to train workers at every level, from sewing and cutting skills for the garment industry to advanced engineering and scientific education for high-technology industry.

Large-scale immigration of low-wage workers (especially undocumented workers) into Southern California is also a problem. The lower expectations of many immigrants regarding wages and working conditions squeeze blacks out of labor markets in which they might otherwise have a strong presence. This situation helps to keep a ceiling on wage levels, thus enabling Southern California manufacturers to compete with foreign producers, but at high social cost. It also highlights major unresolved issues concerning the 1986 Immigration Reform and Control Act. Vigorous enforcement of the act, by penalizing manufacturers who employ illegal immigrants, would drive up production costs and hence reduce competitiveness, but continued tolerance of infractions will deprive many blacks and other legitimate citizens of much needed employment. No easy solution of this dilemma is evident.

Federal Contracts

The economy of Southern California is nowhere more vulnerable than in its heavy dependence on federal defense and space contracts. Changes in the political climate, such as budget crises, shifts in macroeconomic policy, or international agreements to reduce armaments, can and do cause severe downswings in local employment. The problem is intensified by the large numbers of suppliers to defense and space prime contractors; the negative effects of cutbacks are multiplied many times over. Although much of the economy of Southern California is extremely competitive internally, externally it faces a monopsonistic buyer in the federal government.

This dependence on military and space program markets creates a further weakness. The economic security of these markets, with cost-plus pricing for major contractors, entices many firms away from the pursuit of less lucrative forms of business (Reich 1987), and reduces the variety and innovative capacity of the local manufacturing system. Policies designed to wean the economy of the region away from its dependence on defense contracts should be on the political agenda. The booming markets of the Pacific Rim countries provide a major opportunity for the expansion of non-defense-related production in Southern California.

Problems of Governance and Regulation

Most of the problems of Southern California have their roots in market failures and in the inadequacy of established mechanisms of governance and regulation. These problems are particularly pressing in view of the size of the economy of the region.

First, the effective operation of business communities and local labor markets depends on a subtle but potent balance between competition and cooperation (Storper and Scott 1989). The Southern California economy has a surplus of competition and a serious deficit of cooperation. Institutionalized coordination of economic activity is underdeveloped, whether by voluntary organizations or governmental agencies. An example of voluntary organization is the SPRINT telematic network in Prato, Italy; all participants in the Pratese woolen textile industry are tied together into an efficient transactional system. An example of governmental agencies is the CRITT program in France; local innovation centers provide money and advice to small and technologically inventive firms.

Second, the Southern California manufacturing system depends on collective intervention in such matters as infrastructure provision, land-use controls, traffic management, and the coordination of development. The industries of Southern California have a strong propensity to form localized industrial districts and dense technopoles. Some areas gain property tax windfalls due to growth, but other areas suffer negative externalities from the very same growth. The most serious negative externalities are traffic congestion, housing shortages, and intensifying land-use conflicts. These have sparked active slow-growth political movements in the region. Local municipal government is so fragmented that it cannot deal with these spatial imbalances at an appropriate scale. The counties—in conformity with California practice—have only those functions that cities reject. Locally federated structures (e.g., the Southern California Association of Governments [SCAG] and the San Diego Association of Governments [SANDAG]) lack legal authority to undertake development programs or to regulate minor jurisdictions.

The region needs an agency with powers of governance and regulation to steer the economy and the human settlement system toward a prosperous, orderly, and equitable future.

The rapid growth of the industrial system of Southern California over the last couple of decades has been based in large degree on post-Fordist, flexible forms of industrialization, and above all on revitalized craft specialty production and high-technology industry. Despite their varied sectoral makeup, these two production ensembles share important structural traits. Significant groups of producers within them have flexibly specialized production techniques, deep social divisions of labor, and volatile local labor markets. These ensembles also have a marked tendency to locational agglomeration, as demonstrated by a system of dense industrial districts in and around the central core of Los Angeles, and by a set of burgeoning technopoles scattered across Southern California. These two industrial ensembles, along with services, represent the major driving force of the post-Fordist economy of Los Angeles.

Southern California has evolved into the premier industrial region of North America and the major focus of immigration into the United States, but it is divided by deep socioeconomic cleavages. Great citadels of international capitalism lie cheek-by-jowl with squalid sweatshops employing undocumented immigrants, and great power and privilege are alongside poverty, powerlessness, and marginality. The inequalities and tensions have intensified since the 1970s, and we might well ask if this situation does not contain the seeds of future explosions like the Watts riots of 1965. Can effective policies be put into place to ensure continued rapid economic growth and a more equitable distribution of the benefits of that growth? These goals are not incompatible; they can be reinforcing.

Southern California is the most advanced case of post-Fordist industrialization in the United States, if not in the world. Its economic and social development, and the policies that steer its course, are a great experiment in the construction of new geographical realities. We have described some of the economic foundations of this experiment, and some of the policy problems that it poses. There remains the more intractable and equally important question of the logic of social life in the post-Fordist megalopolis and its cultural and ideological representation.

APPENDIX

Calculation of Employment Growth

Three establishment size categories were defined: small (1–99 employees), medium (100–499 employees), and large (500 and more employees). Manufacturing employment growth for the period 1970 to 1985 was computed from the public-use computer tapes of *County Business Patterns*, which list the number of establishments in employment size bands in each county. Total employment for each size band (except the largest) was estimated for each county by multiplying the median value of its band by the number of establishments. Employment in the largest (and open-ended) size band was estimated as the residual $x_L = E - \Sigma X_i$, where E is total employment in manufacturing (as given by *County Business Patterns*) and X_i is estimated employment in the ith band. The computed results were then aggregated into the three size categories. This method overestimates employment in small size categories and underestimates in the large. We should be cautious in using the data (Table 11.6, Figure 11.7), but any bias presumably is fairly constant from year to year for each size category, and the general trends are probably reliable.

ACKNOWLEDGMENT

This paper was originally commissioned by the Institute of Industrial Relations, University of California-Los Angeles, and presented at the Institute's conference "Can California Be Competitive and Caring?" It was supported by National Science Foundation grant SES 8812828.

REFERENCES

Aglietta, M. 1976. *A theory of capitalist regulation*. London: New Left Books.

Bailey, T. R. 1987. *Immigrant and native workers: Contrasts and competition*. Boulder, Colo.: Westview Press.

Becattini, G. 1987. Introduzione: Il distretto industriale marshalliano: Cronaca di un ritrovamento. In *Mercato e forze locali*. Edited by G. Becattini. Bologna: Il Mulino.

Berger, S., and M. Piore. 1980. *Dualism and discontinuity in industrial societies*. New York: Cambridge University Press.

Birch, D. L. 1979. *The job generation process*. Cambridge, Mass.: MIT Program on Neighborhood and Regional Change.

Boyer, R. 1986. *La théorie de la régulation*. Paris: La Découverte.

Cohen, S. S., and J. Zysman. 1987. *Manufacturing matters: The myth of the post-industrial economy*. New York: Basic Books.

Daniels, B. 1982. Capital is only part of the problem. In *Mobilizing capital: Program innovation and the changing public/private interface in development finance*. Edited by P. J. Bearse. New York: Elsevier.

Harvey, D., and A. J. Scott. 1989. The practice of human geography: Theory and empirical specificity in the transition from Fordism to flexible accumulation. In *Remodelling geography*. Edited by W. MacMillan. Oxford: Basil Blackwell.

Johnson, C. A. 1982. *MITI and the Japanese miracle: The growth of industrial policy, 1925–1975*. Stanford, Calif.: Stanford University Press.

Kochan, T. A., H. C. Katz, and R. B. McKersie. 1986. *The transformation of American industrial relations*. New York: Basic Books.

Maram, S. L., S. Long, and D. Berg. 1980. *Hispanic workers in the garment and restaurant industries in Los Angeles County*. Working Papers in United States-Mexican Studies, No. 12. San Diego: University of California Program in United States-Mexican Studies.

Markusen, A., G. Clark, C. Curtis, S. Deitrick, G. Fields, A. Henny, E. Ingersoll, J. Levin, W. Patton, J. Ross, and J. Schneider. 1985. Military spending and urban development in California. *Berkeley Planning Journal* 1: 54–68.

Morales, R. 1983. Transitional labor: Undocumented workers in the Los Angeles automobile industry. *International Labor Migration Review* 17: 570–96.

Muller, T., and T. J. Espenshade. 1985. *The fourth wave: California's newest immigrants.* Washington, D.C.: The Urban Institute Press.

Noyelle, T. J. 1987. *Beyond industrial dualism.* Boulder, Colo.: Westview Press.

Noyelle, T. J., and T. M. Stanback. 1983. *The economic transformation of American cities.* Totowa, N.J.: Rowman and Allanheld.

OECD. 1986. *La politique d'innovation en France.* Paris: Organization for Economic Cooperation and Development.

Piore, M., and C. Sable. 1984. *The second industrial divide.* New York: Basic Books.

Reich, R. B. 1987. *Tales of a new America.* New York: Times Books.

Schiesl, M. J. 1984. Airplanes to aerospace: Defense spending and economic growth in the Los Angeles region, 1945–60. In *The martial metropolis: U.S. cities in war and peace.* Edited by R. W. Lotchin. New York: Praeger.

Schmandt, J., and R. Wilson. 1987. *Promoting high technology industry: Incentives and policies for state governments.* Boulder, Colo.: Westview Press.

Scott, A. J. 1988a. *Metropolis: From the division of labor to urban form.* Berkeley, Calif.: University of California Press.

———. 1988b. *New industrial spaces: Flexible production organization and regional development in North America and Western Europe.* London: Pion.

Soja, E. W., R. Morales, and G. Wolff. 1983. Urban restructuring: An analysis of social and spatial change in Los Angeles. *Economic Geography* 59: 195–230.

Soja, E. W., and A. J. Scott. 1986. Los Angeles: Capital of the late twentieth century. *Environment and Planning D: Society and Space* 4: 249–54.

State of California. 1982. *The effect of increased military spending in California.* Sacramento: Department of Economic and Business Development, Office of Economic Policy, Planning, and Research.

Storper, M., and C. Chrisopherson. 1987. Flexible specialization and regional industrial agglomeration: The case of the U.S. motion picture industry. *Annals of the Association of American Geographers* 77: 104–17.

Storper, M., and A. J. Scott. 1989. The geographical foundations and social regulation of flexible production complexes. In *The power of geography: How territory shapes social life.* Edited by J. Wolch and M. Dear. Boston: Allen and Unwin.

Teitz, M. B. 1984. The California economy: Changing structure and policy responses. *California Policy Responses* 1: 37–59.

U.S. Department of Commerce. 1979. *Final Reports.* Advisory Committee on Industrial Innovation.

TWELVE

Futures of American Cities

John R. Borchert

With their richly varying views of the country's urban settlement fabric, the preceding chapters in this volume have suggested the themes of my essay—American cities are much bigger and more complex than ever; we have entered a new epoch in the evolution of the American urban system in which complexity is growing at an increasing rate; and that fact poses an endlessly exciting need for geographical study.

THE EVOLVING URBAN SYSTEM

The American settlement system, like any open system, has structure, flows, and a process of structural change. The geographical structure is described and defined on maps that show resources, places, and routes of circulation on the face of the earth. Geographical flows are depicted on maps of trade and travel. Maps of resources, routes, and places at successive times show the process of change in geographical structure; and maps of flows of resources and population reflect underlying causes of the change. Maps define the geographical settlement system at many scales, ranging from local to regional to national to continental and global.

In a way, maps of the settlement system are diagrams at geographical scales of a large, complex machine created to facilitate the human use of the earth. The settlement machine is distinctive, of course, because its internal parts include people, whose innovations make the machine self-redesigning in evolutionary, unpredictable ways. The immediate purpose of the machine is to produce goods, services, and knowledge, but the ultimate purpose is to improve the quality of human life on earth.

American places are nodes at junctions of routes in the circulation network. They range in size from farmsteads and viewpoints in wildlife preserves, or one- or two-person hamlets such as Node, Wyoming, or Alzada, Montana, to the more than three hundred metropolitan areas, to the conurbations of metropolitan areas surrounding New York and Los Angeles. I will focus on the metropolitan areas and conurbations. Measures of the importance of these places are their size, their functions in the system, their wealth, and many other related characteristics of their populations.

The sizes and functions of urban nodes in the circulation network are sensitive to changes in the technology of transportation and communication because cities are centers of assembly, processing, exchange, and distribution (Borchert 1967). Several innovations have had profound effects on the location of growth within the national system and on the pattern of growth within individual metropolitan areas—the large-scale introduction of steam power in both land and water transportation around the 1830 census; the onset of low-priced, large-scale steel production, followed by central-station electric power, in the 1870s and 1880s; and the large-scale application of the internal combustion engine around 1920. Those events were in no sense simple determinants of all that followed, but they are major landmarks in the complex development of the system.

The innovations in circulation technology are reflected in critical points on curves of rail mileage, general cargo tonnage on the inland waterways, production of primary energy from water power, coal and oil, motor vehicles, highway mileage, and many other measures of the national circulation system (Figure 12.1). These critical dates marked times of transition between distinctive epochs in American urban development, which I labeled Wagon-Sail, Iron Horse/Steam Packet, Steel Rail, and Auto-Air (Borchert 1967). From the early applications of steam through the end of cheap domestic oil in the 1960s and 1970s, the epochs were marked by American energy self-sufficiency and gradual reduction in the real cost of energy raw materials. The auto–air–cheap oil epoch also saw the large-scale introduction of radio and intercity telephone, which, for the first time, liberated mass media and two-way communication from transportation technology. Both became essentially instantaneous and to some extent independent of traditional literacy.

A pattern of metropolitan areas evolved along with the national circulation system (Figure 12.2). By 1870 the rail-waterway network of the pre–Civil War North had opened the rich resources of the Pennsylvania coal fields and the Midwestern glacial drift plains; all of the great twentieth-century cities of the northeastern quadrant of the country were on the map. By 1920 a nationwide steel rail network had opened every resource region, and today's system of cities was in place (Figure 12.3). By 1970 the greatest internal

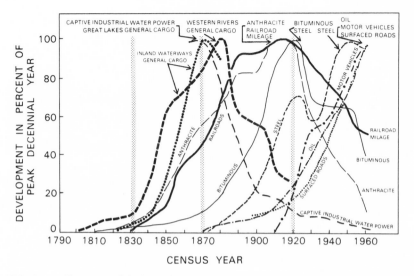

FIG. 12.1 The rise and decline of ten indicators of the technology of transport and industrial energy. Peak values concentrate around the census years 1870 and 1920. Source: Borchert 1967, 302.

migration in American history had shifted sixty million people from rural areas to cities. The Census Bureau had officially recognized metropolitan areas, and more than one hundred urban areas had grown to metropolitan size. Meanwhile, some of the larger and more closely spaced metropolitan areas expanded into one another's commuter reaches to form massive conurbations. At the end of the 1970s, twenty-seven major conurbations were on the map, with about 16 percent of the nation's land and nearly two-thirds of its people (Figure 12.3, Table 12.1).

A kind of prototype, or average, internal metropolitan geography evolved during this same series of historical epochs. A primary node developed at a historic convergence point of regional transportation routes. Age rings reflected the amount of growth around the primary node in the periods dominated by different circulation technologies, with coincidental distinctive characteristics of the population. The rings are suggested on the map that shows the population increments at major metropolitan areas during each epoch (Figure 12.4). Sectors were differentiated along and between the routes that radiated from the primary node toward distant places. New secondary nodes were defined by the intersections of radial and circumferential routes. Eventually new realms focused on the newer nodes and created a new, truly multicentered, metropolis (Vance 1991). These development patterns, in turn, have provided the framework for migration and commuting; neighborhoods, communities, segregation, and congregation; succession, turnover, filtering, and vacancy chains; work and recreation; deterioration, abandonment, preservation, clearance, redevelopment, and environmental management (Palm 1981; Johnston 1982). The result is the evolution of a schematic map of land use, land values, and population with our well-known patterns, labels, and images of urban places.

While these patterns were evolving, the population grew, but, more important, the aggregate national wealth grew even faster. The greatly increased accessibility of everyplace to everyplace else accelerated exchange, resource use, productivity, and gross national product per capita.

In the railroad epochs, both the national and the internal geographic patterns were conducive to rather simple schematic description. Cities were ordered by size and spacing based on their position in the rail pattern. The rail pattern, in turn, reflected natural resource concentrations—natural harbors and waterways, fertile plains, mineral wealth, forests, and, as wealth increased, beaches and scenery. The urbanizing population had to concentrate at major rail nodes, and these locations were stable. Local farm trade centers were limited in spacing by the range of wagon transportation from the railways. This range was essentially constant, independent of advances in railroad technology. Inside the cities the pattern was organized by the regional railroad and internal streetcar corridors, focusing on the central business district. The whole system was strongly hierarchical, stable, self-reinforcing. Furthermore, the geometry of the system provided a convenient framework for organizing information and theorizing about migration and social stratification.

That system received its first severe jolt in the auto-air-cheap oil epoch, for well-known reasons. Mobile heavy machinery, the dense, ubiquitous road network, air transport, and affluence were major culprits. In concert they refocused the resource-based settlement from primary production to recreation. They reversed the values of rough and flat land for many development purposes. The highway network came to provide direct connections between each place and all others virtually everywhere in the country. Automotive circulation shattered the hierarchies that had been based on railroad and streetcar corridors, networks, junctions, and wagon cargo collection points. Ubiquitous radio and telephone communications added strength to this initial assault on hierarchy.

A NEW EPOCH

In this framework of transportation and communication technology we apparently entered a new epoch in the 1970s. The key elements were more costly energy together with electronic and jet propulsion technologies.

America's historic energy self-sufficiency and long-term decline in outlay for energy raw materials reversed dramatically after 1970. Political events in the Middle East in the early 1970s focused the timing, but well-known, long-term changes in the geography of global oil reserves had set the

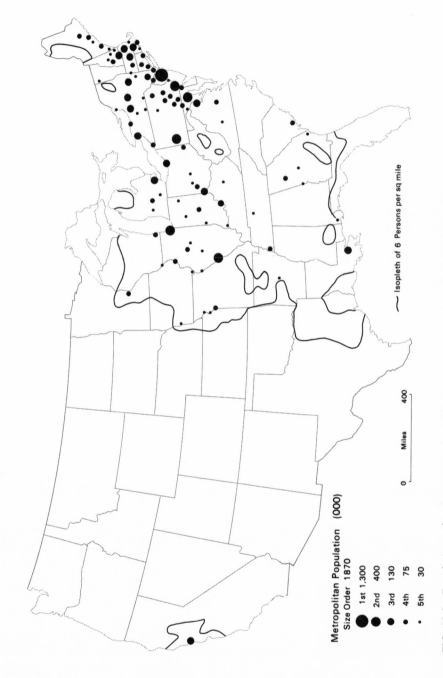

Metropolitan Population (000)
Size Order 1870

1st 1,300
2nd 400
3rd 130
4th 75
5th 30

~ Isopleth of 6 Persons per sq mile

0 ____ Miles ____ 400

FIG. 12.2 Populations of major cities and neighboring counties, 1870. Source: Borchert 1967, 317.

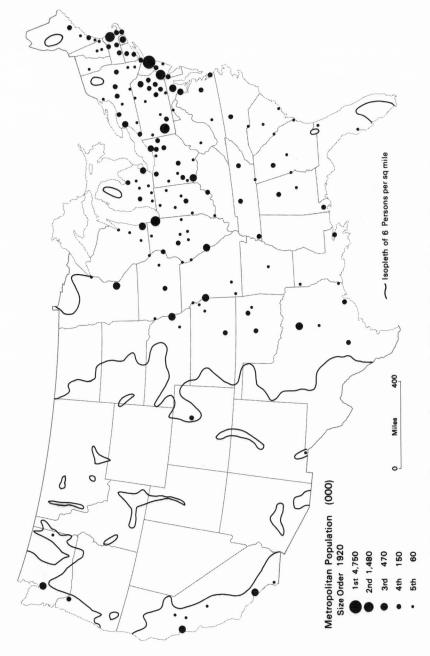

Metropolitan Population (000)
Size Order 1920

1st 4,750

2nd 1,480

3rd   470

4th   150

5th   60

— Isopleth of 6 Persons per sq mile

0   Miles   400

FIG. 12.3   Populations of emerging metropolitan areas in 1920, at the end of the steel rail epoch. Source: Borchert 1967, 318.

TABLE 12.1   Populations of the 1980 High-order Conurbations at the Censuses for 1920, 1970, 1980, and 1987, and Projected Populations for 2025

High-Order Conurbation	Populations in Millions				
	1920	1970	1980	1987	2025
Atlanta	1,106	2,492	3,083	3,594	5,224
Baltimore–Washington	1,939	5,563	5,974	6,539	7,992
Boston	5,003	8,107	8,247	8,439	8,941
Buffalo–Rochester–Syracuse	2,438	3,115	3,010	3,995	5,300
Carolina Piedmont	1,600	3,589	4,208	5,470	8,250
Chicago–Milwaukee	5,142	10,981	11,215	11,323	11,859
Cincinnati–SW Ohio	2,199	4,447	4,631	4,774	5,268
Cleveland–Pittsburgh	4,932	7,892	7,683	7,420	6,747
Dallas–Ft. Worth	964	2,588	3,212	4,055	6,223
Denver–Colorado Piedmont	542	1,440	2,350	2,699	4,557
Detroit–Southern Michigan	3,452	8,862	9,092	9,044	9,391
Houston	678	2,936	3,979	4,567	6,977
New Orleans	1,420	3,530	4,263	4,576	6,126
Indianapolis	1,338	2,334	2,431	2,464	2,662
Kansas City	1,196	1,934	2,026	2,107	2,367
Los Angeles–San Diego	1,302	11,603	14,100	16,098	22,751
Miami–Ft. Lauderdale	75	2,316	3,372	3,961	6,390
Minneapolis–St. Paul	1,117	2,344	2,610	2,820	3,527
New York	9,818	19,376	18,798	19,367	19,410
Phoenix–Southern Arizona	190	1,458	2,236	2,819	4,827
Philadelphia	5,180	7,989	8,129	8,360	8,929
Portland	589	1,728	2,164	2,254	3,033
St. Louis	1,406	2,536	2,492	2,513	2,486
San Francisco–Oakland–San Jose	1,518	6,405	7,489	8,548	11,722
Seattle–Tacoma	777	2,195	2,592	2,911	3,971
Tampa–St. Petersburg	318	2,734	4,110	5,270	9,012
Virginia Tidewater	731	1,773	1,926	2,226	2,898
Total High-Order Conurbations	56,970	132,231	145,422	158,213	195,608
Total "Isolated" Metro Areas	19,686	37,605	43,409	46,702	68,567
Rest of United States (Nonmetro)	29,805	35,216	38,926	38,858	39,663

Note: The projections assume that the average decennial rate of change in share of U.S. population in each conurbation from 1970 to 1987 will persist until 2025. United States population for 2025 was assumed to be the Middle Series projection by the U.S. Bureau of the Census, published in the *Statistical Abstract of the United States 1987*, Table 14. Conurbations are outlined in Figure 12.4. Isolated metropolitan areas are the census Metropolitan Statistical Areas outside the high-order conurbations. Census areas for the isolated MSAs have been modified to include counties inside the 5 percent commuting lines of Berry and Gillard (1977).

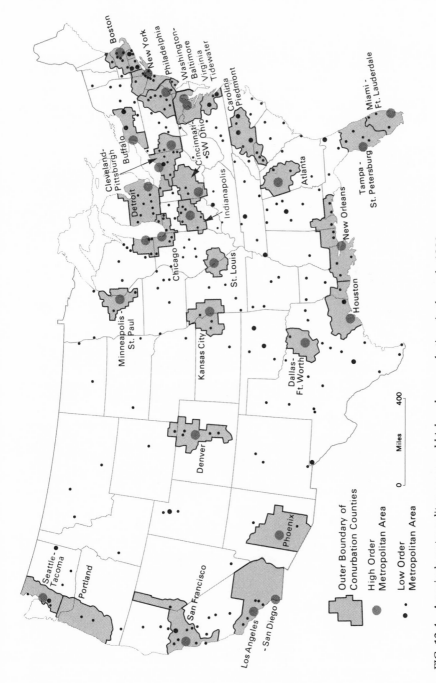

FIG. 12.4 America's metropolitan areas and high-order conurbations in the early 1980s.

Boston
New York
Philadelphia
Washington-
Baltimore
Virginia
Tidewater

Carolina
Piedmont

Miami-
Ft. Lauderdale

Cleveland-
Pittsburgh
Buffalo

Cincinnati-
SW Ohio

Atlanta

Tampa-
St. Petersburg

Detroit

Indianapolis

New Orleans

Chicago

St. Louis

Houston

Minneapolis-
St. Paul

Kansas City

Dallas-
Ft. Worth

Denver

Seattle-
Tacoma

Portland

Phoenix

San Francisco

Los Angeles
-San Diego

Outer Boundary of
Conurbation Counties

High Order
Metropolitan Area

Low Order
Metropolitan Area

0   400
   Miles

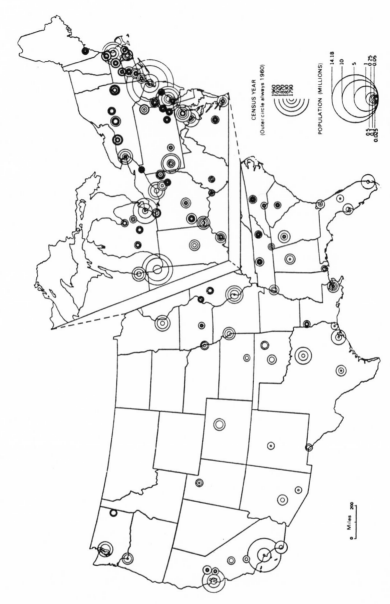

CENSUS YEAR
(Outer circle always 1960)

POPULATION (MILLIONS)

14·18
10
5
0.25
0.05
0.1
0.05

o Miles 200

FIG. 12.5   The varied historical layering of American metropolitan areas in 1960. Source: Borchert 1967, 326.

stage (Schurr et al. 1960; Cook 1971; Darmstadter 1972). Increased efficiency in processing and distribution has so far sheltered consumers from the higher cost of energy raw materials, but the trend during the 1970s and 1980s suggests that the energy raw material price curve reversed even more sharply than projections indicated at the time of the 1970s oil crisis (Figure 12.5). The shift to massive global imports and the adoption of very large vessels and port facilities have been accompanied by well-known environmental costs, by increases in development and transportation costs, by indirect costs of enlarged sensitivity and fear in the American people's image of their military and diplomatic position in the Middle East, and by costs of uncertainty, false starts, and failures in the development of alternative energy sources.

The country appears to be well into a period of relatively high-cost transition in energy technology. The transition is likely to last at least into the second or third decade of the next century. It will surely but fitfully stimulate the replacement of fossil fuel technology and eventually lead to yet another new epoch. Meanwhile, the uncertainty of future energy resources resulted almost immediately in greater efficiency of automotive fuel use (Figure 12.6), and it probably will be reflected in a multiplicity of experiments in energy-related urban development styles.

A sharp increase in the importance of the country's overseas commerce has followed a long transition to self-sufficiency both in commodities and in industrial products during the period of complacent isolation in the auto–cheap oil epoch (Figure 12.7). World War II briefly interrupted the complacency but not the self-sufficiency, although it surely hastened the end of the epoch. Energy imports account for only about half of the growth of overseas trade in the new epoch. The rest reflects the general increase in international interaction of all kinds in the satellite-electronic-jet propulsion age.

A major information explosion has coincided with developments in satellite and electronic technologies. The rapid emergence of global, two-way conversation, video, and color image transmission has brought an unprecedented acceleration of global interaction. Look, for example, at the growth of American overseas cable, radio, and phone messages since 1970 (Figure 12.8), and the growth of interaction between cities on the domestic scene (Figure 12.9), or the consumption of paper for record keeping, correspondence, magazines, and advertising circulars that has accompanied television, computing, word processing, and desktop publishing (Figure 12.10).

The information explosion has produced a massive information overload at all levels—individuals and organizations; advanced societies and those less developed; and institutions responsible for managing the resource and settlement system, from the simplest tribes to the most sophisticated national governments and business corporations. All institutions, cultures, and conceptual frameworks have been opened to question. Institutions and individuals can use only a fraction of the information that buries them. They have

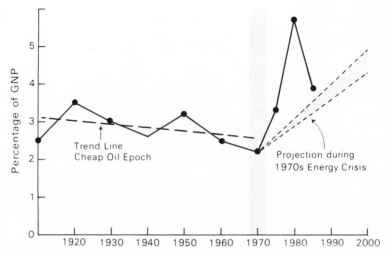

FIG. 12.6   Long-term trends in the cost of U.S. energy raw materials. Sources: for 1970 and earlier, Borchert 1981, 43; after 1970, *Statistical Abstract of the United States 1988*, Tables 910, 1159, and 1165.

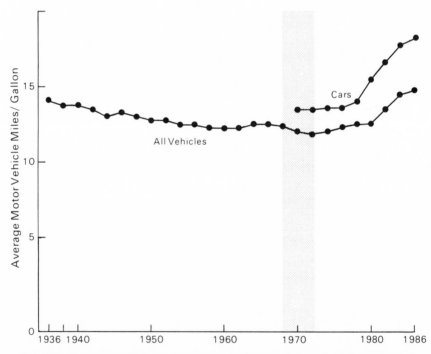

FIG. 12.7   Increased efficiency in response to the uncertain outlook for motor fuel cost and supply. Sources: 1970-1986, *Statistical Abstract of the United States 1988*, Table 1003; 1936-1969, *Historical Statistics of the United States*, Series Q 148-162.

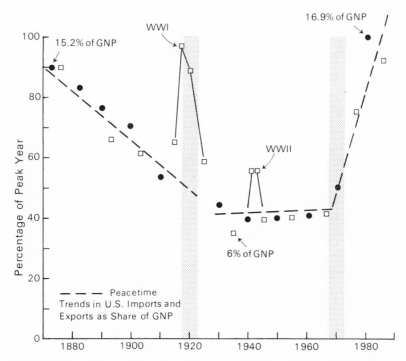

FIG. 12.8   Peacetime trends and wartime anomalies in total value of U.S. imports and exports expressed in percentage of gross national product. Sources: *Historical Statistics of the United States*, Series U 317-352; *Statistical Abstract of the United States 1988*, Table 1349.

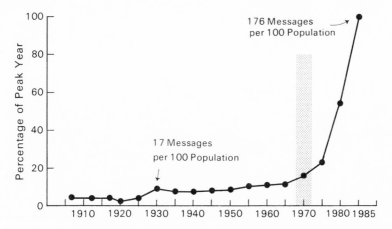

FIG. 12.9   Long-term trend in overseas messages (cable, radio, telephone) per capita of resident U.S. population. Sources: *Historical Statistics of the United States*, Series R 75-88; *Statistical Abstract of the United States 1988*, Table 881.

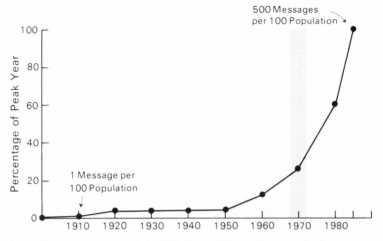

FIG. 12.10   Long-term trends in U.S. domestic long-distance telephone messages per capita of resident population. Sources: *Historical Statistics of the United States*, Series R 1-12; *Statistical Abstract of the United States 1988*, Table 881.

rather suddenly become visibly functionally inadequate to a much greater degree than before.

Meanwhile, efforts to order the new, vastly enlarged mass of information tend to be plural, uncoordinated, specialized. For any individual or organization the absolute amount of information and understanding surely is greater than it ever was, but the knowledge and understanding possessed relative to the total amount available has surely diminished. A temporary but probably protracted ignorance explosion has accompanied the information explosion, and none of us is exempt. Uneven ability to select and use the avalanche of information surely threatens to widen further the gap between the most advantaged and disadvantaged, both within American society and worldwide.

Through probes of space, jet propulsion has added to the information overload and erosion of conceptual frameworks by exposing the human race to unprecedented empirical observations and questions about the global environment and the wider celestial environment of the earth itself. The jet age has sharply increased the frequency of direct personal contact among a greatly enlarged range of cultural and natural environments. It has accelerated the diffusion of goods for satisfying basic human needs and follies—from simple consumer goods to sophisticated military weapons. Together with the satellite-electronic revolution, jet propulsion has been a major factor in internationalizing business ownership, management, and labor. Like the energy transition, these forces underlie the striking rise in American overseas trade.

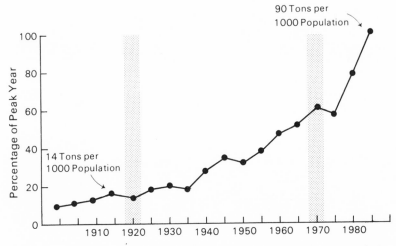

FIG. 12.11   Long-term trend in U.S. per capita consumption of paper, excluding newsprint, packaging, industrial, and tissue. Sources: *Historical Statistics of the United States*, Series L 178-191; *Statistical Abstract of the United States 1988*, Table 1129.

They also underlie the growth of overseas travel (Figure 12.11) and the resurgence of foreign immigration (Figures 12.12 and 12.13).

It seems likely that the forces set in motion by the satellite-electronic-jet propulsion revolutions will endure as long as those associated with the energy transition—well into the next century.

BUILDING A NEW COUNTRY

The layer of new development and redevelopment in the electronic-jet propulsion age is the latest in the historical accumulation of buildings and other works represented by the cultural features on the topographic maps of the United States. Those features represent the real property assets on the national balance sheet. In constant 1970 dollars their estimated book value has risen from less than thirty billion dollars in 1840 to nearly four trillion today (Figure 12.14). Although the rise has been fitful from year to year, only the combination of the Great Depression and World War II has profoundly interrupted the long-run accumulation. It took thirty to forty years to get back on the projected pre-1929 trend line after 1945.

Normally new construction in each decade exceeds the amount required by new growth. The surplus is then available to replace the oldest or most deteriorated stock of buildings, which then may be abandoned. Unfortunately it is virtually impossible to estimate the amount of total replacement con-

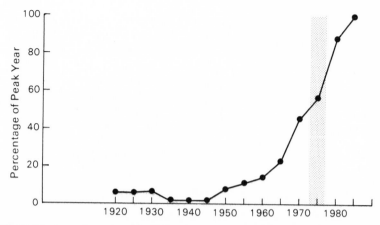

FIG. 12.12   Long-term trend in U.S. overseas travel, excluding military travel, cruise ships, and travel to Canada and Mexico. Sources: *Historical Statistics of the United States*, Series H 921-940; *Statistical Abstract of the United States 1988*, Table 387.

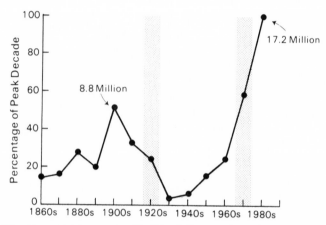

FIG. 12.13   Long-term trend in numbers of immigrants admitted to the U.S., expressed in percentages of peak decennial immigration. Actual numbers are indicated for two peak decades, 1900s and 1980s. Sources: *Historical Statistics of the United States*, Series C 143-157; *Statistical Abstract of the United States 1988*, Table 392.

struction, but it is possible to estimate housing replacement (Borchert et al. 1983; Gleeson 1981).

Until well after the end of the Civil War, I estimate, there was virtually no replacement construction in the country (Figure 12.15). A very small percentage of the housing was more than a century old, and essentially everything built was needed for new growth. Replacement construction slowly climbed

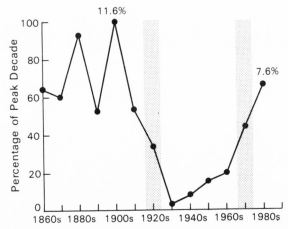

FIG. 12.14   Long-term trend in immigration in each decade expressed as a share of the resident U.S. population at the beginning of that decade. Sources: *Historical Statistics of the United States*, Series C 143-157; *Statistical Abstract of the United States 1988*, Table 392.

during the steel rail epoch. By the end of the 1920s boom the country had finally built enough to replace all of the stock that had been built before 1830. Household growth exceeded new dwelling units built during the Depression and World War II years, so there was negative replacement and doubling up. By the end of the 1950s boom we had only recovered the 1930 position.

The replacement rate since 1950 has been unprecedented. By the 1970s Americans were in a position to abandon the equivalent of all housing built before 1880. By 1990 we could be abandoning much housing built before 1900, and by the turn of the next century we could be abandoning most housing built before the rise of the automobile epoch in the 1920s, if recent rates of replacement continue. In 1920, at the end of the steel rail epoch, the frontier had finally closed, and the national pattern of cities and towns we take for granted today was completed. Two decades into the new satellite-electronic-jet propulsion epoch, the nation is well along toward abandoning virtually all of the structures that existed in 1920. No replacement of similar magnitude has happened before in our history.

To be sure, the geography of the replacement process is a complex set of compromises. On the one hand, structures are very seldom replaced where they stand. The replacement for an obsolete building has almost certainly been in another block, another part of the metropolis, or another region of the country. Cost and sheer mechanical inconvenience, as well as changing locational advantages, have usually discouraged replacement of obsolete structures on site. On the other hand, the replacement process has not been entirely footloose geographically. Limitations on the savings and credit avail-

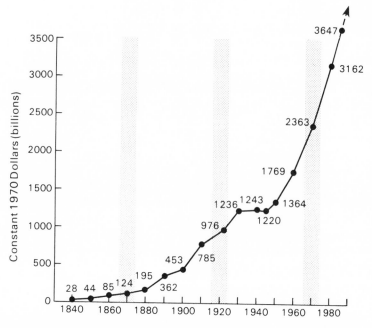

FIG. 12.15   Long-term trend in the net cumulative value of structures in the
United States. Values are expressed in constant 1970 dollars, based on the implicit
price deflator for fixed investment. Values before 1880 are estimated from the
value of output of all fixed capital. I have assumed that the increase in accumulated
value of structures during those years was proportional to the output of all fixed
capital. Sources: 1839–1879, *Historical Statistics of the United States*, Series F
238-249; 1880–1922, ibid., Series F 446-469; 1925–1985, *Fixed Reproducible
Tangible Wealth in the United States 1925–1985*, 164, 227; 1986, *Statistical
Abstract of the United States 1988*, Table 722.

able for new construction in any decade mean that new building must be
incremental. Most development decisions are constrained by the locations of
major highways, energy transmission lines, airports, and electricity generating stations, or by ignorance or fear of alternatives. Furthermore, both monumental and flimsy structures have life expectancies far different from the
average.

Nevertheless, in the new epoch America is abandoning most of the
structures put into place during the steel rail epoch. Since 1970 the new
patterns have been literally taking over. Both by design and by default the
nation is slowly learning how to make unprecedented decisions about what to
save, what to destroy, and where. New patterns have emerged as much more
than an aberration to be somehow cured within the framework inherited
from the rail-streetcar era. They have become dominant at the national and

intracity levels. New cities are outpacing old; new neighborhoods are eclipsing old. The older settlements have most favored nuclei for preservation, rehabilitation, and redevelopment: the most durable architectural monuments and the homes of the most durable institutions or social groupings, at the most durable nodes in the circulation network. Elsewhere, in many kinds of locations, railroad-era structures lie as accumulations of architectural solid waste—abandoned by the socioeconomic descendants of their builders, consumptively used by those with no other choice, or vacant, vandalized, and disintegrating.

In this process, the nation is not simply replacing an inventory of buildings. Because of changed locational advantages, it is also replacing the major part of the fabric three generations have taken for granted as the bedrock geographic pattern of American settlement. Observers have fully recognized, at least since the 1950s, the obsolescence of rail-era locations, cities, and regions, not only individual structures, but the extent to which we have been building a new settlement pattern and abandoning the older one has not been clearly described, nor have the consequent capital shifts been measured.

PATTERNS IN THE NEW EPOCH

The National Map

The national metropolitan system was a historical legacy in 1970 (Figure 12.3). Each metropolitan area was a critical location on the natural resource, railroad, and steamship circulation maps of the nineteenth and early twentieth centuries. Their population sizes reflected both their initial advantage in the railroad era and their subsequent advantage or disadvantage in the massive redistribution of population during the auto–air–cheap oil epoch.

The high-order metropolitan areas (generally more than 1.2 million in 1970) had grown at the great ports of the iron horse epoch or at the national and regional nodes of the steel rail epoch (Borchert 1972). Development of the modern highway network greatly expanded the commuter ring around each metropolitan area, and the commutersheds of twenty-five high-order central metropolitan areas in 1970 had grown to overlap or include the commuter zones of neighboring low-order satellite metropolitan areas (Berry and Gillard 1977). Those clusters of interlocking metropolitan commuter sheds are "high-order conurbations" (Figure 12.3). Two other conurbations—the Carolina Piedmont and Tidewater Virginia—contained no high-order metropolitan area, but their populations in 1970 were larger than the smallest conurbations centered on the high-order cities. I refer to all twenty-seven conurbations as high-order.

In addition to the high-order conurbations, with their central and satellite metropolitan areas, are the isolated metropolitan areas outside the major conurbations and the nonmetropolitan area of the country—the smaller cities, towns, and rural territory (Figure 12.3). In 1970, the high-order conurbations had 64.5 percent of the country's total population (Table 12.1), the isolated metropolitan areas 18.3 percent, and the rest of the country 17.2 percent. These three settlement classes provided the framework for successive, quite different population redistributions in the auto–air–cheap oil epoch between 1920 and 1970 and in the new epoch since 1970.

In the 1920 to 1970 epoch there was a strong, clear population shift right up the hierarchy that had been inherited from the railroad era. The net shift from the nonmetropolitan areas was unequalled in history, and all of the net gain was in the metropolitan areas of the emerging high-order conurbations.

Trends have been quite different in the new epoch (Figure 12.16) (Dunn 1980; Noyelle and Stanback 1984; Frey and Speare 1988; Abler, Adams, and Lee 1976; Adams 1987). From 1970 through 1987 the net outflow from nonmetropolitan areas has slowed, in spite of continued outflow from the extensive farming areas, because of growth concentrations in high-amenity districts and major trade centers. At the same time, existing isolated metropolitan areas—many of which are new—have absorbed most of the net growth. The high-order conurbations have had only a small net growth be-

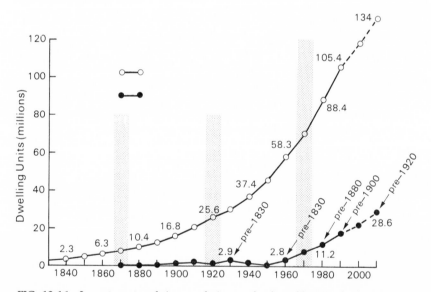

FIG. 12.16 Long-term trends in cumulative total value of housing built and replaced, by decade. Total dwelling units were estimated for years before 1940 from numbers of occupied units and assumed 5 percent vacancy rates. Farm dwelling units were estimated by assuming that each new farm household required one new dwelling unit. Sources: Tables showing numbers of dwelling units and number of households at each decennial census, and number of new dwelling units constructed during each decade (including mobile homes after 1950), in *Statistical Abstract of the United States* for 1958, 1962, 1966, 1971, 1980, and 1987; and *Historical Statistics of the United States*.

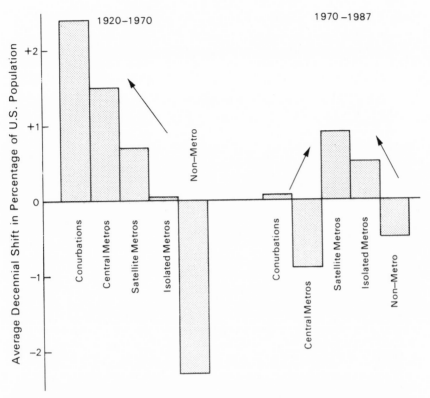

FIG. 12.17   Shift from strong centralization to focused decentralization in the new epoch; contrasts between settlement classes in the auto-air and jet-electronic epochs. Source: Table 12.1.

cause large net losses in the central metropolitan areas offset gains in the satellites. The variability of metropolitan growth rates, both geographically and over time, increased in the 1970s compared with previous decades (Borchert 1983a). Smaller centers are more specialized and thus more sensitive to fluctuations in the fortunes of a particular class of employment. It seems likely that the spread of the country's growth over a larger number of smaller centers will sustain the increased instability of metropolitan growth rates.

Of course, these trends are for general size classes regardless of region or age. Although the growth of the great conurbations slowed overall, it was much greater in the conurbations of the South and California. The population of the eight southern and California conurbations increased nearly twice as much as the other nineteen, and nine new conurbations—which attained high-order after 1920—had far higher percentage increases than the eighteen old ones (Figure 12.17). The newer areas were also in the South and

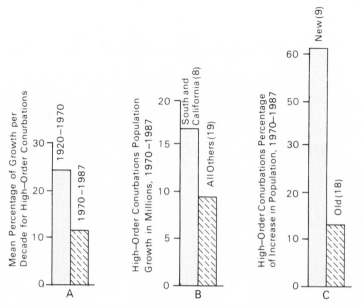

FIG. 12.18   Growth of major conurbations in the new epoch has slowed overall
(A), but it has favored the southern, western (B), and newer (C) regions of the
country. "Newer" conurbations center on metropolitan areas that attained high-
order status after 1920, including Atlanta, Carolina Piedmont, Denver, Houston,
Indianapolis, Miami–Ft. Lauderdale, New Orleans, Portland, and Tampa–St.
Petersburg. The eight southern and western conurbations that dominated 1970–
1987 growth include Atlanta, Carolina Piedmont, Miami–Ft. Lauderdale, Tampa–
St. Petersburg, Dallas–Ft. Worth, Houston, New Orleans, Los Angeles–San Diego,
and San Francisco–Oakland. Source: Table 12.1.

West. In fact, for metropolitan populations generally, the upland and Gulf
South, Texas, and the West had consistent relatively high growth rates in
booms, depression, and war from the 1920s through the 1960s, whereas the
1920s, wartime, and postwar booms had frequently sustained growth in the
older metropolitan areas. In the 1970s, fast metropolitan growth finally concentrated unequivocally in those regions (Figure 12.18).

In summary, there has been a revolutionary increase in information,
knowledge of alternatives, and exercise of options. The communications revolution has accelerated the weakening of hierarchies, the population redistribution, and the instability that had already seriously undermined the
geographical legacy from the railroad era. More specific trends observable
since 1970 reflect the jet-electronic revolution more directly and are likely to
continue. Take a few important examples:

1. The surge in immigration and global interaction has promoted growth around the major centers of international air transportation, international educational or financial services, or immigration across the Mexican border.
2. The emergence of an international labor pool has either reduced wages and overhead expenditures or increased automation in the American production of factory goods and routine business services in the international market. As a result, urban growth dependent on those functions has been dispersed or weakened except in centers of heavy immigration from the Third World.
3. Much easier and more frequent international contact surely reduces the need for traditional military force, but fear and uncertainty stemming from unstable energy supply lines and the growth of relative ignorance work in the opposite direction, which suggests a continuation of the highly variable but downward secular trend in the share of national income spent on the military since World War II. In periods of military cutback, metropolitan areas highly dependent on traditional bases have been especially vulnerable to decline, while centers of defense research and development have shown much more adaptability.
4. Expenditures for welfare, social services, and public improvements—mainly roads, utilities, and environmental quality—can be a significant factor in the distribution of growth within the national system. Large expenditures from the national budget in those fields could redistribute income and equalize growth. On the other hand, financing from local sources tends to reinforce differences among cities in wealth, communality, and comparative locational advantage. Struggle and uncertainty over priorities and methods, under a growing barrage of information, is likely to add to the instability and uneven pattern of growth rates.
5. Finally, increasing knowledge of environments and cultures further reinforces the drift of footloose population to centers of amenity—especially amenable climates. It also increases the frequency and geographical range of innovations and entrepreneurship.

The net results are (1) an accelerated drift away from the constrained hierarchical patterns of the steel rail epoch, and (2) a further increase in short-term fluctuations in growth, related to chance locations of new ideas, the impacts of shifting experiments and compromises in the policies of individuals, markets, and organizations, and the distribution of population among a larger number of smaller metropolitan areas.

The Metropolitan Map

Like the shifts between cities, the shifts within the metropolitan areas also reflect both the approaching demise of railroad-era locational legacies

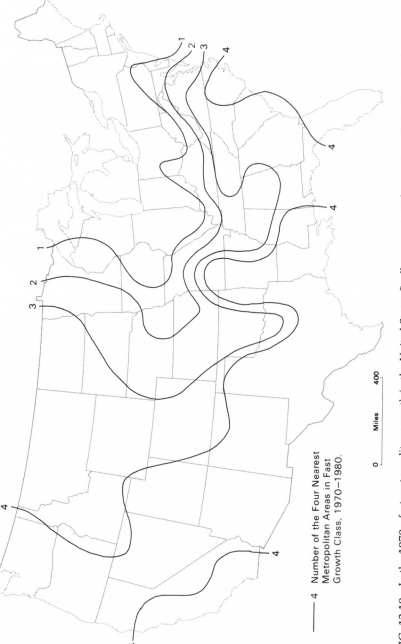

FIG. 12.19 In the 1970s, fast metropolitan growth in the United States finally concentrated unequivocally in the upland and Gulf South, Texas, and the West, after hesitantly drifting toward that pattern in the preceding half-century. Those regions had the most consistently high growth through booms, depression, and war from the 1920s through the 1960s, but localized boom times in Midwestern, Northeastern, and some Plains cities during the 1920s, World War II, and the immediate postwar period sustained intermittent growth in those older and more northeasterly metropolitan areas before the 1970s. Source: Borchert 1983a.

—— 4 Number of the Four Nearest
        Metropolitan Areas in Fast
        Growth Class, 1970–1980.

0   Miles   400

and the explosion of information and locational options. Compared with the auto–air–cheap oil epoch, the share of national population growth in the central metropolitan counties of the high-order conurbations declined sharply (Figure 12.19). The central counties of the major conurbations in the South and California were exceptions. They gained a share of national population, while the others lost heavily. The suburban commuter counties and the satellite metropolitan areas in all of the conurbations continued strong gains in their share of national growth, but there was a shift from the commuter counties of the central metropolitan area to the commuter counties of the satellite cities (Figure 12.20). In the isolated metropolitan areas, as well, growth shifted from the central counties to the commuter ring.

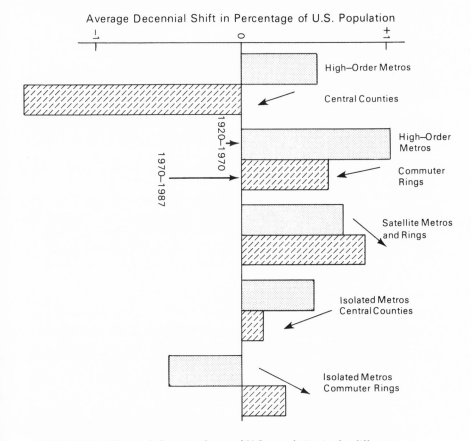

FIG. 12.20   Observed changing shares of U.S. population in the different metropolitan development rings, 1970–1987 compared with 1920–1970. Source: Table 12.1.

Thus, in each metropolitan area a new age ring is growing in the new epoch, and the faces of the older rings are changing. Visualize the landscapes that bring to life the legend on the accompanying schematic maps of the old and new age rings in a generic high-order metropolitan area.

The pre-rail core was built up before 1830 (Figure 12.21A). The site of initial development was at the mouth of an estuary facing eastward toward the sea. In 1970, that area of the city had been the central business district for almost a century. The 1830 to 1870 ring was built up during the iron horse epoch (Figure 12.21B). Beyond the edge of the built-up area, pioneer regional rail lines radiated toward distant centers in the emerging national system. Near the city, a handful of early railroad suburbs had been injected into the array of older farm trade centers, mill sites, and fishing ports. In 1970, the iron horse ring contained the rail terminals, the original port, obsolescent rail-industry corridors, and arterial streets bordered by commercial strips that had developed originally along horsecar routes. Those corridors defined the sectors within the ring.

The 1870 to 1920 ring developed during the steel rail epoch (Figure 12.21C). Industrial corridors reached out farther, at larger scale, along the rail lines, and a belt railway and a new larger port were developed near the outer edge of the ring. Outlying industrial corridors developed along the belt line, and the first large central power generating stations rose where the belt railroad met the bay. Commercial strips extended along the arterial streets with electric streetcar lines. The original sectors grew and widened toward the periphery, and developers strung two dozen railroad suburbs like beads along five of the main radial rail lines. The earlier rail suburbs were enveloped by massive streetcar-era urbanization.

The 1920 to 1970 ring was a product of the auto–air–cheap oil epoch (Figure 12.21C). Low-density commercial strips lined the arterial highways and older parts of the freeway system. Large malls, industrial parks, and office parks sprawled near the freeway interchanges. They dwarfed the areas of the railroad-era central business district and rail-industry strips. At the 1970 frontier, or a few miles beyond it, the electric utility had built five massive new generating stations at critical locations in the rail and water networks. Contiguous development pressed near the 1950s metropolitan airport, and some major commercial projects had leaped beyond it. Half of the steel rail epoch suburbs were now islands in the sea of auto-era growth. The old rural farm trade centers and fishing ports had gained a new lease on life as the new wave of exurbanites basked in their quaintness and added almost randomly to the minimal infrastructure.

Even in this gross generalization, by 1970 the pattern had become extremely complex. (To be sure, it was not disorderly in a scientific sense; everything was explainable in its historical-geographical context.) Growth in each ring surrounded islands of earlier urban development that had preempted land that once lay beyond the edge of the city. Pre-rail villages were embraced within the iron horse city. Pre-rail villages and iron horse suburbs were surrounded by the steel rail city. Settlements from all three earlier epochs lay within the auto ring.

Furthermore, there had been continuous, although piecemeal, replacement. The core in 1970 contained monumental buildings from every epoch, especially from the steel rail and auto ages. The iron horse ring was the 1970s "gray zone." Obsolescence, vacancy, and spotty demolition dominated the landscape, but almost no original structures survived. They were mostly replacements from the steel rail and even the early auto epochs. The steel rail ring had become the inner city—almost entirely within the central municipality of the metropolitan area. Built up in the streetcar days, most of its older structures were nearing the lower end of the vacancy chain and eligible for abandonment. The 1920 to 1970 auto ring was the least disturbed by new development, obsolescence, or abandonment. It was the most comfortable ring.

Cultural complexity had grown apace. Communities of interest spawned, mutated, splintered, and multiplied as an exponential function of population growth and information growth. Their geographic patterns spread and coalesced and dissolved or persisted kaleidescopically in the continuous processes of immigration, diffusion, turnover, succession, congregation, segregation, filtering, abandonment, and replacement. The cultural complexity extended to the map of municipal governments and all that implied for management of the public business. The auto ring and the adjacent fringe were a political geographic crazy quilt. Small municipalities dated from the days of rail suburb development, and large municipalities had been created from rural towns in the recent epoch of auto commuting. A political-bureaucracy-based community of interest coalesced around each city or town hall. Each community was searching for a unique history that legitimated its boundaries and its separation from other municipalities in the same metropolitan system. Each was trying to find and develop its downtown amid the miscellaneous collection of metropolitan components that chanced to lie within its historically accidental boundaries. Still other communities of interest gathered around maps that displayed the entire collection of features and activities as a metropolis; and those groups became yet another part of the culture. Of course, memberships of all these cultural groups overlapped, and group memberships had different mixes and priorities in the lives of individuals.

Age Rings in the New Epoch

Yet another ring is being added in the new epoch, from 1970 to 2000 and beyond (Figure 12.21C). It will be still more complex. The variety of new housing is likely to be greater. The new outer ring of development covers a

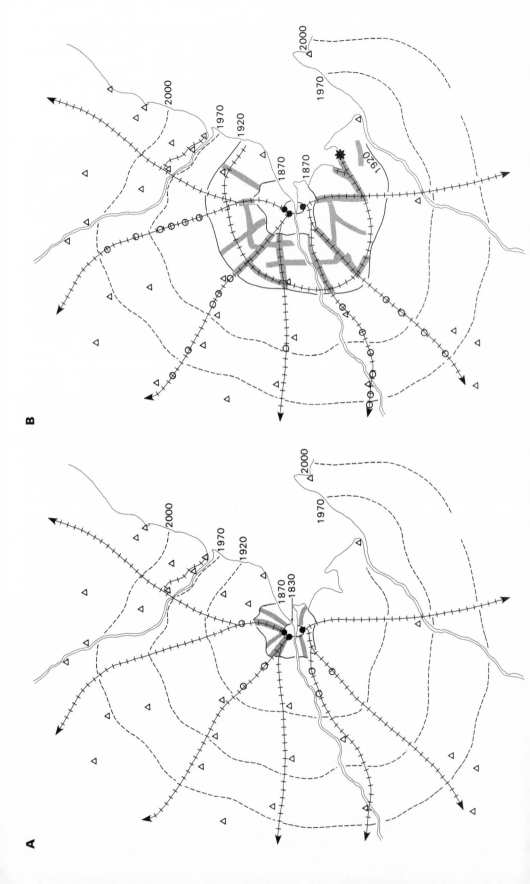

A

B

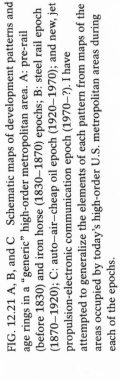

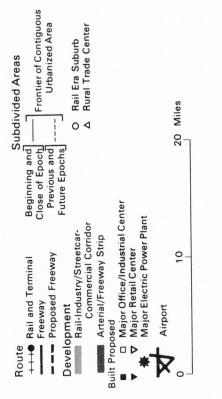

Route

+━━━+ Rail and Terminal

━━━ Freeway

━ ━ ━ Proposed Freeway

Development

▨ Rail-Industry/Streetcar-
Commercial Corridor

▬ Arterial/Freeway Strip

Built Proposed

■ □ Major Office/Industrial Center

▼ ▽ Major Retail Center

✹ Major Electric Power Plant

✈ Airport

Subdivided Areas

Beginning and ⎤
Close of Epoch ⎦ Frontier of Contiguous
Previous and ⎤ Urbanized Area
Future Epochs ⎦ - - -

O Rail Era Suburb

△ Rural Trade Center

0   10   20 Miles

FIG. 12.21 A, B, and C Schematic maps of development patterns and age rings in a "generic" high-order metropolitan area. A: pre-rail (before 1830) and iron horse (1830–1870) epochs; B: steel rail epoch (1870–1920); C: auto–air–cheap oil epoch (1920–1970); and new, jet propulsion-electronic communication epoch (1970–?). I have attempted to generalize the elements of each pattern from maps of the areas occupied by each of the epochs during today's high-order U.S. metropolitan areas during each of the epochs.

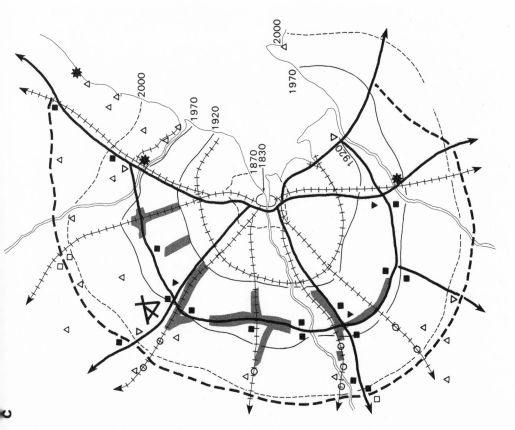

c

much larger area than did the earlier rings. It contains a much wider variety of locations and sites, but there are other factors. Recent trends on the periphery have tended toward fewer and larger units for the housing dollar. Meanwhile, the need grows for better housing at low price and low cost. Eventually there must be a response in the form of manufactured or modular housing of some kind. Open land is still relatively inexpensive in the outer ring. Jobs are becoming more accessible as development continues to intensify near the freeways, and the alternative supply of land available for low-priced housing in the inner city will shrink.

Fitful highway improvements will also add to the complexity of the outer ring. The second circumferential freeway, planned to accommodate the continuing new round of office-industrial parks and retail centers, will be stalled intermittently and only partly completed. Freeway and arterial highway construction has fallen behind population and economic growth and threatens to continue to lag in competition for public improvement funds, while public improvement funds compete with still other, multiplying demands. Suburban gridlock apparently will become somewhat worse and more widespread before it lessens.

Airport expansion or relocation poses large, unresolved questions. The energy uncertainty, the growing potential for competitive new technologies, and the lagging outlay for public infrastructure cloud large-scale transportation planning (National Council on Public Works Improvement 1988; NAS/NRC 1988). Noise will blight extensive suburban residential areas if the airport is not moved. Weakening of housing demand and prices in those relatively new areas may well accelerate minority residential expansion. If the airport is moved the present site will become an abandoned area half as large as the pre-1870 central city, and it probably will take decades to bring that much new development into one location.

Also complicating the scene in the future outer ring are the salvage yards and dumps essential to the metropolis but absent from the master plans, and several large controversial electric generating stations completed before the 1980s. Built in the 1950s and 1960s by engineers who assumed that they were safely out of sight of the city, they now are resented by newly arrived exurbanites who find them looming in their bucolic backyards (Borchert 1983b).

While the new outer ring is taking shape, the earlier rings are being reshaped. Increasing variation in the social and economic geography of the aging 1920 to 1970 ring is likely. In the new epoch, most of it will continue to be firmly in the middle of vacancy chains for all types of uses, yet there will probably be substantial change as the epoch advances. The leading edge of deterioration and abandonment could reach the inner part of the auto epoch ring by the 2010s. The lower socioeconomic stratum of the metropolitan population would be moving in. Quality of life could improve for those newcomers as a result of lower density, or it could deteriorate if they cannot maintain structures and grounds—if the gap between the advantaged and disadvantaged is stable or widening. Much will depend on job growth and on the effectiveness of education, welfare and social services, housing subsidies, and public improvements.

The pre-1920 rings outside the central business district will be reshaped in a different pattern. Most of the structures will be replaced, mostly elsewhere in the metropolis. At the outset extensive land areas lie unused, especially in the railroad corridors, and the amount will grow, yet that land will be closer to all of the outer realms than any of the outer realms are to most of the others in a period of uncertain energy cost. The potential value of these inner-city locations will continue to grow. There will be a great variety of site conditions—bluff and waterfront land attractive for residential, office, and institutional use and for public open space; interior land attractive for industry and warehouses; and clusters of old, monumental buildings worth rehabilitating.

For a long time many tracts will be unimproved. Long-run opportunities will continue to tempt the central city to provide subsidies to encourage new development and rehabilitation, but fiscal pressure will surely keep increasing, with heavy competing metropolitanwide demands for public improvements and maintenance of all kinds. Understanding of the vast commitment of money and time needed to rebuild a large part of a city will continue to grow, and emphasis may well shift to a more varied mixture of monumental buildings and low-cost, transition uses, including simply landscaped open spaces that have become ripe for abandonment but not for redevelopment.

Heterogeneity in the pre-auto ring of the metropolis, like the younger rings, is likely to increase for several decades of transformation. The second or third decade of the next century may well see a metropolis in which the average age of structures is newest in the central ring and oldest in the pre-1970 suburbs, with average population density in the central ring lower than that of the 1970s. The market position of the historic central business district will be strengthened as the central realm of the metropolis becomes relatively newer.

GROWING COMPLEXITY

The net result of these changes in the new epoch is increasing heterogeneity of physical structures in every ring. The growing heterogeneity will result in the first place from the continuing process of aging, expansion, filtering, replacement, abandonment, and redevelopment, but additional factors are at work. The overlay of cultural communities and neighborhood centers on the map of the physical city also will grow more intricate. Social networks and nodes have been based on work, health, sports, arts, hobbies, ideas, skills, mating, beliefs, power, and control. In every one of these topical areas, at every scale, organizational variety is multiplied and splintering, accelerated by the information explosion and the resulting outpouring and fragmentation of organizational activity.

While the social, cultural, and economic geography becomes increasingly variegated and fragmented, the need for physical infrastructure continues to grow. The systems include not only transportation, utilities, and open space, but also waste disposal and recycling. Locational issues will become more complex as the metropolis becomes increasingly the source of its own industrial raw materials, as pressure mounts to locate waste processing near the metropolitan source and market. These physical systems must be planned and organized over large areas. The question may well arise whether officials of general units of government, responsible to increasingly fragmented constituencies, can effectively plan and operate sophisticated integrated regional and national systems.

In the face of growing tasks of managing and coping, some individuals and organizations will surely continue to emigrate to smaller metropolitan areas elsewhere in the conurbation or in a different region of the country. The goal then, as now, will be to optimize their particular requirements for accessibility and amenity. The internal changes in each metropolis are both cause and effect of changes in the larger system.

For those who persist in the management task in the big conurbations, the challenge to understand and prescribe is further complicated by physical reality. I have been talking about a schematic map of a generic high-order American metropolis. Now overlay the scheme upon the actual map of the United States. Transform the coastline into that of Seattle, San Francisco, Portland, San Diego, Houston, New York, Tampa, or Miami. Transform the regional and national location of the rail and highway corridors into those of Chicago, Dallas–Fort Worth, or Atlanta. Transform the ocean embayment into the channel of the Mississippi at Minneapolis–St. Paul, St. Louis, or New Orleans, or the Missouri at Kansas City or the Ohio at Cincinnati or Pittsburgh, or the Delaware at Philadelphia or the Willamette and Columbia at Portland. Transform the historical rings into those of Boston, New York, Philadelphia, or New Orleans; or, in contrast, into those of Miami or Phoenix, or even San Diego, Houston, or Tampa Bay. Transform the shoreline facing Europe into one that faces the Caribbean and Latin America, or East Asia, or into a land border with Mexico. Or think about the different ocean shorelines during a significant rise in sea level, under global warming. The results will be additional sets of relationships among all of the variables.

As the inhabitants of these cities and of the system seek to understand their options and their actions, a regular outpouring of atlases and interpretation is essential. To contemplate the task is sobering indeed. More observations and more minds for the study of geography will be sorely needed. The resulting effort and body of knowledge will surely be just as fragmented as the system it is trying to describe. Although the scale will be unprecedented, the task of that enlarged population of students will continue to have the same few basic components it has always had: to describe the settlement system in terms of evolving structure, flows, and process; to understand how each place is linked to others in the system; and to anticipate evolving future patterns. Generalized geometries can help, but explanation and forecasting will depend mainly upon the application of location principles and analytic techniques to empirical knowledge of changing specific places and the linkages between them.

REFERENCES

Abler, Ronald, John S. Adams, and Ki-Suk Lee. 1976. *A comparative atlas of America's great cities.* Minneapolis: University of Minnesota Press.

Adams, John S. 1987. *Housing America in the 1980s.* New York: Russell Sage Foundation.

Berry, Brian J. L., and Quentin Gillard. 1977. *The changing shape of metropolitan America.* Cambridge, Mass.: Ballinger Publishing Company.

Borchert, John R. 1967. American metropolitan evolution. *Geographical Review* 57: 301–32.

———. 1972. America's changing metropolitan regions. *Annals of the Association of American Geographers* 62: 352–73.

———. 1981. Geographical shifts in midwestern population in the twentieth century. In *Population redistribution in the Midwest.* Edited by Curtis C. Roseman. Ames, Iowa: North Central Center for Rural Development.

———. 1983a. Instability in American metropolitan growth. *Geographical Review* 73: 127–49.

———. 1983b. American land use in a national perspective. In *Geography and regional policy: Resource management by complex political systems.* Edited by John S. Adams, Werner Fricke, and Wolfgang Herden. Heidelberg Geographical Works. Heidelberg: Geographical Institute of the University of Heidelberg.

Borchert, John R., David Gebhard, David Lanegran, and Judith Martin. 1983. *Legacy of Minneapolis: Preservation amid change.* Part V. Minneapolis: Voyageur Press.

Cook, Earl. 1971. The flow of energy in an industrial economy. In *Energy and power.* Edited by Gerard Piel et al. San Francisco: W. H. Freeman.

Darmstadter, Joel. 1972. Energy. In *Population, resources, and the environment.* Edited by Ronald G. Ridker. Research Reports. Volume 3. Washington, D.C.: Commission on Population Growth and the American Future.

Dunn, Edgar S., Jr. 1980. *The development of the U.S. urban system.* Baltimore: Johns Hopkins University Press for Resources for the Future.

Frey, William H., and Alden Speare, Jr. 1988. *Regional and metropolitan growth and decline in the United States.* New York: Russell Sage Foundation.

Gleeson, Michael E. 1981. Estimating housing mortality. *Journal of the American Planning Association* 7: 190–91.

Johnston, R. J. 1982. *The American urban system.* New York: St. Martin's Press.

NAS/NRC. 1988. *A look ahead: Year 2020.* Washington, D.C.: National Academy of Sciences/National Resource Council, Transportation Research Board.

National Council on Public Works Improvement. 1988. *Fragile foundations: A report on America's public works.* Washington, D.C.

Noyelle, Thierry J., and Thomas M. Stanback, Jr. 1984. *The economic transformation of American cities*. Totowa, N.J.: Rowan and Allenheld.

Palm, Risa. 1981. *The geography of American cities*. New York: Oxford University Press.

Schurr, S. H., B. C. Netschert, V. F. Eliasberg, J. Lerner, and H. H. Landsberg. 1960. *Energy in the American economy*. Baltimore: Johns Hopkins University Press for Resources for the Future.

U.S. Bureau of the Census. 1975. *Historical statistics of the United States: Colonial times to 1970*. Washington, D.C.

————. 1988. *Statistical abstract of the United States*. Washington, D.C.

U.S. Department of Commerce. Bureau of Economic Analysis. 1987. *Fixed reproducible tangible wealth in the United States, 1925–1985*. Washington, D.C.

Vance, James E., Jr. 1991. Human mobility and the shaping of cities. In *Our changing cities*. Edited by John Fraser Hart.

CONTRIBUTORS

John S. Adams is a professor of geography, planning, and public affairs at the University of Minnesota. He is the author of *Housing America in the 1980s*.

Brian J. L. Berry is Founders Professor, Professor of Political Economy, and Director of the Bruton Center for Developmental Studies at the University of Texas at Dallas. His recent books include *Market Centers and Retail Distribution* and *Long-Wave Rhythms in Economic Development and Political Behavior*. He is a member of the National Academy of Sciences and a Fellow of the American Academy of Arts and Sciences, of the American Association for the Advancement of Science, of University College London, and of the British Academy. He has been awarded the Anderson Medal by the Association of American Geographers and the Victoria Medal by the Royal Geographical Society.

John R. Borchert is Regents' Professor Emeritus of Geography at the University of Minnesota. He is the author of *America's Northern Heartland: An Economic and Historical Geography of the Upper Midwest*. He is a member of the National Academy of Sciences and the American Academy of Arts and Sciences. He has received the Van Cleef Medal from the American Geographical Society and an Honors Award from the Association of American Geographers.

William A. V. Clark is a professor of geography at the University of California, Los Angeles. He has authored and edited *Human Migration, Residential Mobility and Public Policy*, and *Modelling Housing Market Search*.

He has received an Honors Award from the Association of American Geographers.

Larry R. Ford is a professor of geography at San Diego State University. He is working on a book on urban architecture and the geography of the city. He has received an Outstanding Teacher Award from the National Council for Geographic Education and a Guggenheim Fellowship.

Reginald G. Golledge is a professor of geography at the University of California, Santa Barbara. He has co-edited *A Ground for Common Search* and *Behavioural Modelling in Geography and Planning*. He is a Fellow of the American Association for the Advancement of Science, and has received a Guggenheim Fellowship and an Honors Award from the Association of American Geographers.

John Fraser Hart is a professor of geography at the University of Minnesota. He is the author of *The Look of the Land* and *The South*, and edited *Regions of the United States*. He served as Editor of the *Annals of the Association of American Geographers* from 1970 through 1975.

David Harvey is Halford Mackinder Professor of Geography in the University of Oxford. His recent books include *The Limits to Capital, the Urbanization of Capital*, and *The Condition of Postmodernity*. His awards include a Guggenheim Memorial Fellowship, the Gill Memorial Medal of the Royal Geographical Society, the Anders Retzius Gold Medal of the Swedish Society for Anthropology and Geography, and an Honors Award from the Association of American Geographers.

John C. Hudson is a professor of geography at Northwestern University. He is the author of *Geographical Diffusion Theory*, and his *Plains Country Towns* was awarded the John Brinckerhoff Jackson Prize by the Association of American Geographers. He has been a John Simon Guggenheim Fellow. He served as editor of the *Annals of the Association of American Geographers* from 1976 through 1981.

Richard L. Morrill is a professor of geography and environmental studies at the University of Washington. His monographs include *Spatial Organization of Society, Political Redistricting and Geographic Theory*, and *Spatial Diffusion*. He has received a Guggenheim Fellowship, an honorary fellowship from the American Geographical Society, and a meritorious achievement award from the Association of American Geographers.

A. S. Paul is a doctoral candidate and a Chancellor's Fellow at the University of California, Los Angeles.

Allen J. Scott is a professor of geography at the University of California, Los Angeles, and acting director of the Lewis Center for Regional Policy Studies. His most recent books are *Metropolis* and *New Industrial Spaces*. He has been awarded a Guggenheim Fellowship and an Honors Award by the Association of American Geographers.

James E. Vance, Jr., is a professor of geography at the University of California, Berkeley. He is the author of *Capturing the Horizon, The Con-*

tinuing City, and *The North American Railroad*. He has received the Van Cleef Memorial Medal from the American Geographical Society and an Honors Award from the Association of American Geographers.

Julian Wolpert is Henry G. Bryant Professor of Geography, Public Affairs, and Urban Planning in the Woodrow Wilson School at Princeton University. He is a Fellow of the American Association for the Advancement of Science and has received fellowships from the Center for Advanced Study in the Behavioral Sciences, the Guggenheim Foundation, and the Woodrow Wilson Center. He has received an Honors Award from the Association of American Geographers.

Index